Hand-coloured engraving from *Twelve New Designs of English Butterflies* (1742) by Benjamin Wilkes.

Published by Little Toller Books in 2019
Lower Dairy, Toller Fratrum, Dorset

Text © Peter Marren 2019

The right of Peter Marren to be identified as the author of this work
has been asserted by him in accordance with the Copyright, Design and
Patents Act 1988

Typeset in Caslon and Perpetua by Little Toller Books

Printed in India by Imprint Press

All papers used by Little Toller Books are natural, recyclable products
made from wood grown in sustainable, well-managed forests

A catalogue record for this book is available from the British Library

ISBN 978-1-908213-71-6

EMPERORS, ADMIRALS AND CHIMNEY SWEEPERS

The weird and wonderful names of butterflies and moths

PETER MARREN

A LITTLE TOLLER BOOK

The caterpillar-festooned title page of *Twelve New Designs of English Butterflies* (1742) by Benjamin Wilkes.

Contents

A plate from *Index Entomologicus* by William Wood, published in 1839,
showing an assortment of snouts, fan-foots and Pyrales.

To Michael McCarthy

"What sort of insects do you rejoice in, where you come from?" the Gnat inquired.

"I don't *rejoice* in insects at all," Alice explained, "because I'm rather afraid of them – at least the large kinds. But I can tell you the names of some of them."

"Of course they answer to their names?" the Gnat remarked carelessly.

"I never saw them do it."

"What's the use of their having names," the Gnat said, "if they won't answer to them?"

"No use to them," said Alice; "but it's useful to the people that name them, I suppose. If not, why do things have names at all?"

"I can't say," the Gnat replied.

Through the Looking-Glass and What Alice Found There
by Lewis Carroll, Chapter 3, Looking-Glass Insects

The Emperor Moth (Female).

Red Admiral (*Pyrameis Atalanta*).
Under side.

The Chimney Sweeper (*Tanagra chærophyllata*).

Introduction

Perhaps it was because I was a bookish sort of boy, but once I became aware that butterflies existed, I found their colourful names almost as entrancing as their beautiful wings. Red Admiral, Purple Emperor, Green Hairstreak, Orange-tip, Clouded Yellow: these were butterflies caught in poetry. But while the names seem bright as a rainbow, are they not also strange? How, for example, did a butterfly get promoted to an admiral, let alone an emperor? What exactly is a 'hairstreak'? (My dictionary tells me it's a butterfly, so round we go in a circle.) Why was a little chequered butterfly named after the Duke of Burgundy – and who was he anyway? Why was one blue butterfly called a 'mazarine' and another an 'adonis'? I don't suppose my ten-year-old self tried very hard to find out. After all, they were just names, like tench or chaffinch or weasel. Maybe they didn't mean anything. From the rather few butterfly books available back then, you would be forgiven for thinking so. None of them hinted that behind a name there might be a story, a little nugget of wisdom from the past.

And then I discovered moths. Although I loved butterflies with a passion, I had never paid much attention to their nocturnal cousins until the day I bought *The Observer's Book of Larger Moths* from the village shop. It cost five bob (25p, that is). Five bob to change your life! Probably I had been attracted by the Red Underwing on the cover. It resembled a big, dusky butterfly, but with its bright wings tucked unexpectedly beneath mottled grey forewings, like a party frock hidden under a raincoat. I opened the book, which began with the hawk-moths, far more substantial and animal-like than any butterfly, and proceeded through a gallery of wonderfully named winged beings: kittens, prominents, tussocks, eggars, tiger-moths, lutestrings, footmen … One big moth was named after a lobster, and another after an old lady, and a big plump one at the back named after a goat. I remember a flash of realisation that my inner world – the one you stock like an iPad with all the good things in life: stories, songs, pictures – had just experienced a seismic shift. I felt like John Keats when he opened Chapman's Homer: 'Then felt I like some watcher of the skies/When a new planet swims into his ken.' Weird and homely at the same time, these mothy names seemed to catch something about the personality of each species even when, on the face of it, they made little sense. Even when the moth was called a Lackey or a Vapourer or a Ghost Swift.

The author of *The Observer's Book* did not attempt to explain how these funny names came about. He was far more concerned to tell you where to find the moths and how to rear their caterpillars. In his concentration on strictly scientific pursuits, he was in no way unusual. *The Observer's Book* was the prototype of field guides that illustrate all the butterflies and all the moths, and tell you where to find them, and at what time of year, but they rarely display the slightest interest in why a moth should be called 'a drinker', or what kind of imagination lay behind names like Beaded Chestnut or Brindled Green or High Brown Fritillary (did that mean it flies high, or what?). Perhaps there was an unspoken sense that common names were unscientific, and not particularly helpful. If butterflies and moths were to be named afresh, we would probably dispense with all the emperors and admirals and goats, and go instead for the baldly descriptive approach taken by whoever named the Large Blue or the Small White or the Poplar Hawk-moth. The Beaded Chestnut, for instance, would be reinvented as the Spotted Brown.

For proper lepidopterists, common names were always a bit, well, common. Among your scientific peers you would use the scientific 'Latin' name, whose meaning would have been more familiar because Latin and Ancient Greek were on the curriculum of every public school. But few bothered to delve into the meaning of the Latin names either. They might have realised that certain butterflies were named after characters in Homer or Virgil or Ovid. But they were only names – that is to say, labels, a simple necessity to enable you to talk butterflies and do science. No one seemed much interested in finding out why the Red Admiral was called Vanessa, or why a harmless little bee hawk-moth was named after the terrible giant Tityos.

That was, until Emmet came along. Lt. Colonel A. Maitland Emmet (1908–2001) was a rare combination of expert lepidopterist and classical scholar. He specialised in the difficult species, the so-called Microlepidoptera, and especially the smallest of them all, the fingernail-sized Nepticulidae or 'neps'. He studied Greats (Latin, Greek and Philosophy) at Oxford, and later taught Latin, English and Ancient Greek at St Edward's School in that city. He was therefore perfectly placed to explore and explain the Greek- or Latin-based scientific names of butterflies and moths, and he did so in great detail in his scholarly work, *The Scientific Names of the British Lepidoptera. Their History and Meaning*, published in 1991, the book that inspired A. S. Byatt to write her novella *Angels and Insects*.

A friend remembers Emmet as a 'larger than life' character: intelligent, phenomenally hard-working, and generous with his knowledge. He was also a man with a 'wicked' sense of humour, and mildly addicted to sherry. A perfect combination of traits for a writer about esoteric and often humorous names.

To elucidate what Linnaeus and his followers were getting at, Emmet went back to the original texts and manuscripts, offering his own interpretations wherever there was room for doubt. Some Latin names, he discovered, were anything but straightforward. They were akin to cryptic crossword clues, and to solve them it helped to understand the puzzler's mind-set. Names could contain word-games and even jokes, little squibs of laughter surviving from different times and other places. Emmet's study was characteristically thorough. He has been my lodestone and guide when it comes to the meaning of scientific names, although I am proud to say I have been able to add to, or modify, his explanations here and there.

Emmet also happens to be the main authority on the English names of butterflies, which he outlined, species by species, in *The Moths and Butterflies of Great Britain and Ireland, Vol. 7, Part 1* (1989), the section dedicated to butterflies alone, which Emmet edited with the late John Heath. At the end of each species account, Emmet wrote a section on 'The vernacular name and early history,' to explain, in effect, where butterfly names came from and who came up with them. Once again, he was characteristically thorough.

When it came to working out the English names of moths, I can claim more originality. Here, I was on my own. I have studied all the main sources, from the Elizabethan Thomas Moffet onwards, and have also explored their social and cultural context. I discovered that the craze for butterflies and moths began not with science, as you might expect, but with art: with the admiration felt by watercolourists and pattern designers and amateur poets for these most beautiful of insects. The names they came up with are their legacy. We are lucky that in most cases we use the same names today, and throughout the English-speaking world. For the names of our butterflies and moths are old, and not invented by sober scientists but by creative people with a gift for touching on exactly the right word.

This book is in two parts. The first is a historical overview of how and when butterflies and moths began to be named, beginning with the remote origins of the words 'butterfly' and 'moth'. It explores the background to the naming of names in the learned societies of Georgian England and the sumptuous butterfly books illustrated by artists for a relatively wealthy clientele. Again and again one finds that the common names, and to some extent the scientific names too, were coined in a feeling of admiration, and with an artist's eye for the beautiful and the bizarre. It was as though the Lepidoptera were living examples of art. But it also says something about the conservatism of amateurs and collectors that we continue to use names from the past without, in so many cases, really understanding them. It was as if we were still calling rabbits 'conies' and thrushes 'throstles'.

The second part is an A to Z of topics: the extraordinary variety of words and objects from which butterflies and moths have drawn their names. They range from birds and beasts to a surprising array of household objects, not to mention the curious number of moths named after weddings. This section can be read in any order. I hope it will amuse. I also hope that, by the end, you will not see a Red Admiral or an Oak Eggar in quite the same way. It seems to me that knowledge of how and why a species acquired its name can deepen our interest and understanding of these most lovely of insects quite as much as knowing about their caterpillars, or foodplants, or month of appearance.

This has been a fun book to write. I hope you will find it a fun book to read.

Peter Marren
Ramsbury, 2019

A note on names

The Latin names of moths in this book are taken from the two standard field guides, *Moths of Great Britain and Ireland* by Paul Waring & Martin Townsend (BWP, 2003) and *Micro Moths of Great Britain and Ireland* by Phil Sterling and Mark Parsons (BWP, 2012). The butterfly names are from *The Butterflies of Britain and Ireland* by Jeremy Thomas and Richard Lewington (BWP, 2010). All these names are, in turn, based on the standard checklist by J. D. Bradley (2000), since updated by David Agassiz and co-authors (2013). Similarly, the English names are those used in the standard field guides, although in some cases I have added a discrete 'the' to conform to older texts. The omission of the definite article is a grave discourtesy to the species.

BOOK ONE

Butterflies & moths
acquire their names

Butterfly-collecting in the Middle Ages.

In the Beginning

Δll the birds and beasts of the world once lived in the Garden of Eden. Each one, says the Book of Genesis, was given a name – not by God but by his creation, Adam:

> And out of the ground the Lord God formed every beast of the field, and every fowl of the air; and brought them unto Adam to see what he would call them: and whatsoever Adam called every living creature, that was the name thereof. (Genesis 2:19)

Unfortunately, it seems that Adam omitted to name any insects. Perhaps he did not regard them as beasts or fowls. Later on, the Bible does mention a few insects but, with the exception of honeybees, they are invariably malign forces of nature, appearing as devouring swarms – more like tempests than living entities. One of the plagues of Egypt was a vast cloud of locusts that arrived on the east wind and 'covered the face of the whole earth, so that the land was darkened.' Moths are mentioned too, but they are almost invisible, not so much flying insects as grubs that turn garments into dust.

Strangely, the Bible doesn't mention butterflies even once. For that matter no surviving ancient text does, not until we reach Aristotle in the fourth century BC. Aristotle lists a lot of insects, but most of them are generic rather than specific; his 'fly' could be any winged insect. Aristotle was also familiar with beetles, cicadas, mayflies – and butterflies. His name for the last was *psuche*, which is the same word in ancient Greek as 'soul' or 'spirit', and from which we get words like 'psyche' and 'psychology'. That seems unlikely to be coincidence. Aristotle knew that butterflies were insects, and he also knew something about their life cycles. He knew that the

The cabbage white: the original butterfly?

winged insects originated as caterpillars and that they went through a dormant stage – the pupa or chrysalis – before the butterfly emerged. (Yet he didn't know that butterflies laid eggs. He believed, as did everyone else for centuries to come, that caterpillars emerged miraculously from inanimate matter in the form of condensed dew). Presumably the Greeks thought that the life cycle of butterflies was akin to the journey of humans from cradle to grave and to the afterlife, which every Greek philosopher believed in. If the caterpillar was the equivalent of our earthly existence, the butterfly represented the spirit released from the body. That might explain *psuche*, the spirit-cum-butterfly.

Aristotle had no names at all for individual butterflies, although Pliny recognised the cabbage white. Until early modern times, insects seem to have been known by their group names. Aside from a few familiar species such as the cockchafer or the glow-worm or the firefly, beetles were just beetles. Bees were just bees, although the larger kinds could be distinguished as humblebees or bumblebees (most references to bees, however, are to just one species, the honeybee). Wasps were just wasps, or *wæps* in Old English, apart from the biggest kind, which was a *hynete* or hornet. Even butterflies were sometimes just 'flies' – because they flew. And moths were just moths, apart from the silk-moth, which was a bombyx.

In general, the oldest names were based on what the creatures do. Humblebees 'hum' over the meadow – Tennyson's 'murmur of innumerable bees', though the hum of midsummer is all too rarely heard now. 'Beetle' (*betel* in Old English) is derived from an old word meaning 'biter' – for biting is what beetles do, with a large and projecting pair of mandibles. An alternate beetle name was 'chafer', taken from a linguistic root meaning 'to chew or gnaw'; *Käfer* is still the German name for a beetle. Spiders spin webs to trap their prey; their name comes from another antique word meaning 'spinner'. 'Cricket' comes from the Old French *criquet*, in imitation of their most familiar characteristic: their chirp. 'Insect' comes from the Latin *in secare*, meaning 'cut into'. Insects have bodies divided into segments, rather like lego bricks.

Observant people must have been well aware that there was more than one kind of beetle or spider or butterfly. They would have seen with their own eyes how butterflies came in different colours and sizes, and that a small blue butterfly was obviously not the same thing as a giant swallowtail. People not only noticed butterflies but took delight in them too. The fourteenth-century chronicler Jean Froissart recalled how as a child he and his mates would catch butterflies, tie fine threads of flax to their bodies and stick the other end in their hats so that the butterflies would flutter around their heads like tiny living kites. Butterflies galore appear in the margins of medieval manuscripts, sometimes accurately depicted so that it is easy to recognise cabbage whites, clouded yellows, fritillaries and peacocks, among other species. The Red Admiral was a favourite, as it was with Dutch still-life artists later on. They would have been just as familiar to our distant ancestors, too. Perhaps they even had explanations for those eyes on the Peacock or the interesting blood-red bands on the Admiral.

We also find moths on the pages of old manuscripts, especially the colourful day-flying burnets and tiger-moths, and also the large Emperor Moth with four glaring eyes on its wings. Did some of these faithfully rendered moths and butterflies have folk names? (If so, they would probably have differed from place to place, like the eighty-odd recorded local names of woodlice). If such names existed, it was our bad luck that no one ever bothered to write them down. Maybe if the fathers of natural history such as Ulisse Aldrovandi in Bologna, or Conrad Gessner in Zurich, or even Edward Wotton at the court of Henry VIII, had paid more attention to the views of their countrymen and less to Aristotle or Pliny we might know what name they gave to the Red Admiral in Reformation England.

Such passing references as there are in pre-scientific texts are less concerned with biological truth than with moral instruction. A church congregation might be warned to beware the 'gilded' butterfly, for, just as pride comes before a fall, so chasing a butterfly might result in a broken leg (and serve you right). You were invited to observe the butterfly, clothed like Joseph in brilliant colours, but in truth worth nothing at all. Chaucer knew the phrase 'as worthless as a butterfly'. In his 'Nun's Priest's Tale', he mentions a butterfly, presumably a cabbage white, flitting over the vegetable garden, but its place in the narrative serves only to distract the cock,

The original moth: a clothes moth.

Chanticleer, while the fox jumps out and grabs it: another instance of how watching butterflies can lead to disaster.

We do know that Chaucer and his countrymen used the word 'butterfly' (or, in Middle English, *boterflye*, variously spelt). In fact it seems that much of northern Europe, whether in England or Holland or Germany, knew butterflies by that name. But what exactly does 'butterfly' mean? Is there a link between butterflies and butter, and if so, what is it? For centuries dictionary-makers have been guessing. For Samuel Johnson a butterfly was 'an insect which first appears in the season for butter' – that is, in the summer season when the grass is green and growing. Others suggested that 'butter' might be an allusion to a colour, perhaps the yellowish tint of some of the whites or the full-on yellow of the male Brimstone. As one of the first butterflies to appear in early spring, the Brimstone would also herald the 'butter season'. Or perhaps 'butterfly' was based on the old word *buda*, meaning a 'grub', and so, in effect, meant 'the fly that comes from a caterpillar'. Others have suggested it comes from *beatan*, Old English for 'to beat'; butterflies are 'flies' that beat their wings rather than buzz – the 'beat-flies'. I have also heard it suggested that the original word wasn't related to butter or bugs or beating but beauty: the 'beauty-flies', for butterflies are, after all, very comely. We can dismiss with a wave the suggestion that 'butterfly' is a rearrangement of 'flutterby'. True, butterflies do 'flutter by', but 'flutterby' is a modern word; a cheerful bit of spoonerism. 'Butterfly' isn't modern: Chaucer knew the word and so did Aelfric, who was writing Christian homilies during the reign of Aethelred the Unready.

Even when Aelfric was around, the butterfly, rendered in Old English as *butorfleoge*, was a familiar insect needing no further introduction. It reappears in Middle English, variously as *buterflie*, *butterflye*, *boterflye* or *buddeflye*, but in each case pronounced something close to 'butterfly'. The word first appears in its modern form in the work of the Elizabethan Thomas Moffet, as translated into English in 1658. 'Butterfly' is clearly, then, a word of deep antiquity. As to its meaning, no one bothered to explain, assuming anybody knew, but there are a few clues from etymology. In Low German (the dialect spoken in parts of northern Germany and Holland), butterflies are also *botterlicker*, or 'butter-lickers'. The name suggests that butterflies were attracted to fresh butter, slurping up fatty liquid exuding from the pat with their long, straw-like tongues. In Dutch, an earthy variant name is *boterschijte*: 'butter-shit', a libel on the butterfly, which scarcely shits at all (though caterpillars certainly do). There are further links to dairy products in the common German name for a butterfly, *Schmetterling*, from *Schmetter*, a dialect word for 'cream'. Still more suggestive is a folk name from southern Germany, *Milchdieb* or 'milk-thief'. It seems that people thought that butterflies were attracted to dairy products in general, whether milk, cream or butter. It does seem that white butterflies are indeed attracted to fresh milk in the pail, possibly by its colour, possibly by some attractive pheromone.

To understand why they were named 'butter-flies', we probably need to forget about the way we see them now, with all the advantages of knowledge and hindsight, and try to imagine how they might have seemed to a primitive, illiterate culture that knew almost nothing about them. The ancient tribes of northern Europe had every reason to fear the natural world. Insects were nearly always troublesome and, as possible agents of the devil, also fearsome. Knowing little, people suspected much. Why should butterflies have been any different? They might look pretty but what were they up to? Stealing milk or whey is one of the activities attributed to witches; they crept out at night in spirit form and robbed the honest farmer by tweaking the udders of his cows. If butterflies were suspected of doing the same thing, might they not be evil spirits in league with witches? Especially since these same butterflies came from grubs that attacked the poor crofter's kale and turnips.

On the evidence, I think that fear is the most likely explanation for the word 'butterfly'. The original butterfly was probably the one that bothers us most: the cabbage white. It was akin to the locust by damaging crops, and to witches by their unhealthy interest in milk and butter. Few insect names were coined in an affectionate spirit. People may have seen something fairylike in butterflies, but the fairies of the distant past were not carefree innocent beings. They were spirits from beyond, with secret powers and unknown, possibly malign, purpose. They were closer to our idea of ghosts. I think, therefore, that the word 'butterfly' originated as a term of abuse, rather like the names of the first political parties, the Tories and the Whigs, or the Roundheads and the Cavaliers – or, for that matter, the Suffragettes.

What about the moth? Does that name have a kinder meaning? No indeed, though here we are on firmer ground. The original moth, the moth of the Bible, was the

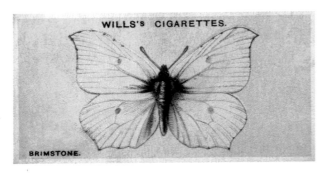

A butter-coloured butterfly: the Brimstone as featured on the Wills cigarette cards 'British Butterflies', 1927.

clothes moth, and not so much the winged adult (which does not feed) but its tiny grub. Everyone suffered from that kind of moth, from the king in his palace to the peasant on his patch. In ancient texts the moth seems less a living entity than a corrosive force. 'Thou makest his beauty to consume away like a moth' (Psalms 39:11). 'Lay not up for yourselves treasures upon earth, where moth and rust doth corrupt,' teaches Jesus (Matthew 6:19). In the Book of Job, the moth appears like some awful devouring spirit. What is man, Job is told, compared with the might of God. Man dwells in houses of mere clay, 'whose foundation is in the dust, which are crushed before the moth' (Job 4:19). The metaphor is about the reduction of something precious to dust and nothingness.

The Hebrew word for a moth and its larva, rendered as sh/v or 'ash', comes from a root meaning 'to fall away'. In the Greek New Testament the word is transliterated as 'ses', a name that survives in Latin as *sesia*, and, as Sesiidae, is now the family of the wholly innocent clearwing moths. The word 'moth' itself originated, like 'butterfly', in the Germanic languages of northern Europe, whether rendered as the Old English *motthe*, or the German *motte*, or the Old Norse *motti*. The earliest form of the English word was spelt with a letter known as a thorn, a hard 'th' as in 'this', and so *motthe* was pronounced rather like 'mother' but with a short 'o'. (This word-form has recently returned: latterday moth recorders often refer to themselves as 'mothers', though with a soft 'th'.) 'Moth' shares the same root word as 'maggot' and possibly 'midge'. It was not, obviously, a word born from a love of nature.

In pre-scientific times, a moth could be almost any small pest that chewed up domestic items. It was named not so much for what it was as for what it did. Hence in Thomas Moffet's *Theatre of Insects*, first written in Latin in the 1590s, the 'moths' included crickets, bookworms and even 'Moths called Blattae', or cockroaches. The clothes moth appears in that text as 'the Garment-eating Moth'. And the medieval tradition of using the natural world as a source of Christian homilies still continued. Moffet urged his readers to 'think himself to be like a garment that Moths eat,' for then he would surely 'lay aside all pride, and blush, and fall lowly upon his knees unto Almighty God.' In other words, moths taught us humility. No doubt that was why God had created them. (Thomas Moffet, it might be worth adding, was a Puritan.)

The clear distinction between butterflies and moths is peculiarly English. In German a *Schmetterling* or a *Falter* can be either, even though it is usually translated as 'butterfly'. It is the same in Dutch, where all of the Lepidoptera are encompassed by the word *vlinder*. In French they are *papillons*, although moths can be differentiated as *papillons de nuit*. These names are fully justified by science, for butterflies are in truth just one group within the much larger order of scaly-winged insects, the Lepidoptera, albeit a very distinctive one. Even in England before Linnaeus and his followers got to work on insect orders, little distinction was made between butterflies and the larger and more colourful moths. They were all 'papilios'. One is reminded of that other peculiarly English practice of differentiating mushrooms from toadstools. On the continent they are all one and the same, whether as *champignons*, *pilze* or *funghi*.

A FOOTNOTE ON ANCIENT BUTTERFLIES

I am told by a leading scholar of ancient Greek texts that no one ever mentioned butterflies before Aristotle – not once, despite the rich surviving literature of plays and histories and philosophies. This, surely, is surprising. Greek writers from Homer onwards mention many other forms of nature: birds, seasons, flowers, fish, even insects such as bees and cicadas. Butterflies would have been familiar inhabitants of this world, and indeed Greece has one of the richest butterfly faunas in all Europe; they must have been even more abundant in the distant past, when there was far more undeveloped land. Butterflies would have been impossible to ignore. When, in about 340 BC, Aristotle came to describe the butterfly's progression from caterpillar to emergent flying insect, he was evidently setting out some familiar, readily observed facts. So why didn't his equally learned predecessors, who included Homer, Hesiod and Plato, ever mention butterflies?

In his wonderful *Birds in the Ancient World*, Jeremy Mynott runs through some possible explanations, only to dismiss them one by one. Were there fewer butterflies back then? Unlikely. Did butterflies enter the literature but in disguise, as 'little birds' for instance? Also unlikely. The Greeks had a perfectly good word for butterflies – *psuche*. Or perhaps the Greeks did in fact write about butterflies but only in texts that have been lost. That isn't very likely either. The mountain of literature that does survive suggests that, for whatever reason, butterflies were simply not on the literary agenda.

Why is that? The most plausible explanation is that butterflies were in some way a taboo subject. That they were perhaps seen as 'spiritual' is suggested by their Greek name, *psuche*, which, as we have seen, is the same as their word for 'soul' or 'spirit'. However, Mynott is sceptical of this explanation, as the Greeks did not seem at all inhibited about discussing anything. They were too rational to have taboos. Comic writers such as Aristophanes made fun of all sorts of sensitive issues: religion, sex, family, race, politics. Xenophon went so far as to suggest that *psuche* would make a good name for a dog!

So the mystery remains. We can be sure that butterflies were familiar, but are forced to assume that, cabbage whites aside, they did not impinge much on human affairs. Ancient people were practical. Things with names usually had a use, or at least had an impact on human lives. Bees were useful; clothes moths were actively harmful. Butterflies, as Chaucer reminded us, are useless. Yes, they are pretty, but their attractiveness is merely aesthetic. They could be enjoyed without requiring knowledge – or names. The one group name they had was quite sufficient: *psuche*, or, in Latin, *papilio*, or our English *butterfly*. No one bothered to explain those names either.

The Theatre of Insects

The first published work in English on creatures without backbones was the *Theatrum Insectorum* by Thomas Moffet. Actually to say it was 'by' Moffet is an oversimplification. Much of the work had been amassed by two slightly earlier English naturalists, Edward Wotton (1492–1555) and Thomas Penny (1532–89). In fact the whole work might well have been completed by Penny had he not died and left the manuscript in Moffet's hands. Penny in turn had borrowed material and anecdotes from the Swiss naturalist Conrad Gessner (1516–65). In truth, the *Theatrum* was a composite work, a compilation which Moffet edited in his best Latin (its vivid language may well be his personal contribution). Moffet spelt his own name in as many ways as his contemporaries spelt 'butterfly': Moufet, Mouffet, Moffat. His name was probably pronounced as '*muff*-ett', as in 'Little Miss Muffet sat on a tuffet.' Some believe that the original Miss Muffet was Thomas's daughter Prudence. And that the rhyme originated as a satire on Moffet's interest in silk and spiders.

The version of the *Theatrum* available to scholars who lacked Latin is a translation by Edward Topsell that was eventually published in 1658, half a century after Moffet's death. It forms part of a larger work called *The History of Four-Footed Beasts and Serpents*, a 1,130-page treatise on all the known living animals, of which pages 889 to 1,130 are devoted to the 'Insects or lesser living Creatures'. There are pictures and brief descriptions of roughly half the British butterflies, plus a scattering of moths. In the published work these are woodcuts, not a medium that allows much detail; they are based on far superior watercolour paintings that have never been reproduced in print. The watercolours are pasted into Moffet's manuscript (now in the British Library). I have examined it and discovered to my surprise that

Moffet's woodcut of the Privet Hawk-moth's 'chief Caterpillar which hangs upon the Privet'.

nearly all the specimens depicted in these watercolour images are easily identifiable. Whoever painted them must have had actual specimens to copy from.

Turning the pages of the *Theatrum* one finds a whole chapter devoted to butterflies, which in Moffet's sense included some of the larger moths. Despite the crudity of the woodcut illustrations, it is easy to recognise the Swallowtail, Red Admiral, Peacock, Brimstone, Clouded Yellow, Small Tortoiseshell and Comma among the true butterflies, and the Emperor, Oak Eggar, Leopard Moth and various tiger-moths and hawk-moths among the moths. There are separate chapters on caterpillars, divided into silkworms, which were Moffet's special interest, plus 'smooth worms' and 'rough and hairy' ones. Once again the hawk-moths are well represented, along with the unmistakable caterpillars of the Puss Moth, Emperor and the 'bear-worm' of the Garden Tiger-moth. The Lobster Moth caterpillar is there too, but in a different chapter, for Moffet thought that this grotesque beast was some kind of beetle.

Moffet's winged 'butterflies' and crawling caterpillars are in separate chapters, as if they were separate forms of life. He would have been aware that caterpillars change into butterflies, but he did not seem to know which caterpillars turned into which butterflies; or at least he made no such connections in the *Theatrum*.

Moffet described his butterflies vividly, in language reminiscent of Shakespeare. He clearly admired them, but he had no names for them. The few individualised names he did mention belong not to the adult insects but to their caterpillars. He knew the big, fleshy caterpillars of hawk-moths as 'horn worms', from the prominent spike on the caterpillar's tail. In northern England, he noted, hairy, wandering caterpillars were known as 'oubuts', whereas in the south they were 'palmer-worms', for they could be encountered whilst walking on beaten paths, like palmers or poor pilgrims. Palmer-worms, continued Moffet, had no dwelling place but 'pass on boldly, and taste of all plants and trees and feed where they please.'

INSECTORVM
SIVE
Minimorum Animalium
THEATRVM:
Olim ab
EDOARDO WOTTONO.
CONRADO GESNERO.
THOMAQVE PENNIO
inchoatum:
Tandem
THO. MOVFETI Londinâtis operâ sumptibusq; maximis concinnatum,
auctum, perfectum :
Et ad vivum expressis Iconibus suprà quingentis illustratum.

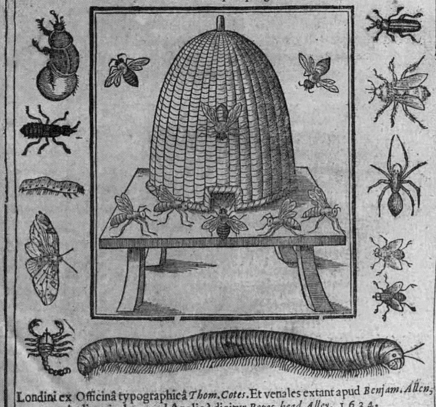

Title page of *The Theatre of Insects* published in 1658 as part of Edward Topsell's *History of Four-footed Beasts and Serpents.*

Londini ex Officinâ typographicâ *Thom. Cotes.* Et venales extant apud *Benjam. Allen,* in diverticulo, quod Anglicè dicitur *Popes-head Alley.* 1634.

'My word, what a lovely Caterpillar!'
Woodcut of the Puss Moth caterpillar
in Moffet's *Theatre of Insects*.

Of course, he knew the word 'caterpillar', which is a folk name that originates from the Norman-French word *chatepelose*, or 'hairy cat'. Cats were the model for all kinds of fluffy, hairy things, such as the catkins of the pussy willow. Not all caterpillars are hairy, but those that are tend to steal the show. Perhaps the original *chatepelose* was the 'woolly bear' of the Garden Tiger-moth. Another French word for caterpillar is *chenille*, a hairy dog. In English the same word describes a kind of thick, fluffy yarn – yarn that, in other words, looks a bit like a caterpillar!

Moffet greatly admired the strange caterpillar of the Puss Moth, which he called *Vinula* (it is the same caterpillar that sits on a mushroom smoking a hookah in *Alice's Adventures in Wonderland*). '*Elegans mehercule Eruca et supra fidem speciosa,*' he wrote: 'By Jove, an elegant caterpillar and handsome beyond belief!' *Vinula* was named after vines, or rather their product, wine, and the name refers to the reddish saddle-shaped marking on the creature's back. Moffet had found the thing on a willow branch, 'feeding greedily'. But he did not illustrate the adult moth; perhaps his *Vinula* caterpillar died before it could complete its cycle.

He also knew *Porcellus*, the little pig, the caterpillar of the elephant hawk-moth. Moffet probably meant the Small Elephant Hawk-moth, for he found this little pig 'feeding on the leaves of the meadow Trefoil [ie clover], devouring them with wonderful swiftness'; the larger Elephant Hawk-moth prefers to feed on willowherb. Both *Vinula* and *Porcellus* are still the scientific names of these moths four hundred years later, for Linnaeus had consulted Moffet and decided to keep his names.

Another old name is *Cossus*, which Moffet borrowed for the large and plump caterpillar of the Goat Moth (*see* Goats in the A to Z). He might have got it from a remarkable 'stinking Caterpillar' described by Conrad Gessner, which, when angry, 'sent forth a filthy smell' and raised its forefeet threateningly into the air. He also mentions *Pityocampes* or 'the pine-caterpillar', which spins a silken nest in the trees

Opposite: Small Tortoiseshell and Dark Green Fritillary, watercolours commissioned by Thomas Moffet around 1590. These are among the first reasonably accurate pictures of British butterflies.

gratiorem reddunt ━━━━ intus vero maculis nigerrimis, scutis

effigiem imitantibus foedantur Verùm sicut foris nimius speciosa, ita inte-

rior internarum alarum pars, albo vivore nitens, guttulis vero argen-

teis superinductis resplendet: et quæ extra ovales margaritæ videbantur,

intus argentum purum putum non mentiuntur.

11ª. speciosam radiantium in cærulo margaritarum insititam ostentat. alæ

superiores ex flammeo flauescentes ignem referunt, seu nigerrimis pannis

infecta internarum radix anthracina, deinde flauo in igneum corus-

cant. corpus fuscis capillamentis hirsutum, quem colorem cornicula

cum pedibus imitantur.

12ª. eximiæ et pulcritudinis: ale leuiter cruenta et maculis nigris tinctæ,

radiolis micant aureis filatim ad lacinis usq ambitum dispsis. hæc vero

xerampelina serratim desinens, intus aureis lineis lunatim ductis orna-

tur Corpus ex nigro purpurascei oculi aurei videntur, pedes

&c.

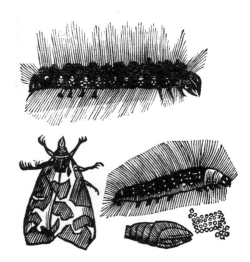

Woodcut of the woolly bear caterpillar from Moffet's *Theatre*: 'The bear-worm will not be tied to any kind of flowers or leaves, but they pass on boldly, and taste of all plants and trees and feed where they please.'

'like spiders, drawing and disposing their threads with their forefeet'. Today we know it as the Pine Processionary Moth, named from the caterpillars' habit of following-my-leader down the trunk to pupate on the ground. *Pityocampes*, too, is an ancient name dating back two millennia to the works of Galen and Pliny, and *pityocampa* is the moth's species name to this day. It is a southern European species with only a few records from Britain. Again, Moffet was probably drawing his information from Conrad Gessner or Ulisse Aldrovandi.

Moffet mentions receiving two different caterpillars from across the Channel which he calls *Neustriae*, from Neustria, the ancient name for northern France. From his picture and description, one of them is The Lackey moth, which still bears the species name of *neustria*. The other one, which has curious tufts of long, stiff, black hairs, he calls the 'sayl-yard', or, at another point, 'the Pensill'. It appears to be the caterpillar of the Vapourer Moth.

With the same idea of naming a species after its supposed foodplant, the caterpillar of the Emperor Moth became Moffet's 'Cranesbill-eater', though nowadays it prefers heather and hawthorn to 'the Crowfoot Cranesbill in the Marishes' – whatever that may have been.

Moffet's 'Cabbage Catterpiller' is unmistakably the Large White butterfly. According to him, the thing was 'venomous' (that is, poisonous), and Moffet recounts a story (which he got from Gessner) of a woman who, after accidentally eating a handful of the caterpillars with her cabbage, immediately vomited and suffered painful swellings in her belly. Moffet also knew the spiky 'nettle caterpillar' of the Peacock butterfly, which supposedly had a sting 'hard to be endured'. He distinguished that one from another spiky one which he called 'the Urchin Catterpiller', that is, the Hedgehog Caterpillar. To judge from the illustrations, they are the caterpillars of the Small Tortoiseshell and the Comma. Less easy to identify are Moffet's 'Bramble Catterpiller', his 'Nut-tree Catterpiller, Corylaria', and 'St John's Wort Catterpiller'. These were simply caterpillars he had found feeding on those plants.

Yet despite naming these few caterpillars, neither Thomas Moffet nor his informant Thomas Penny knew any names for adult butterflies or moths, with the possible exception of the 'cabbage white'. But, as in ancient Greece, the woods, meadows and river banks of Tudor England must have teemed with butterflies; and on summer nights you would hardly be able to light a candle without attracting a moth. Without names there could be no real progress: no record-keeping, no serious study, perhaps not even much conversation except in the most general terms. Even Shakespeare mentioned butterflies only occasionally, and only in a moralistic way. Presumably they all felt that what was good enough for Aristotle was good enough for them. They did not seem all that interested in finding out more.

In these early days no distinction was made between butterflies and moths. Apart from the tiniest ones, they were all 'butterflies' or 'papilios'. But night-flying moths were also known by folk names such as 'owls' or 'buzzards', or, perhaps by the more educated, as 'phalenes' or *phalenae* (in his *Natural History of Selborne*, Gilbert White referred to night-flying moths as *phalenae*). The latter name comes from an old French word meaning, in effect, 'the shining ones' from the way the flying moths shine in reflected light. The word 'moth' was still reserved for that least prepossessing creature, the clothes moth.

Pap. fusco Albo & Rubro maculati.

M.F. 315. Tab. 4. f. 1 & 2. Smal. Teckadou

1384. 85

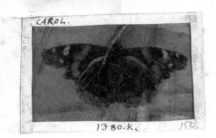

CAROL.

1380. K. 152

1380.

M. PET. 327. Tab. 2. f. XI. English

admiral. 1380.g. 192

1378. a. 36

1380. i.

MARYL. american. 152

Pap. Oculati.

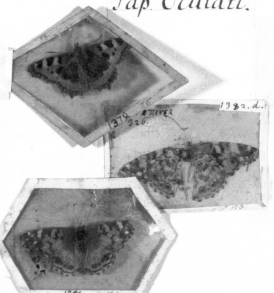

1378. 36. 326.

ANTIVER

1382. d.

1385. 154

1407. 173.

At last! Naming begins

For nearly a century after the death of Thomas Moffet in 1604, butterflies and moths were only individualised in a few learned tomes, and not with proper names but with short Latin tags. These might have been helpful to scholars, but they were obviously not intended for field use or everyday discourse. The first printed text to list all the British butterflies known at the time was the *Pinax Rerum Naturalium Britannicarum* (*Tablet of Nature in Britain*) by Christopher Merret (c.1614–95), a tract of all the living species and geological specimens then known. Merret was a physician; a difficult man apparently, and prone to melancholy. He had the terrible bad luck to place his *Pinax* in the hands of a London bookseller just in time for the Great Fire of 1666, in the course of which the entire first edition went up in smoke.

Merret knew about twenty kinds of butterfly, much the same ones as Moffet. The most intriguing was one whose wings were said to be *externis purpurascentibus* – 'becoming purple at the edges' – which does not fit any known British butterfly but does suggest the Continental Purple-edged Copper. Did it once occur here, or (more likely) had Merrett got in a muddle? Today Christopher Merret is better known for his observations on glassmaking, and for his notable discovery that adding sugar to fermenting wine produces a sparkle suitable for weddings and other celebrations.

And so on to a much greater English naturalist, John Ray (1627–1705). Ray brought to natural history a new and deeper sense of enquiry allied to a resolute determination to find order amid the chaos of nature. He found ways of classifying forms of plant and animal life by shared characteristics that strongly influenced

Opposite: James Petiver's collection of specimens mounted between sheets of mineral mica. In a sense these were the *original* Admirals, Peacocks and Painted Ladies, specimens taken by the man who first used these names.

Engraving of John Ray based
on a contemporary portrait.

Linnaeus three-quarters of a century later. But Ray was primarily a botanist. He came to insects late in life, and his main work, the Latin *History of Insects* (based partly on notes from Ray's deceased companion Francis Willughby) was left unfinished at his death (it was published posthumously in 1710). Ray could at least claim to be the first person to distinguish between a butterfly and a moth. The former not only flew by day but possessed a 'sure and characteristic mark' in their clubbed antennae. Ray's classification of British butterflies was less surefooted. He listed twenty-nine kinds, arranged by colour. He began with butterflies with yellow or yellow-and-black wings and proceeded through the whites, then those with a reddish background, including the fritillaries, followed by the browns and finally those with dusky or black wings – which resulted in the Purple Emperor seated uneasily next to the Grizzled Skipper.

Ray described more than two hundred kinds of moths – far more than Moffet or Merret had – but since they are not illustrated, and we only have his short Latin tags to go on, they are not all easy to identify. He obtained many of the specimens locally, at his home at Braintree in Essex. Ray's band of helpers included his four daughters. 'My little daughters caught many of this species flying at dusk in our garden,' he would write of a moth which, years later, would be called the Burnished Brass. His daughters' own names are found in Katherine's Oak-Geometer (possibly the Lunar Thorn) and Jane's Chickweed Caterpillar (not identified). His third daughter Margaret found for him a marvellously pretty green-and-black moth, later named the Merveille du Jour. His wife helped him to rear the Peppered Moth from its sticklike caterpillar, and they marvelled at how quickly the newly emerged moth, a female, attracted the attention of two males.

Ray had one clear advantage over Thomas Moffet. Moffet had depended on the teachings of Aristotle and other classical authors, plus a bit of updating from a handful of Renaissance scholars, and not much else. Since then the Dutch scholar Jan Swammerdam had demonstrated beyond any reasonable doubt that caterpillar, chrysalis or pupa, and winged insect were all stages in the life of the same creature. Insects did not, as previous generations had supposed, spring to life out of inanimate muck but from an egg laid by a parent. As Benjamin Wilkes phrased it a century later, the butterfly, like us, 'partakes the Toys of Love'. The 'pregnant female,' added Wilkes, 'with unerring Sagacity lays her eggs under secure Concealment, where the Infant Brood may find as soon as hatch'd, immediate and proper Sustenance.' The discovery that humans and butterflies have things in common, such as lust and maternal instinct, perhaps made them more appealing than if they were mere products of 'spontaneous generation'.

It was also becoming clear that 'butterfly' consisted of many entities, each with different life cycles and diets. The new name for an entity was a species, and John Ray himself produced a working definition of what that was: a self-perpetuating unit of life. The Scotch fir, the codfish and the human being, for instance, were species. Butterflies and moths, on the other hand, were not: each consisted of a great many species. Even so, butterflies and moths were an identifiable group, an order of insects with coloured wings made up of tiny scales. Later on they would acquire a name: the Lepidoptera, or 'scale-winged insects'. Ray reckoned that there must be at least several hundred species of butterflies and moths in the world. In fact there are, so far, about 180,000. In Britain there are about 2,500 species of moths but only 70 of butterflies.

Ray also had an answer ready for those who asked (as it seemed they did), 'What is the use of butterflies?' 'I reply,' wrote Ray, 'to adorn the world and delight the eyes of men: to brighten the countryside like so many golden jewels. To contemplate their exquisite beauty and variety is to experience the truest pleasure. To gaze enquiringly at such elegance of colour and form devised by the ingenuity of nature and painted by her artist's pencil is to acknowledge and adore the imprint of the art of God.' In other words, butterflies were an inspiration.

Like Merret, Ray individualised his nameless butterflies with short tags. His Ringlet is easily recognisable as the 'Butterfly, middle-sized, all dusky, the undersides of the wings marked with eyes' – though he wrote that in Latin. Nor could one easily mistake the 'Butterfly, small with white upper wings marked with bright orange' – soon to be known as the Orange-tip. This habit of using labels or tags instead of proper names persisted for a long time. As late as 1740, the Austrian naturalist and artist Johann Rösel von Rosenhof was labelling his beautifully illustrated butterflies and moths, and their caterpillars, with short descriptions, beginning with a 'big social thorn caterpillar with gold-red spots'.

Fortunately, proper English names were soon on the way. It was James Petiver (c.1665–1718) who, at long last, decided to label his specimens with names people could remember and use in records and conversation. It took him a little time to get there. Petiver was first and foremost a collector of natural objects. Among many other things he collected butterflies and moths, both on expeditions with friends around London and from specimens brought to him by the crews of trading ships. From his jumbled home museum near the Barbican, he made a practice of listing and illustrating items from Britain and around the world in printed catalogues, which he first called *Centuries* (because they each contained a hundred objects) and later called *Gazophylacia*, or 'treasure-chests'. He found ways of obtaining and preserving natural objects which were then novel. In the case of butterflies this meant mounting the dead insect with outspread wings between transparent sheets of mica. The result looked a bit like an old photographic slide with a butterfly in the middle. It was at least one up on the previous practice of squashing them flat in a book, like pressed plants.

Petiver's first bash at common names were variations on Ray's Latin labels. The Gatekeeper butterfly entered history as 'the Hedge Eye with double Specks'. The Wall was 'the golden marbled Butterfly, with black Eyes'. Species new to the collection tended to carry the name of the person who procured them. Thus the Dingy Skipper became 'Handley's small brown Butterfly' and the Grizzled Skipper 'Dandridge's midling black Fritillary'. The first Purple Hairstreak became 'Mr Ray's purple Streak'. Where Petiver had himself procured the specimen, it became 'ours', as in 'Our Half-mourner', now the Marbled White, 'taken in a wood near Hampstead'. His first Swallowtail was caught, improbably if appropriately, in the Royal Garden at St James 'by my ingenious friend Mr Tilleman Bobart' in 1699. Petiver named it The Royal William, after the reigning king, William III, perhaps in the hope of his patronage.

Nonetheless, Petiver was the first to use certain words that are still found in the names of butterflies, despite their archaic nature. He possibly coined the word 'hairstreak' (originally spelt with a hyphen) for small, dark butterflies with a white line running along the length of their underwings. I have held in my hands Petiver's own specimen of the Brown Hairstreak, a female which he called 'Our Golden Hairstreak', obtained from the London area in 1704. He also came up with the word 'argus' for small butterflies with numerous little eyespots set into their wings. Those with larger eyespots became, simply, 'eyes', as in his 'Brown Meadow-eye', known today as the Meadow Brown. Petiver was also the first to use the word 'fritillary' in print for the pretty dappled butterflies that abounded in the woods and heaths around London.

Many of Petiver's invented names, such as his variously coloured, spotted or 'speckt' butterflies, were seldom seen again outside his catalogues. But at least one of them deserved a better fate. 'Hog' was his inventive name for the Small and Large Skipper. The bodies of these plump little butterflies are undeniably porcine, with their beady eyes and plump, hairy bodies. Petiver might have pronounced the word ''og', for he refers somewhere to 'an hog'. The flying pigs had only a brief life. The skipping flight of the butterflies attracted someone's eye, and so they became 'skippers'.

The most intriguing of Petiver's names are those which diverge from his usual formulae and sound like folk names. They include the Admiral (later the Red Admiral) and the Lesser and Greater Tortoiseshells. He also introduced the Brimstone in the first of his *Gazophylacia*, printed in 1699. More surprisingly, he named a much less conspicuous butterfly the Small Heath, a name it carries to this day. Another was the Comma, although Petiver thought there was not one but three different species, which he distinguished as the Silver, Pale and Jagged-winged Commas (they correspond to different forms of this twin-brooded species). Apart from the Small Heath and the Greater Tortoiseshell, which was clearly much commoner then than now, these are all common, brightly coloured butterflies that visit gardens. They are the butterflies that people first came to notice.

How long people may have called them admirals and tortoiseshells and painted ladies is anyone's guess. The Admiral was known by the same name in other countries too, such as Holland and Sweden. The name Tortoiseshell is unlikely to date from before Petiver's lifetime, since objects made of tortoiseshell had only recently been imported to Britain. It made a perfect name for butterflies with similarly variegated orange-and-black colours.

Petiver's last word on butterflies was published in pamphlet form in 1717 as *Papilionum Britanniae icones, nomina*, or *Pictures and Names of British Butterflies*.

James Petiver's 'Golden Hairstreak': a female Brown Hairstreak 'taken by B. Harris near Croydon, August 1702'.

It is a highly creditable effort, recording more than eighty different butterflies, although many of them are males and females of the same species. His copperplate engravings of specimens, both at rest and with outspread wings, are the first decent illustrations of British butterflies, and most are easily identifiable even without Petiver's helpful text alongside. Each one is given Ray's Latin tag, followed by Petiver's English name, with a few remarks about the butterfly's appearance and habits, and an index to its page in the works of Moffet and Ray. The Admiral, for instance, is categorised as 'a beautiful Fly, and eminently distinguished [with] a red Last cross [in] the upper Wing'. He adds that it is 'often seen in Gardens and Fields from the End of July till Autumn'.

Table 1 (*see* page 230–2) is the full list of butterflies in the *Papilionum Britanniae*. It will be noticed that only a few bear today's common names: White Admiral, Brown Hairstreak (though only the male butterfly was called that). Others, however, such as Tunbridge Grayling and Brown Meadow-eye, are close to their modern equivalents. Confusingly, Petiver's 'Small Tortoiseshell' is today's Small Copper; the actual Small Tortoiseshell was his 'Lesser or Common Tortoiseshell'.

For all their imperfections, Petiver's names set a precedent. He was not the only learned gentleman to take an interest in butterflies and moths. The names of at least twenty contemporary enthusiasts are known. Lepidoptera were coming into fashion, and people had begun to rear them from caterpillars, to catch them with homemade nets, and to proudly display their collections in attractive patterns. This first generation of butterfly people forms an interesting cross-section of educated, middle-class society at the time. Petiver himself was an apothecary, a peddler of herbal potions and drugs, and was in charge of the Chelsea Physic Garden. His friends and acquaintances included an Eton schoolmaster, Robert Antrobus (uncle of the poet Thomas Gray), several clergymen and physicians, various artists and silk-pattern designers, and others in the cloth or silk trade. Among them were three Fellows of the Royal Society: John Ray, the physician David Kreig, and the natural philosopher William Derham, as well as Petiver himself. Among them is a lone woman, the renowned Eleanor Glanville, whose name is remembered in the Glanville Fritillary, a butterfly she discovered on a visit to Lincoln (*see* Glanville in the A to Z).

What caused this sudden interest in butterflies? It was in part a burgeoning interest in science, a curiosity about the natural world and its phenomena encouraged by the Royal Society. Men like David Kreig were deeply interested in chemistry, in forecasting the weather, and in the revelations of botany both in Britain and abroad. They were, in a sense, the new Renaissance men, the scholars of new learning. But butterflies and moths seem to have had a peculiar appeal to contemporary artists and designers. Their patterns and colours were an obvious inspiration, and added to that were their miraculous 'transformations' that could be studied at home by finding caterpillars and rearing them through. Collecting natural objects was in fashion, and once the means were found to preserve butterflies and moths in lifelike postures, they held a fascination hitherto confined to shells, fossils and stuffed birds. Butterflies also appealed strongly to gardeners, especially those in charge of botanic gardens, or those wealthy enough to afford a fashionable glass conservatory. Flowers and butterflies went naturally together, linked not only by mutual dependence but by beauty.

It was only a matter of time before this growing interest, and all the talk it must have engendered, would be formalised into a society. James Petiver's pamphlets provided the means to identify known species of butterflies and larger moths. But the growth of the first entomological society began elsewhere. If it is possible to pinpoint a moment when amateur entomology began, it happened not in the universities, nor in the great institutions such as the Royal Society, but in the coffee shops and taverns of the City of London. There, amid the steaming pots and flowing tankards, men discussed the wonderful new world of insects, and slowly the swarms and flutterings of creatures in the mass transmuted into individualised, identifiable beings with names.

Enter the Artists

Butterflies needed a champion. As early as the sixteenth century, Dutch artists were incorporating butterflies and moths into their compositions, rarely as the main subject but shown realistically, fluttering and settling on gorgeous arrangements of flowers and fruit. The butterflies were accurately depicted and recognisable – Red Admirals and Large Whites were among the favourites. Sometimes they seemed to carry moral messages: red for danger or sin, white for innocence and Christian virtue, in an ironic reversal of the butterflies' real habits. These painted butterflies were never named. Perhaps they did not yet have names.

There were also artists – just a few – who painted insects as objects of interest in themselves. Georg Hoefnagel painted all kinds of bugs for Emperor Rudolf of Austria in the 1590s, and so realistically that they practically crawl or fly off the page. But the first artist to paint the life cycles of butterflies and moths, with their caterpillars posed on the correct plants, was the remarkable Maria Sibylla Merian (1647–1717). The art critic Andrew Graham-Dixon called her 'the godmother of modern scientific illustration'. The German-born Merian had been fascinated by insects since she was a girl. The full 'transformation' of butterflies and moths from egg to crawling caterpillar, and on to winged insect, had been demonstrated only recently, and therefore had the bonus of novelty (it enabled the poet and dramatist John Gay to define a butterfly as 'but a caterpillar drest'). Another incentive was that, as a woman, Merian was forbidden by the guilds to paint in oils. Despite her obvious talent, she was therefore unable to set up as a painter of portraits or standard

Opposite: A plate from Maria Merian's *Metamorphosis of the Insects of Suriname* (1705) showing two species of hawk-moths, known in the New World as Sphinxes: the Vine Sphinx and the Satellite Sphinx, and their early stages. Merian was the first artist to show butterflies and moths in accurate, lifelike poses, together with their correct larval foodplants.

Engraving of Maria Merian in old age.

still-life compositions. Instead she turned to watercolour and practised her skill on flowers and caterpillars, and finally in her most famous work – the pictures that put her own portrait on a 500 Deutsche Mark note – the *Metamorphosis or Transformations of the Insects of Suriname*.

Merian's 'long dreamed of' journey to South America was facilitated by the Mayor of Amsterdam, who owned a large collection of stuffed animals and preserved insects from both the West and East Indies. The gorgeous butterflies of the tropics were starting to reach Europe via commerce and trade, and there were already wealthy private collectors who would pay good money for birdwings, morphos and other fine specimens. Maria sailed for Surinam in 1699; by the time of her return two years later, she had the materials for a large folio volume of coloured engravings based on drawings made from life. The plates of her *Metamorphosis* illustrate the life cycles of 186 species of insects, especially butterflies, along with a wild assortment of spiders, frogs, lizards and other creatures. But more important than the content was Merian's technique. Her pictures borrow something from the formal compositions of Dutch still-life artists, except that in her case the life is never 'still'. Her insects buzz and flutter and crawl. Even the plants on which they settle and feed seem alive, with the coiled tendrils of her passion flowers matching the curly tails of her lizards and chameleons. These pictures made a great impression in England as well as in Holland. They raised the status of insects from petty annoyances to exotic wonders. King George III bought a complete coloured set of her engravings. So did Sir Hans Sloane, the foremost English collector of the age.

The Large White butterfly plate from Eleazar Albin's *A Natural History of English Insects*, published in 1720, was 'humbly dedicated' to Caroline of Anspach, Princess of Wales and the future Queen. No irony was intended. Maybe the Princess just liked white butterflies.

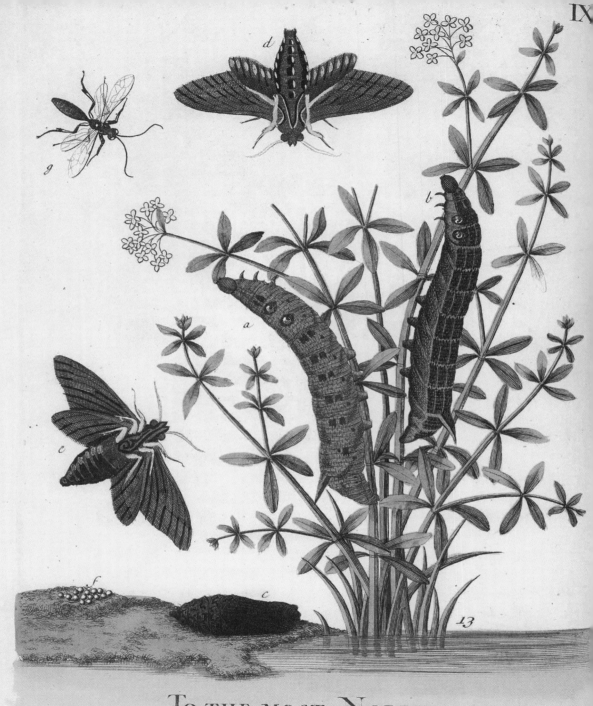

IX

TO THE MOST NOBLE
Mary Dutchess of Ormond
this plate is humbly dedicated by Eleazar Albin.

E. Albin del.

JJ. Seniſson, Sculp. London 1712.

Merian seems to have inspired another ambitious, German-born artist, who, after immigrating to England, changed his name from Weiss to Albin: Eleazar Albin. A jobbing painter with a growing family to support, Albin would not have turned to natural history as a subject unless it was likely to prove profitable. As it was, he embarked on an ambitious plan to illustrate British insects, especially butterflies and moths, in all their stages. He sold his coloured engravings as 'fascicles' of plates that could be bound into book form. Albin's *A Natural History of English Insects* was published in 1720, and introduced the public to the glories of our own insects.

Looking through Albin's hundred coloured plates, 'curiously engraved from life', two things strike you. One is that every plate has a patron, among them a large number of titled men and

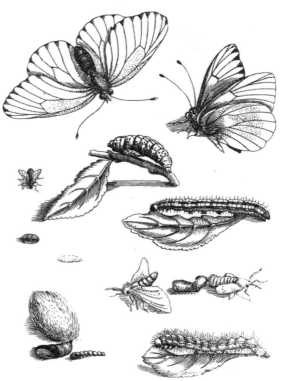

Merian's drawing of the Black-veined White butterfly, its early stages and its parasites: a comprehensive portrait made in c.1670, though not published until 1717.

women (the Princess of Wales got the cabbage white) and an equally impressive number of Fellows of the Royal Society. Clearly insects were already sufficiently in fashion for aristocrats and intellectuals to underwrite Albin's project. Interesting, too, is that many of his subscribers were women. Albin paid particular tribute to the Duchess of Beaufort, who had encouraged him to embark on the project. The cost of the hand-coloured edition was three guineas (£600 in today's money) with

Opposite: Albin's Elephant Hawk-moth, also from *A Natural History of English Insects*, shows its life cycle along with an ichneumon wasp parasite, suggesting that he had reared the moth. If so, he unfortunately illustrated the wrong foodplant: the caterpillar feeds on willowherb, not bedstraw as shown.

The mysterious 'Albin's Hampstead Eye', engraved by Petiver.

half down and the other half paid on delivery.

The other thing is their quality. Albin engraved and coloured his butterflies and moths with an exacting eye, and they were easily the most impressive depictions of English insects so far. However, he had names for only a few of his butterflies and moths. His notes occasionally hint at a name – often the one the insect would ultimately assume. A moth 'with a double spot of a Yellowish White like a Figure of Eight' would soon become the Figure of Eight moth. A mighty caterpillar with 'Flaps or Lappets on every Joint' would morph into The Lappet. Another that 'came at the latter End of December' was later called the December Moth.

Yet the butterfly Albin is most remembered for was probably a mistake. Among those that are drawn and labelled in Petiver's *Papilionum Britanniae* is one called Albin's Hampstead Eye. It sits next to another eyed butterfly, the Peacock, along with a note that it had been caught on Hampstead Heath 'by this Curious Person [Albin], and is the only one I have yet seen'. ('Curious' in this sense meant 'enquiring', not 'odd'.) The specimen, which amazingly still survives, is known today as *Junonia villida*, the Meadow Argus, but it is an Indo-Australian insect and does not occur in Europe, let alone Hampstead Heath. No doubt Albin, in Maitland Emmet's words, had 'muddled his specimen'. (*See* Table 2 on page 232 for list of Albin's names.)

The Aurelians

Three hundred years ago, the most flattering thing you could say about a naturalist was, as Petiver noted of Eleazar Albin, that he was 'curious'. Like the scientists of a later age, these would-be 'natural philosophers' needed a hyperactive sense of enquiry. They observed, questioned, and looked for answers. But for insects this presented problems. There were few books to consult, and those that existed were either in Latin or another foreign language – or were extremely expensive. Some collectors even went to the trouble and expense of hiring an artist to paint their best specimens, as did the Duchess of Portland and the London silversmith Dru Drury. Or they could create their own DIY field guide, as did the silk trader and amateur botanist Charles Dubois, whose butterfly notebook still survives in the Natural History Museum.

There was a further drawback for the seeker of truth, and that was that he or she was likely to feel rather lonely. Pioneers need colleagues to talk things over, to compare notes, to stoke the fires of enthusiasm, and simply to enjoy their hobby in congenial company. Yet such things were becoming possible, even in the 1690s. John Ray, out in the wilds of Essex, and bedridden much of the time, relied on his daughters and neighbours to hunt for specimens, but he was also lucky enough to enlist the services of a learned and like-minded neighbour, the physician Samuel Dale. Ray could also draw on the help of a web of correspondents further afield. When in town, he could attend one of several formal gatherings. There was, of course, the Royal Society, of which he was a Fellow. Or he could join one of the meetings or excursions of the Society of Gardeners, who met in Newhall's Coffee House in Chelsea, close to the physic garden. And, from 1689, there was also the Temple

Engraving of Peter Collinson, one of the first generation of Aurelians.

Coffee House Botanic Club, which met on Friday evenings and dined at the nearby Swan Tavern. Crucially for the development of entomology, it held summer 'herberising' excursions – that is, collecting trips – to the countryside surrounding London, which was never far away in those pre-industrial days.

Some forty original members of the Temple Coffee House Botanic Club are known. Heading the list is Sir Hans Sloane (he of Sloane Square), whose vast collection of artifacts and natural objects formed the nucleus of the British Museum. It also included James Petiver and the lofty and quarrelsome Leonard Plukenet, Royal Professor of Botany and gardener to Queen Mary (wife of King William III). There was also Adam Buddle, who, like John Ray, was a parson-naturalist, one of the first to take a serious interest in mosses (he is remembered today in the butterfly bush, or buddleja). Yet another member was Martin Lister, a physician and prototype naturalist who was perhaps the first Englishman to take a scientific interest in spiders. Botany was their nominal pursuit, but men like Plukenet, Buddle and Lister also took a much broader interest in natural history, including insects – especially butterflies and moths. Adam Buddle took this link to its logical conclusion by pressing butterflies along with his plants on carefully arranged folio pages. Others saw the possibilities of painting butterflies and flowers together in lifelike compositions.

Opposite: Moses Harris's composition of the Clouded Yellow, Oak Eggar and Brimstone Moth. He dedicated this plate to Richard Bateman, rector of Fulham, who died before the work was complete.

To the Honᵇˡᵉ
This Plate is humbly Dedicated by his most

Richard Bateman
Obedient Servant Moses Harris.

The chrysalis or 'aurelia' of a butterfly gave its name to the Society of Aurelians, the world's first entomological society.

At some stage (probably no earlier than 1720 but certainly not later than 1738), some of these gentlemen decided to establish another club dedicated to the study of insects. They called it the Society of Aurelians. They took the name, which means 'the golden ones', from the *aurelius* or chrysalis of a butterfly. Some species, such as the Red Admiral and the Small Tortoiseshell, have gold or silver markings on their chrysalids that make them shine like jewels. Perhaps there was a sense that knowledge, like a gilded butterfly, was breaking forth from the chrysalis of superstition. But these were men (like members of all learned societies then, they were men only) who were classically educated and often artistically inclined. Calling themselves Aurelians reflected their admiration for the elegance and beauty of butterflies, and also created a kind of identification with them. A contemporary caricature shows an 'Aurelian Macaroni', an entomological dandy with a butterfly hat, a wig made of live caterpillars, and coiled snails for buttonholes.

We know the names of some of the members of the first Society of Aurelians. Their founder and leading light was Joseph Dandridge (1664–1746), who has been called the greatest English naturalist no one has ever heard of – for, although he left innumerable drawings and paintings, he never published a word. Dandridge, like several other Aurelians, was a professional artist, a silk-pattern designer, and an early illustrator of birds and insects (and spiders). To paint these objects he required a collection, and no doubt he borrowed Petiver's methods to build up the substantial assemblage of butterflies and moths which he generously made available to the society. Some ninety-six drawers of his insect collection were rescued by Sir Hans Sloane after Dandridge's death at the grand old age of 82, and they were later donated to the British Museum – only to perish in the bonfires of a curator who regarded them as outdated rubbish. A colleague and fellow Aurelian, Emanuel Mendez da Costa, remembered Dandridge as a generous-spirited man, 'thick and of a middle size', 'very merry and chatty' and full of yarns of the old collectors. (It appears that as early as the 1740s there was already nostalgia for the good old days in the field).

The Aurelians seem to have been socially inclusive. A shared interest in insects transcended social barriers. Some were professional artists and pattern designers for the silk trade. James Leman, for instance, was an artist who manufactured fabrics with his own designs, some of which are now in the Victoria and Albert Museum. There was Peter Collinson, a cloth merchant and Fellow of the Royal Society, whose Quaker philosophy encouraged enquiry into the ways of the natural world. There was room for amateur poets such as Henry Baker (another FRS), an early enthusiast for the microscope. Later members included the Royal Society's Jewish librarian, Emanuel Mendez da Costa; Daniel Solander, the Swedish apostle of Linnaeus and cataloguer of natural objects at the British Museum; and Henry Smeathman, a Quaker physician who was the first to investigate the

natural history of Sierra Leone. These were all men who left their mark on the world. Other members are now little more than names. Elias Broadsword was a stationer at Budge Row in the City. Stephen Austin and Samuel Lee were 'esquires', and therefore considered to be gentlemen. Of apparently lower social rank were Samuel Hartley, Ephraim Bell, Walter Blackett, Thomas Grace and William Wells. But at Society meetings they were all 'worthy Aurelians', offering a true cross-section of the cosmopolitan society of early Georgian London.

We know all too little about what they did and discussed. We do know that they

Portrait of Henry Baker, Aurelian, amateur poet and early promoter of the microscope.

A composition of Painted Ladies and Marbled Whites and their early stages on their correct foodplants, a plate from *The Aurelian* by Moses Harris. Painted Ladies are attracted to thistles which often grew on rubbish heaps in eighteenth-century London, hence Harris's careful placement of broken pottery, clay pipe and glassware. The mussel shell was used by artists for mixing colours.

met regularly at The Swan in Change Alley, in the Cornhill district of London, the sociable bookselling and coffee-house quarter. They had premises at The Swan that housed the Society's collections and library, and they dined there too, probably in a private room heated by a coal fire. They held collecting expeditions around London, and perhaps further afield. The shared interests of members were very wide: botany and gardening, shells and fossils, art and design, microscopy, and the general advancement of science. They exchanged views on collecting, cultivating and rearing, and all kinds of philosophical topics. They were interesting people. One likes to think they had a lot of fun.

Georgian Imaginations

Most of what we know about the Aurelians comes from two works that they helped to sponsor and produce, both of them illustrated by one of their members, Benjamin Wilkes. The first, published in 1742 and dedicated to the 'Worthy Members of the Aurelian Society', was a set of twelve designs of 'English butterflies' (including a few moths), with a short introduction. The second and more significant was *The English Moths and Butterflies*, completed in 1748. This was a work of beauty as well as an elegant summation of what was known at the time. It is a significant advance on Albin's work, both in artistic merit and in the range of species depicted. Wilkes described himself as a painter 'of History Pieces and Portraits in Oil'; he painted the 120 designs, which were engraved on copper plates by a fellow artist, Henry Roberts. It seems that Wilkes had known nothing about insects until he was shown the Society's collections by Henry Baker, the poet and microscopist. Wilkes became inspired, he wrote, by 'Nature's admirable Skill in the Disposition, Arrangement and contrasting Colours' of butterflies and moths. Assisted by the redoubtable Joseph Dandridge, he became a hunter and rearer of caterpillars, and resolved to paint every detail of the life cycles of butterflies and moths, including (as Albin had) their parasites. Wilkes's collection was kept at the Horn Tavern on Fleet Street, where 'any gentleman or lady' could arrange to see it.

Like Albin's, Wilkes's book was sold by subscription. The hundred-plus 'encouragers' on his list included four dukes, three duchesses and the Archbishop of Canterbury. Among other subscribers were a future Prime Minister, the Third Earl of Bute; Horace Walpole, the renowned man of letters; and a certain Lady Diana Spencer. Nearly a quarter of the subscribers were women, despite the fact that

Engraved self-portrait of Moses Harris.

they were barred from learned societies. One wonders about Mr Hodges, who bought three copies, and Mr Dodesly, who bought four. The coloured edition of *The English Moths and Butterflies* cost £9, or £1,820 today (the individual plates, many destined for framing, cost 2/6 each). Worn out, perhaps by his labours, Wilkes died suddenly, shortly after publication. It transpired that many of his plates were based on drawings by the Continental artists Georg Dionysius Ehret and Jacob van Huysum. As for the text, Henry Baker let out that the work was 'in some sort my own child' – for Wilkes, though indefatigable in his observations and skill as an artist, was 'for want of learning quite incapable of writing a book'.

English Moths and Butterflies illustrated some thirty kinds of butterflies and more than a hundred moths. It took Wilkes ten years to complete. Some of the compositions were fanciful: as Wilkes admitted, his butterflies and moths flutter around arrangements of flowers and fruits that would not have interested them in real life. Artistic variety was still more important than scientific fidelity. What is notable is that nearly all of his subjects now had accepted common names, some of them the ones we still use today. Here for the first time we meet such famous moths as the Kentish Glory, the Clifden Nonpareil, the Buff-tip, the Puss Moth, the Angle Shades and the Peach Blossom. Much of what we might call the vocabulary of moth names is already in place: words such as 'Ranunculus', 'silver-lines', 'sword-grass', 'ermine', 'satin', 'dagger', 'tussock', 'brindled' and 'beauty'. The names of butterflies, too, had come a long way since Petiver's clumsy labels. The two cabbage whites are now the Large and Small Whites; the Royal William has become the Swallowtail; the Orange-tip is so-named for the first time, although it was also known as the 'Lady of the Woods'. The 'Peacock's Eye' has been reduced to a plain Peacock; and 'Small Tortoiseshell' transferred from the Small Copper. On the other hand, the

1. The Cock Emperour. See this Moth describ'd in Plate the 4.th N.º 1. 2. The Burnet. 3. The Forester. The Caterpillar of these Moths feed on Hay-Grass, change to Chrysalis the beginning of May and appear in the Fly State
the end of the same Month. 4. The Small PearlBorder, a Fritilary, taken in the Fly State in Tottenham Woods
the end of May. 5. The Admirable Butterfly. See it describ'd in Plate the 2.º N.º 3. 6. The Great Fritilary
Butterfly. To be taken in the Fly State near Comb Wood, the middle of July.

Printed for Carington Bowles, N.º 69 S.t Pauls ChurchYard, London.

Hand-coloured engraving of butterflies and moths from *Twelve New Designs of English Butterflies* (1742) by
Benjamin Wilkes, suggesting how contemporaries might have displayed butterflies in cases in their drawing rooms.

Wall is still the Great Argus, the Common Blue the Blue Argus (the Aurelians were still very uncertain when it came to distinguishing the various blues), and the Green Hairstreak a mere 'Green Butterfly'. The Camberwell Beauty joins the British list for the first time, but as 'the Willow Butterfly'. The Admiral has suffered a name change and is now 'The Admirable'.

Where did all these new names come from? Almost certainly from the shared experiences of the Aurelian Society members over the past couple of decades. Perhaps a member had suggested a name based on some attribute that others agreed with, and so entered it on their labels. We surely have the Aurelians to thank for the poetic flavour of so many of the names of butterflies and moths still used today. Fortunately, Benjamin Wilkes, or his factotum Henry Baker, went out of his way to explain the *modus operandi*. Since it is rarely mentioned in historical texts, I will quote this important statement in full, with corrections for modern spelling and grammar:

> Names are arbitrary, and if remembered, and the intent of them well understood, may, whatever they are, serve the purpose of giving them. But here, as in everything else, a propriety is to be aimed at, and the names given ought to denote some distinguishing particularity, and that the most obvious, in the subject on which they are bestowed, so as to make the name, if possible, descriptive of the thing. Which rule has been followed as strictly as might be in naming the Moths and Butterflies contained in this work; that is to say, the shape, the colour, the markings, the food, or the place where found, is what they are named from.

Wilkes and Baker add that where there were existing names, these were retained. They bestowed new names only on species that either lacked them, or where the previous name was 'not sufficiently denotative'. (For a full list of Wilkes's names *see* Table 3 on pages 232–5.)

We would know more, perhaps a great deal more, were it not for a terrible accident that robbed posterity of the formal records of the Society of Aurelians. They all went up in flames on the night of March 25, 1748 in a great fire that consumed the whole of the City of London between the Royal Exchange and Lombard Street. It nearly consumed the Aurelians too, who were sitting late at The Swan on Exchange Alley, perhaps after a long and companionable dinner. Moses Harris was given an account of events by his uncle of the same name, a member and perhaps an eyewitness:

Within the engraving:

An exact View of the Ruins, of the Houses burned down, by the late dreadful Fire in Cornhill the 25th of March 1748. Taken from Sam's Coffee House in Exchange Alley. Published according to Act of Parliament by J. Cross April 8th 1748. Sold by M. Cooks Printer in Scalding Alley Poultry London.

Eldridge's House in Exchange Alley where ye Fire B. Mr. Eldridge, his Wife, two Children, & ...eyman perished in ye Flames. Michael's Church where it Stopped to ye Eastward. White House opposite ye Royal Exchange where ...ire Stopped to ye Westward.

D. The George & Vulture Tavern in George Yard where ye Fire Stopped on that side. E.B. Cornhill. F.F. The Ruins of two Houses in Birchin Lane. G. The Jamaica Coffee House. This Fire Consum'd 82 Houses.

A contemporary engraving of the ruins of the Cornhill district in the City of London, after the Great Fire.

The great Fire happened in Cornhill [at one o'clock in the morning], in which The Swan Tavern was burnt down, together with the Society's valuable Collection of Insects, Books etc., and all their Regalia. The Society was then sitting, yet so sudden and rapid was the impetuous Course of the Fire, that the Flames beat against the Windows before they could well get out of the Room, many of them leaving their Hats and Canes.

It seems that the society never recovered from the loss of its records, its collection, and its 'regalia' (whatever that was). It is ironic that the end coincided with the publication of Wilkes's book, which encapsulated what the society had stood for, with its marriage of art and science, beauty and truth, and in designs that recalled the Dutch masters of the previous century. As Moses Harris relates, 'Their loss so disheartened them that although they several Times met for that Purpose, they never could collect so many together, as would be sufficient to form a Society, so that for fourteen Years, and upward, there was no Meeting of that Sort, till Phoenix-like our present Society arose out of the ashes of the old.' It seems that the disaster knocked the stuffing

57

Perfect naming: the Silver-washed Fritillary.

out of the fellowship until Harris managed to get it going again.

This second Aurelian Society, established in 1762 with Harris as its secretary, did not last long. Some dissension among its members brought it to a premature close. Its records, too, are lost, but the short-lived revival did bear fruit in one of the most beautiful butterfly books ever published: *The Aurelian* by Moses Harris.

The Aurelian is, by broad consent, the most handsome of all the old butterfly books: the perfect synthesis of art and science. Moses Harris (1730–c.1788) had been entranced by butterflies and moths since childhood. To portray them in a publication, he had to learn the exacting skill of engraving on copper. Like his predecessors, he underwrote the costs by subscription and dedicated each new plate to a sponsor, though by then some of the novelty had been lost and he could not hope to match the Burke's Peerage of subscribers that Albin had enjoyed. Like Wilkes before him, the work took Harris ten years to complete. The full volume was published in 1766, and cost 5 guineas for the hand-coloured version – about £800 in today's currency. Harris also sold the prints individually at 7/6 each. He completed *The Aurelian* in a mood of some bitterness. Apologising for the 'tedious length of time' it had taken, Harris blamed 'the unsteady and fallacious behaviour of a person too nearly connected in my concerns.' That person seems to have been a fellow Aurelian, Emanuel Mendez da Costa, the librarian of the Royal Society. The following year da Costa was discovered to be withholding the Society's subscription fees, was convicted of fraud and served five years in a debtor's prison. Perhaps he had purloined Moses Harris's subscriptions too.

Like Wilkes, Moses Harris depicted butterflies and moths in artistic arrangements with flowers and other objects, but with a better eye, and with greater imagination and artistic integrity. His plate of the 'Olive Shades or Lime Hawk-Moth' included a couple of dead moths pinned and set on boards. His Painted Ladies flew over a Georgian rubbish heap of clay pipes and other debris, for (as he noted) the butterfly liked to visit thistles growing on waste ground. Caterpillars and other early stages

Copper engraving of the Emperor Moth flying around flowering bramble (one of the moth's foodplants) from *The English Moths and Butterflies* by Benjamin Wilkes, published in 1749. His style is more graceful and lively than the work of Eleazar Albin.

Another composition from *The English Moths and Butterflies* showing the Barred Hook-tip moth and its caterpillar. Benjamin Wilkes shows it on wild dog-rose but the caterpillar's true foodplant is beech.

The Scarce Merveille du Jour is a rare French name among British moths. It was evidently a common phrase in Georgian times, and this moth is indeed a 'marvel', a harmony of green, black and white.

were included where known. On his Swallowtail plate, one butterfly is resting on a leaf of milk-parsley in a jam jar of water, whilst close by its big striped caterpillar is about to turn into a chrysalis.

Many of the names of butterflies and moths had changed since 1748. Most of the butterfly names we know today were now in place. Nearly all the fritillaries bore their current names. The Willow Butterfly was now the Camberwell Beauty. The 'hogs' had become skippers, the Tunbridge Grayling was now a plain Grayling, and Wilkes's 'Orange Field Butterfly' had become the familiar Gatekeeper. We also find for the first time the Speckled Wood, the Ringlet, the Common Blue, the Duke of Burgundy Fritillary and (at least in later editions) the Purple Emperor. In some cases Harris offered alternative names: the Small Heath was also known as the Small Gatekeeper, and the Marbled White was also the Marmoress or the Half-Mourner. The White Admiral, too, had an alias, the White Admirable. In every case Harris added the word 'Butterfly'. It is only with this butterfly tag attached that certain names make complete sense. As Harris himself pointed out in the case of the Wall Butterfly, 'wall' is not a noun but an adjective. It is a butterfly that likes to settle on sunny walls. (It might be worth adding that in the eighteenth century a 'wall' could also be a grassy bank, of the kind the Romans called a *vallum*.)

More moths, too, had acquired accepted names. Most of the hawk-moths and tiger-moths now bore their present-day names (although the Spurge Hawk was, amusingly, the 'Spotted Elephant Hawk', named after its polka-dotted long-necked caterpillar). The china-mark moths enter history under that name, and we find many other familiar names for the first time, such as burnet, forester, umber, vapourer, gothic, footman, thorn, snout, swift and arches, as well as the Chimney Sweeper.

The Dot Moth makes its debut, as does the Argent and Sable, the Speckled Yellow and the Grey Scalloped Bar. A few of Harris's names have since been discarded. His Maid of Honour moth is now the Blotched Emerald; his Cream-Dot Stripe or Spotted Buff Moth is the present-day Buff Ermine. And the Rosy Footman was not yet a footman but an 'arches': the Red Arches Moth.

We have Moses Harris to thank for introducing some of the most poetic names of all. 'Silver-washed Fritillary' perfectly captures the silvery runnels and flashes on the butterfly's hindwings. Whether or not you prefer Harris's 'Dishclout or Greasy Fritillary' for today's Marsh Fritillary, his name is undoubtedly imaginative and arguably more apt – for as he says, 'The under Side of the upper Wing always appears greasy.' He also introduces names among the moths that depart from Wilkes's idea that they should be plain and to-the-point. The True Lover's Knot makes imaginative use of looped markings in the moth's wings. 'Marvel de Jour' (now Merveille du Jour) borrows an everyday phrase for a beautifully patterned green-and-black moth. Harris also makes good use of the seasons. Spring Usher is a lovely name for a moth that appears towards the end of winter. Whether he was using names that were already current, or, as I suspect, were his own invention, Harris found names that have stood the test of time. If Petiver was the first to coin names for our butterflies and moths, it was Moses Harris, or his generation of Aurelians, that perfected them. They link us with the artistic milieu of the Georgian artists and natural philosophers, that lost world of silk patterns and gorgeous fabrics, of the curio cabinet, of the first museums and learned societies, of wonder at nature's 'transformations', and the sheer excitement of discovery. (*See* Table 6 on pages 238–9 for the first use of present-day butterfly names).

The Invention of Latin Names

Carl Linnaeus, or Carl von Linné (1707–78), was and is a very famous man. In his lifetime he was hugely admired throughout Europe. Goethe named him, along with Shakespeare and Spinoza, as his greatest influence. Linnaeus's fellow Swede, August Strindberg, considered him 'a poet who happened to become a naturalist'. In London, shortly after his death, they founded a Linnaean Society to further the principles established by Linnaeus, and to house a large collection of his manuscripts and books. With Linnaeus the natural world became a realm of order. What he accomplished was a manner of classification based on natural relationships: his *Systema Naturae* or 'natural system'. Never again would butterflies and moths or any other form of life be presented in random order, as they were in *The Aurelian* (though later editions of *The Aurelian* did include Linnaean names). Every species now had its own place in the grand scheme of nature.

Linnaeus was primarily a botanist. He was more confident working with plants than with animals and insects. Indeed, although he managed to name 3,000 species of butterflies and moths from all over the world, he leaned heavily on the work of previous authorities, including John Ray and Thomas Moffet. Like Ray, Linnaeus tried to sort out the butterflies – his 'Papiliones' – by their most obvious characteristic: their wing colours and patterns. He divided them rather crudely into five 'tribes' whose names were based on classical models suited to his Latin text.

First in the hierarchy came the grandest of butterflies, the swallowtails and birdwings, named after the heroes of Homer and dubbed the 'Equites' or 'knights'. Just below them came the 'Heliconii' or 'Muses', mainly New World species but also including the European fritillaries and Apollos. After them came the 'Danai',

Roslin Eques pinx.   Clementus Bervic Sculp.

CAROLUS a LJNNÉ

Eques Ordinis Reg. Stellæ   Polaris, Regis Sveciæ Archiater,
Medicinæ et historiæ Natur.   Professor in Universit. Reg.
Opsaliensi, Acad. R. Scient-   Stockholm. Upsal. Paris. Londin.
Petrop. Berol. etc. Sociuæ,   Dominus de Hammarby.

1779.

'the daughters of Danaus, King of Argos', which included the Brimstone, Clouded Yellow and the whites; and then the Nymphs ('Nymphales'), a category which includes the tortoiseshells and the Comma. Last in Linnaeus's scheme came a large and ill-sorted group of small butterflies, made up mainly of the blues, hairstreaks and skippers. These were his 'Plebeji', the commoners or 'plebs'. Early on, Linnaeus also found a name for the entire family of butterflies and moths. He called them the Lepidoptera, from the Greek words meaning 'scale-wing'. As he recognised, the colours and patterns of the wings are produced by a mosaic of tiny pigmented scales aligned in neat rows and visible with a magnifying glass. They are unique to the butterflies and moths.

Linnaeus's classification of moths corresponded with modern ideas rather more so than his groupings of butterflies, but it was still very broad-brush. The hawk-moths, he recognised, were a self-contained group, for which he borrowed the old name of 'Sphinges' or Sphinxes, based on the appearance of their caterpillars, which rear up in a sphinx-like manner. All the rest, bar the very smallest, he placed in two broad classes: the Phalaenae, from 'Phalene', the old word for a night-flying moth, and the Geometrae or 'earth-measurers', named from the looping motion of their caterpillars. He subdivided the Phalaenae into the larger Bombyces (from the Latin word *Bombyx*, or silk-moth), which included the tiger-moths and eggars; and the smaller Noctuae, which more or less coincide with today's super-family, the Noctuidae or Noctuids. In all, Linnaeus named 542 species of moths, considerably fewer than his butterflies, and mostly North European species. He would have been very surprised to learn that there are nearly five times that many species in Britain alone.

Linnaeus is credited with the introduction of the binomial system of scientific names. The species name, which convention dictates should always take the lower case, is unique to that particular species. For instance, he chose *coridon*, a mythical shepherd's name, for the Chalkhill Blue, and *ligustri*, based on *Ligusticum*, the scientific name of privet, for the Privet Hawk-moth. Before the species name comes the group name, which came to be called the genus, and that always takes the upper case. Hence the scientific name of the Large White butterfly is *Pieris brassicae*. *Pieris* is the group name of a number of related species, including the Small White and Green-veined White. But *brassicae* is the individual name of the Large White, and, suitably enough,

Opposite: Engraved portrait of Linnaeus after a contemporary painting.

it is taken from the Latin word for cabbage, hence 'the cabbage butterfly'.

Another rule about scientific names is that the original spelling must be retained even when it is wrong. Hence you find the occasional anomaly such as the species name of the Marsh Moth, *pallustris*. As any Latin student will know, that word is in fact spelt with a single 'l' as *palustris*, meaning 'of the marsh'. The same rule applies to names that were subsequently found to be unsuitable. The Horse Chestnut moth got its common name from its scientific one, *hippocastanaria* (from *hippocastanum*, the horse chestnut tree, though the moth has nothing to do with the tree; its caterpillar feeds mainly on heather). Names are names, not scientific facts.

Just as the English names of butterflies and moths are often poetic, so the scientific names, too, can be amusingly allusive, living up to Strindberg's appreciation of Linnaeus as a born poet. Linnaeus's names follow logic, but they have as much to do with history and mythology as sober description. With his classical education, he tended to award names to butterflies that corresponded with their 'tribe'. For example, the Bath White is *daplidice*, after a mythical princess, the daughter of King Danaus, just as the butterfly is, in Linnaeus's scheme, of the Danai tribe. Similarly his names for hawk-moths often derived from monsters, not because he saw anything terrifying about the moths but because their tribe was named after the Sphinx, the riddling monster of Egypt. He wanted to find names to match, although he also felt able to break his own rule where necessary by naming other hawk-moth species after their foodplants.

Playfulness often entered the grand scheme, especially when it came to colourful moths and butterflies. Linnaeus placed some of the most striking butterflies among his 'nymphs', and named them after female figures plucked from mythology: Atalanta the huntress; Camilla the Amazon warrior; Antiopa and Io, both rape-victims of Zeus. In the case of Io, whose name lives on in the Peacock butterfly, *Inachis io* (and in a moon of Jupiter!), there is at least a roundabout connection – for after turning Io into a cow, Zeus placed her under the guardianship of the hundred-eyed Argos, whose eyes were later set into the tail of a peacock. Linnaeus would have known such tales through reading Ovid as a schoolboy, no doubt in the original Latin.

To begin with, the group or genus names of butterflies and moths were left rather vague. It was only after Linnaeus's death that binomial scientific names were formalised into a genus and species. The first specialist to get to grips with the Lepidoptera was Linnaeus's Danish follower, Johan Christian Fabricius (1745–1808). While 'Linn.'

had managed to describe and name some 3,000 species, mostly butterflies, 'Fab.' added another 10,000, mostly moths. He was able to do so because he had access to the many fine collections in public museums and private houses across Europe (Fabricius was an avid promoter of museums, and founded one in his home town of Kiel). He visited London several times to examine the world-class cabinets of Sir Joseph Banks and Dru Drury, as well as specimens taken on the voyages of Captain Cook. In fact it was the much maligned collector – those leisured gentlemen inspired by

Engraved portrait of
Johan Christian Fabricius made in 1805.

the works of Wilkes and Harris – who made such advances possible. Recognising this, both Linnaeus and Fabricius began a tradition of naming species in honour of contemporary naturalists and collectors. Moses Harris, for example, got the White Oak Midget, *Phyllonorycter harrisella*.

Fabricius, like Linnaeus, had a sense of fun. He enjoyed finding names that were informative but also imaginative or mysterious. Some of them are as cryptic as a crossword puzzle. His names incorporate puns and riddles that have tantalised scholars down the ages, for Fabricius left no explanations or solutions. For example, as a group name for a large miscellany of moths, he chose *Zygaena*, which he borrowed from, of all things, the hammerhead shark, *Zugaina*. It seems that Fabricius was looking for a 'monster' name to match that of the hawk-moths. Probably not by accident, the word is also close to the Greek *zugón*, a yoke for cattle, for the various moths have in a sense become 'yoked' to the hawk-moths by their name (so as well as a yoke, it's a joke!). Since then the scope of *Zygaena* has been narrowed, and it is now the genus of the burnet moths alone. In that context the name is meaningless, and anyone searching for a connection between burnets and hammerhead sharks is doomed to fail. It makes sense only in the context of its own time and in Fabricius's fondness for puns.

An equally prolific namer of butterflies and moths was the German scholar Jacob Hübner (1761–1826), who worked specifically on European species. Like Harris, he was a fine entomological artist. Like Fabricius, he had a fondness for allusive and poetic names. Among the many new genera he introduced was *Pyrgus*, for the Grizzled Skipper and its relatives, from the Greek word *purgos*, or battlement – an allusion to the chequered wing-margin of the wings of those butterflies. Harder to unravel is his name for some of the smaller fritillaries: *Melitaea*. The most promising suggestion is that the word relates to honey (from the Greek *meli*) and incorporates word-play both with the butterfly's colour and its love of nectar. The modern name of the Heath Fritillary incorporates the same idea: *Mellicta*, or 'honey-lick'. They slurp up the nectar with their long tongues.

When it came to moths, Hübner coined genera like *Thalpophila* for the Straw Underwing, a word best translated as 'loving the summer heat'. The name is doubly appropriate in that the moth flies during the warmest nights of late summer (its pale yellow hindwings are suggestive of ripening corn). Hübner also seems to have had a thing about bottoms. For the Yellow-tail and Brown-tail moths he coined *Euproctis* or 'pretty bottom'. In similar fashion, the Latin Moth became *Callopistria*, or 'beautiful posterior'. But he was not always so complimentary. He named the Red-necked Footman *Atolmis*, or 'cowardly', perhaps in reference to its retiring caterpillar. His Yellow-line Quaker became *macilenta*, 'lean and meagre', evidently a moth with inadequate markings. His Rosy Marbled, on the other hand, was *venustula*, little Venus, a 'sweet and charming' little moth – 'a tribute,' suggests Colonel Emmet, 'from an artist to a very pretty species.'

Enter the Victorians

The new century, the nineteenth, had a new name for people who studied insects. They had become *entomologists*. In 1801 the Aurelian Society had been revived one last time by Adrian Haworth, but it was soon dissolved after its members proved unwilling to donate specimens for the Society's collection (collectors, it seems, were getting more selfish). In its place rose a new club and a new name: the Entomological Society. Unlike the Aurelians, it published *Transactions*. The change of name is significant: the days of dilettante Georgian curiosity was over; the new science was *serious*.

Adrian Haworth (1767–1833) had inherited a fortune, and so was able to devote much of his time to the study of insects. A devout follower of Linnaeus, he began, in his own words, 'to collect, arrange and describe the natural productions of this fertile and happy island' (Britain, that is), ranging alone on foot, or with like-minded friends, over 'a great variety of woods and lawns, hills and vales, marshes and fens … not fewer than a thousand miles.' Armed with this experience and a sizable personal collection, he set about writing a thoroughgoing guide to all the species of British butterflies and moths then known. He called it *Lepidoptera Britannica*, and dedicated the first volume, published in 1803, to 'the gentlemen of the Aurelian Society'. The Haworth *magnum opus* set the standard for the ensuing century, and was quoted with approval by every subsequent author.

As a devoted Linnaean, Haworth had little time for common names. He reluctantly included them in brackets after the Linnaean name to make his disapproval clear. To make it clearer still, he grumbled that English names, 'as far as they are unobjectionable … are [often] highly fanciful, not to say absurd; and lead to no information: such for

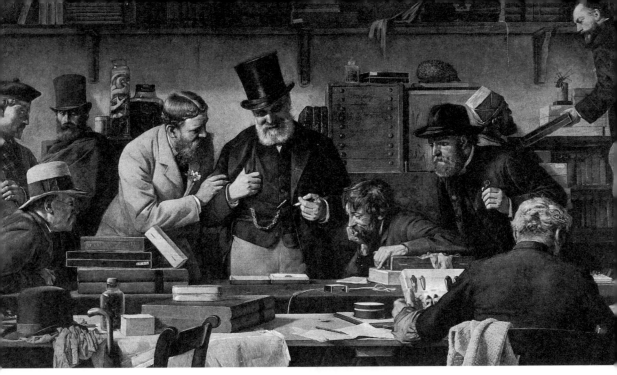

A gentleman looking rather pleased with himself after acquiring specimens for his collection at an entomological auction. This photogravure by Franz Hanfstaengl is in the Wellcome Collection.

instance as The Miller of Mansfield etc.' (There is no longer any moth of that name, though it survives as the name of a pub in Goring.)

The extraordinary thing about the English names recorded grudgingly by Haworth is that they are nearly all the same as today. Such new names as he introduced usually turned out to be different forms of a single variable species. For example, his 'Straw-coloured Footman' is in fact the yellow form of the Dingy Footman; his 'Lineolated Dart' a version of the White-line Dart. There have been minor spelling differences since then. In Haworth's time, writers liked to insert an 'e' into adjectives like 'smokey' and 'rosey', and wrote 'appall'd' rather than 'appalled', and 'scolop' instead of scallop. Only a few Haworthian names have passed away altogether, such as the Mourning Widow for the White-banded Carpet, or the Yorkshire Y for the Scarce Silver Y, or the Ingrailed Wave for the Grass Wave. In general the names for our butterflies and moths back in 1800 are much the same as now. Hence they are not 'Victorian', for Queen Victoria was not even born then. A more accurate description would be 'Aurelian'. They are eighteenth-century period pieces, coined in the smoky rooms of London coffee houses by enthusiastic gentlemen wearing wigs and tricorn hats, and quite possibly after a roast-beef dinner and several passings of port.

A few resident butterflies and a great many moths remained to be discovered. Haworth himself described one new butterfly, the Large Copper, and several moths, some of them quite common and widespread, such as the Black Rustic, Six-striped Rustic and Small Wainscot. They were overlooked because the Aurelians seemed to have experienced trouble distinguishing dull-brown Noctuids. Other species were overlooked because they were rare – or northern (therefore

A contemporary bust of Adrian Hardy Haworth (1767–1833).

equally rare). Fittingly, Haworth is remembered in the names of two moths: *Celaena haworthii*, Haworth's Minor, and *Eupithecia haworthiata*, Haworth's Pug. (*See* Table 5 on pages 236–37 for moths and butterflies first described from British specimens.)

Haworth's lead was followed by three English entomologists, who between them described dozens of new moths: John Curtis (1791–1862), James Francis Stephens (1792–1852) and Henry Doubleday (1808–75). Take the little moths known as pugs. At the outset of his career, Haworth knew only four British species. He himself described six new ones, Stephens three more, and Doubleday another half-dozen species or sub-species. By 1870, some 47 species of pug were known, most of which had been assiduously reared through by British specialists, most notably the clergyman Henry Harpur-Crewe, who published detailed descriptions of the caterpillars in various journals. Like so many nineteenth-century entomologists, Harpur-Crewe was a keen botanist. He needed to be to find the caterpillars on the correct plant; with pugs, as for many elusive small moths, you need to know your wildflowers and trees to have any hope of finding the caterpillars that coexist with them.

The artistic tradition begun a century before by Maria Merian did not disappear altogether. John Curtis was a superb entomological draftsman who made an engraved plate for each new species, often with the caterpillar nibbling on its foodplant (usually the plant was the correct one, but not always). He named one of his new moths Blomer's Rivulet after its discoverer (since it was often found close to a locality of the rare and gorgeous Lady's Slipper orchid, he could not resist depicting the two together). Curtis's sixteen volumes of *British Entomology* included 770 plates of new species. That was another characteristic of nineteenth-century entomologists: they worked hard. In the end Curtis lost his sight.

The last artist who worked within the old aesthetic tradition was Henry Noel Humphreys, who drew lithographically printed colour plates of butterflies and moths for the magisterial works of the Oxford professor John Obadiah Westwood. Each of his compositions was carefully arranged to please the eye as well as inform the mind with its meticulous scientific accuracy. Henceforth species would come to be illustrated in a different way: not as flying or egg-laying butterflies and moths in their natural environments but as drawings (or, later, photographs) based on pinned specimens. The trouble with colour printing was that it was expensive – less so than before, but still seriously depleting the purse of many collectors. Moreover, depicting a species in the old way, flying happily around a blossoming branch or flower arrangement, was not economical with space. The most popular books of the later century were Edward Newman's *An Illustrated Natural History of British Moths* (1869) and the matching *An Illustrated Natural History of British Butterflies* (1871). They were more affordable because they dispensed with colour and substituted austere steel engravings. It is only comparatively recently that field guides have turned away from the Victorian tradition of showing mounted specimens to displaying more lifelike attitudes.

The striking thing about the scores of new species discovered in the nineteenth century is that all except some of the micros were given common names straightaway, as a matter of course. And that these names always fit neatly into the established tradition. For example, when Francis Stephens described a new species that was clearly related to the Heart and Dart moth, he named it in the same spirit as the Crescent Dart: a moth with a black 'dart' and a subtle 'c' or crescent shape in its wings. A new species that shared the same delicate wing tracery as the Gothic Moth was called the Beautiful Gothic (never mind that they are not in fact related). The many new species of footman, or waves, or carpets, retained those names with the addition of a suitable adjective: Dotted Footman, Rusty Wave, Marsh Carpet. In a sense these English names were analogous to the Latin names: a group noun with a qualifying adjective. Footman, for instance, was the group name for a tribe of moths variously distinguished as 'Dotted', 'Orange', 'Dingy', or 'Pigmy'. But with every

Haworth's moth: Haworth's Minor, *Celaena haworthii*, as illustrated by John Curtis for *British Entomology* published in 1823.

Pretty dwarf: one of the many (many) pug moths.

generality there are exceptions. The parade of footmen is interrupted by the Round-winged Muslin and the Dew Moth. They are members of the same group, but someone decided that they were not to be footmen. The sequence of dart moths is similarly broken by a Light Feathered Rustic and a Turnip Moth. There might be historical reasons for some such anomalies. For instance, the Light Feathered Rustic was originally thought to be related to another moth, the Brown Feathered Rustic, now reduced to the Brown Rustic.

Names for some newly discovered species could take a little time to settle. Ashworth's Rustic, for example, was known by some authors as the Welsh Rustic, but Joseph Ashworth of Llangollen, its lucky discoverer, survives in the scientific name as *Agrotis* (now *Xestia*) *ashworthii*. Weaver's Wave once had an alternative name, Greening's Wave. Weaver won, and poor Greening is forgotten. There was also a moth once called Haworth's Carpet. Maybe someone decided that Haworth had been honoured quite enough already, for it is now the Barred Rivulet.

Most moths that carry the names of their discoverers were identified in the nineteenth or twentieth centuries. Haworth's Minor was soon followed by Morris's Wainscot, honouring the Rev. Francis Orpen Morris, a noted author and entomologist who is said to have popularised the bird table. Stephens' Gem is named after the systematicist James Francis Stephens, whilst Barrett's Marbled Coronet is a tribute to Charles Golding Barrett, author of an eleven-volume late-Victorian study of British butterflies and moths. The tradition continues today with such new species as Porter's Rustic, Spalding's Dart and Radford's Flame Shoulder.

The discovery of scores of new species in Victorian England owed much to the railway network, but even more to the eagerness of nineteenth-century collectors, who swung their lanterns along coastal cliffs, painted knots of rushes with treacle, reared caterpillars in sheds and conservatories, took entomological holidays, and wrote up their exploits for one of the speciality's many magazines. The rate of discovery had slowed by the turn of the twentieth century, but new species were still identified from time to time: Sussex Emerald (1902), Slender Scotch Burnet (1907), White-mantled Wainscot and Crinan Ear (1908), Devon Carpet (1917), Sallow Clearwing (1926). Only occasionally was a new species given a name that recalled the inventive spirit of the Aurelians, such as The Silurian moth (1972) or the Jubilee Fanfoot (1976), named in honour of the Queen's Silver Jubilee. Many new species are rare immigrants or newly settled species, but

Most footman moths rest with their wings tightly furled around their body to resemble a stiff little human figure. This is the Speckled Footman.

a few are overlooked residents, such as Lempke's Gold Spot (1966) and Fisher's Estuarine Moth (1970). There was great excitement when a pretty green moth, the Burren Green, was discovered on an entomological expedition to Western Ireland in 1954, and still more when the legendary White Prominent, long thought to be extinct, was re-found in Kerry in 2008.

For butterflies, the nineteenth century was a mopping-up operation. William Lewin's *Papilios of Great Britain and Ireland*, published in 1795, was the first volume dedicated to butterflies alone. (That was not Lewin's intention, but he died suddenly with only the first volume of his prospective survey of insects completed). Lewin was the first to arrange the species in systematic order, by families. He added several butterflies to the British list, including the Manchester Argus, now known as the Large Heath, as well as the Small and Large Blues, and the Brown White Spot, Lewin's name for the Northern Brown Argus (though it was long considered to be a mere form of the Brown Argus and not a full species).

The last butterflies to be discovered made their appearance not in illustrated books but in journals. The discovery of the Scotch Argus was announced in James Sowerby's *British Miscellany* in 1804, though specimens have since been found that backdate the discovery to the 1760s. The elusive Mountain Ringlet, first found in the Lake District in 1809, appeared with a nice illustration in the new *Transactions* of the Entomological Society of London (now the Royal Entomological Society). The discovery of the Black Hairstreak and the Lulworth Skipper were announced in *British Entomology* in 1829 and 1832 respectively, the former with misleading details to put collectors off the scent. The last resident British butterfly was the Essex Skipper, whose discovery – in Essex, needless to say – was reported in *The Entomologist* in 1890; its close resemblance to the Small Skipper had muddled its identity. The other nineteenth-century butterfly discoveries were all rare migrants: the Long-tailed Blue (1859), the Milkweed or Monarch (1876) and the Short-tailed Blue (1885). Our only twentieth century additions were another rare migrant, Berger's Clouded Yellow (1950), and a new Irish species of Wood White, initially identified in 1988 as Real's Wood White, but since re-identified as the Cryptic Wood White, *Leptidea juvernica*.

The stability of our butterfly and moth names owes much to Richard South (1846–1932). As a Londoner of independent means, South was able to spend much of his working life in the service of entomology, as editor of *The Entomologist* and as a special assistant at the Natural History Museum. In the first decade of the twentieth century, he wrote three companion volumes for the Wayside and Woodland 'library' published by Frederick Warne on British butterflies and the larger moths. The huge popularity of these cheap, pocket-sized books was helped by their fine colour plates based on photographs and printed by a new technique forged in America. So successful were they that the three volumes of 'South' ran through numerous impressions almost continually for sixty years. For anyone older than fifty, they were probably the books we cut our teeth on as budding lepidopterists. South, like Haworth, retained and regularised the old common names of butterflies and moths, effectively preserving them in aspic. They were the names we learned, and which, for so many of us, add to the pleasure of our hobby. It would be a brave person who sought to change these names now. Brave or not, they would be completely ignored.

Naming the Tinies

In the early days, no distinction was made between the smaller and larger moths. They were just moths, of whatever size. Among those now in the Microlepidoptera – the 'micros' – were familiar moths that still carry their old names, among them Garden Pebble, Small Magpie and that notorious pest of apple trees, the Codlin Moth. Until the mid-nineteenth century the micros were treated no differently from other moths. Most were given English names as well as Latin ones, although the former tended to change from book to book. Some of these superannuated names were quite imaginative. Noel Humphreys' *Genera of British Moths* (1860) includes such choice examples as the Great Raven-feather, the Bare Cleodora, the Black-cloaked Woollen, the Rosy Day and the Swammerdamian. But gradually English names fell out of favour among micro specialists. For a long time now, a micro specialist will say, 'I have *evonymella*,' and not, 'I have the Bird-cherry Ermine moth.'

The first person to look closely at micros was Linnaeus. By peering at these small moths through a glass, he decided that they consisted of four main groups, which he distinguished by giving their names different endings. Those of the roughly rectangular 'Tortrix' group end in -*ana*, as, for example, the little moth that Linnaeus named *rurinana* – 'from the country' (a name that could apply to almost any moth!). The group shaped like tiny butterflies he named the 'Pyralides', and gave them names that end in -*alis*. The Mother-of-Pearl moth, for instance, is *ruralis*, which is the same name as the previous example but with a different ending. His smallest group, which includes the infamous clothes moths, were the Tineae – the 'gnawing worms'; their names end in -*ella*, for example *Tinea pellionella*, the Case-bearing

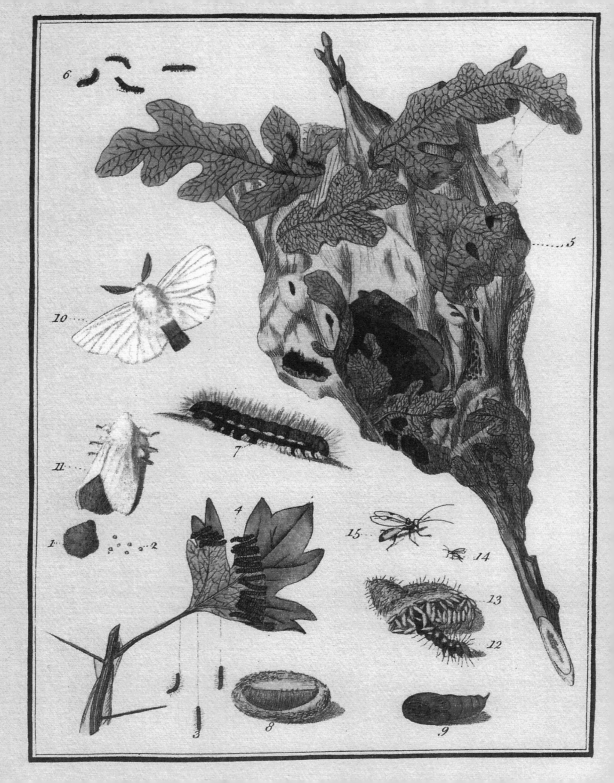

Clothes-moth, whose species name comes from the Latin *pellis*, a 'skin' or 'hide'. His fourth group were very odd-looking moths whose wings resemble tiny feathers; their names end in *-dactyla*, meaning 'fingers' (these oddities have long been known as the plume moths). An example is the Brown Plume which still bears its Linnaean name of *pterodactyla*; it has nothing in common with pterodactyls apart from the name, which means 'feather-wing'. These conventions, though outdated, do make the names easier to remember. In fact any micro specialist will tell you that, thanks in part to these common endings, the scientific names are easier to remember than the English ones.

The Linnaean 'Latin' names soon began to be seen as more respectable than the English ones among the scientifically minded. While larger moths were always given an English name by an established convention, new micros were not. The distinction was cultural rather than scientific. Only a minority of collectors bothered with the micros. They were difficult to identify, exceedingly difficult to set for the collection, and hard to find as adult moths. Micro specialists looked instead for the distinguishing signs of the earlier stages, particularly the caterpillars. Micro specialists needed a whole new skill set: they were gardeners and botanists as well as entomologists, and they spent a lot of time with the microscope.

The handful of tiny moths known to the Aurelians soon became a Victorian swarm: hundreds of new species were identified, and required periodic overhaul in the way they that were classified. From Linnaeus's four tribes emerged dozens of families based on anatomical details, revealing that micros are even more varied, as well as more numerous, than 'macros'. They are also seen as being, in the main, more primitive; that is, they were among the first of the Lepidoptera to evolve. The most primitive micros are ancestral tinies that have functional jaws instead of the usual proboscis.

Britain played an important role in the discovery of Microlepidoptera. By the mid-nineteenth century, several journals catered for the moth-hunter: the *Entomologist's Annual*; the *Entomologist's Weekly Intelligencer*; *The Entomologist's Monthly Magazine*. Many entomologists turned to the micros when they'd had their fill of macros and

Opposite: William Curtis's colour plate from his *Short History of the Brown-tail Moth* (1782), showing the full life cycle of the moth and one of its parasites. This was one of the earliest reasonably accurate studies of a British moth.

A plume moth, one of a natural family of moths whose names end in -*dactyla*, from the Greek word for 'fingers'.

needed a new challenge. The most industrious of them was Henry Tibbats Stainton (1822–92), who inherited a private income and so was able to devote much of his life to the study of moths. Orderly, fastidious, early rising and perpetually busy, he was at the epicentre of Victorian entomology both as a social pursuit and as an advancer of science. He described and named dozens of new species, mostly micros, perhaps helped by the invention of the electric light, which meant that insects could now be studied by night as well as by day. Stainton's names were more workmanlike than imaginative. Typical examples are *weaveri*, named after the entomologist Richard Weaver, *catharticella*, named after the moth's foodplant, *Rhamnus catharticus* or Purging Buckthorn, and *argentimaculata*, 'silver spot', from a distinctive marking. By the time Stainton was through with the micros, he had completely revised their arrangement of genera and families. His monument is the mighty thirteen-volume *Natural History of the Tineina*, written with three colleagues and published in instalments between 1855 and 1873. Illustration remained an important aspect of publishing, and the work is embellished with exquisite lithographed plates of tiny caterpillars by William Buckland, the Moses Harris of his day.

Stainton was succeeded by Edward Meyrick (1854–1938), a classics schoolmaster who over a long lifetime described around 20,000 new species of micro from across the world, and whose collection is possibly the most important ever made by a single individual (it is now split between the national collection in the Natural History Museum and Marlborough College). Unlike Stainton's, many of Meyrick's names are playful. He named one moth *mormopis*, or 'bugbear', either because he thought it an ugly brute, or because the moth has unpleasant habits (it's a nibbler of fur and feathers). He raised a new genus for a single species, *Lathronympha*, which means, rather bafflingly, 'secretly married'. Love appeared once again with *Telephila*, 'far-away love'. Meyrick's *magnum opus* is *The Handbook of British Lepidoptera* (1895), in which the micros finally take their place on equal terms with their larger relations.

How many species of micro there are in Britain is an open question, since new ones are being discovered all the time. By the time of the latest *Field Guide to the Micro Moths of Great Britain and Ireland*, published in 2012 by Phil Sterling and Mark Parsons, there were some 1,627 species of micro-moth on the British list. Most of them are still referred to only by their scientific name – and even those names are subject to change. The rate at which genera and species, even whole families, are being revised in the light of new research, including DNA, has become bewildering.

Small Magpie moth, a micro that bore the same common name from the start.

Common names have been suggested for these tiny moths from time to time, but they have rarely gained general acceptance. A reliance on Latin names only is, after all, normal with insects. That the butterflies and larger moths have English names too, used by the vast majority of us, is because they have long been the most popular insects and among the easiest to identify. Giving these creatures common names was a tradition that began long before Linnaeus devised his Latinate system. It was otherwise with the micros.

One entomologist who took issue with this lack of everyday names for micros was Ian Heslop (1904–70; not to be confused with Ian Hislop of *Private Eye*). He is best known for his lifelong obsession with the Purple Emperor, culminating in his book (co-written with two other experts) *Notes and Views on the Purple Emperor*. Massive and goatee-bearded, Heslop was one of the great characters of twentieth-century natural history, a manic butterfly collector and a crack-shot big-game shooter in Africa (he discovered – and shot – a sub-species of the Pigmy Hippopotamus that was subsequently named after him; it is now extinct). Possessed with a prodigious memory, Heslop left the Colonial Service in Nigeria and, once he returned to England, taught Latin and Greek at various prep schools without requiring a refresher course. Probably not by coincidence, those schools were invariably situated in places that were good for rare butterflies. Heslop's collection is now in the Bristol City Museum.

When still a young man, Heslop set out on what he saw as his life's work, to provide appropriate common names for all the British micros – which even then numbered upwards of a thousand species. In obsolete journals he found a lot of old names that, as he put it, had 'fallen into desuetude'. Where a species lacked a name he provided one on what he called 'established lines'. His first stab at a full list was published in 1947, and it was updated by various supplements published in the *Entomologist's Gazette*. His final word on the subject was published as a 'label list index' in 1964.

Heslop's names were greeted with a mixture of ridicule and amusement by micro specialists – and were completely ignored. He didn't help his case by shunning certain names already in common use, such as Mint Moth for the pretty Pyralid

2146	Caloptilia betulicola Her. Birch Red Slender
2147	Caloptilia azaleella Brants Rhododendron Slender
2148	Caloptilia alchimiella Scop (swederella Thunb.) Sweder's Slender
2149	Caloptilia stigmatella F Triangle marked Slender
2150	Caloptilia hemidactyla F. Mottled Red Slender
2151	Caloptilia falconipennella Hubn. Livid Slender
2152	Caloptilia semifascia Haw. Semi-barred Slender

Epermeniinae

*2153	Cataplecticafarreni Wals. Farren's Lancewing
2154	Cataplectica profugella Staint. Little Lancewing
2155	Cataplectica fulviguttella Zell. (flavimaculella Staint.) Yellow-spotted Lancewing
2156	Cataplectica auromaculata Frey Shetland Lancewing
•2157	Phauiernis dentella Zell. Scale-tooth Lancewing
*2158	Epermenia illigerella Hubn. Large Lancewing
2159	Epermenia insecurella Staint. Chalk-hill Lancewing
2160	Epermenia daucella Pey. Carrot Lancewing
2161	Epermenia testaceella Hubn. (chaerophyllella auct.). Common Lancewing

Plutellinae

*2162	Orthotaelia sparganella Thunb. Veinous Smudge
*2163	Eidophasia messingiella F. R. Bitter-cress Smudge
*2164	Ypsolophusmucronellus Scop. (caudellus L.) Netted Smudge
2165	Ypsolophus xylostellus L. (harpellus Schiff.) Tooth-streaked Hooked Smudge
2166	Ypsolophus nemorelius L. Pale Hooked Smudge
2167	Ypsolophus asperellus L. Chequered Hooked Smudge
2168	Ypsolophus scabrellus L. Wainscot Smudge
2169	Ypsolophus horridellus Treits. Dark Smudge
2170	Ypsolophus lucellus F. Unequal Smudge
2171	Ypsolophus alpellus Schiff. Double-barred Smudge
2172	Ypsolophus sylvellus L. Wood Autumn Smudge
2173	Ypsolophus parenthesellus L. (costellus F.) White-shouldered Smudge
2174	Ypsolophus radiatellus Don. Broad-streaked Smudge
2175	Ypsolophus sequellus Clerck Small Runic Smudge
2176	Ypsolophus vittellus L. Black-backed Smudge
*2177	Anadetia porrectella L. Grey-streaked Smudge
*2178	Plutella maculipennis Curt. (xylostella Hubn. nee L.) Grey Diamond-backed Smudge

Some of Ian Heslop's English names from his *Revised Indexed Check-list of the British Lepidoptera* (1964).

Pyrausta aurata (which he called 'the Small Purple and Gold'). He coined some new names for butterflies, too, and considered them an improvement. For him, and for absolutely no one else, the Brown Argus became the 'Brown Argus Blue', the Large White the 'Large Garden White', and the Orange-tip the 'Orange-tip White'. He renamed the Scotch Argus the 'Northern Brown' and the Essex Skipper the 'New Small Skipper'. One can see where he was coming from. The Brown Argus was in the blue family, ergo it must be a 'blue', and so on. But butterfly names had been hallowed by time. He would have been wiser to leave them alone.

Heslop's names for micros used the same logical framework, giving related species names that broadly corresponded with their genus, and adding an adjectival name corresponding with their species. Hence certain dusky moths were named 'smudges' or 'dowds'; those of a roundish shape 'buttons' or 'bells'. Iridescent ones included 'golds' and 'brights'. Some groups named after the telltale traces of their caterpillars became 'rollers' and 'twists'. Adult moths with distinctive markings could become 'marbles', 'ermines' or 'streaks'. When absolutely stuck, Heslop borrowed from the Latin (e.g. his 'cosmets' and 'conches', from the genus name *Cochylis*: *see* Table 7 on pages 240–41 for a full list of Heslop's names).

At the time, these coinages were regarded as a joke. In fact, among many micro specialists they are thoroughly loathed. None of the standard texts on micro-moths included Heslop's names: not the micro volumes of *The Moths and Butterflies of Great Britain and Ireland*; not *British Pyralid Moths* by Barry Goater, nor the Ray Society volumes on the Tortricidae, nor the new *Field Guide* by Sterling and Parsons. None of these authors even bothered to explain why they had omitted Heslop's common names. 'There was no point in including them,' Mark Parsons told me. 'They just aren't accepted.' As a result, less than ten percent of micros have accepted common names. The main exceptions are the plume moths, which have lately been accorded the status of 'honorary macros', and whose new common names are regarded as respectable.

There are, however, emerging cross-currents. Micros have become more popular since 2000 (most recorders start with the relatively accessible Pyrales and plumes, and go on from there). There has also been a modest surge of interest in social media and on websites, some of which favour common names over Latin ones. In 2002 Jim Porter, author of *Caterpillars of the British Isles*, published a comprehensive online list of micros that consists basically of Heslop's names, plus updates. As more and more recorders get to grips with these tiny moths, it is likely that the use of common names will grow, and even some traditionalists are starting to rethink their position. The latest stage is a 2017 reissue of Heslop's and Porter's names in booklet form by the entomologist Jim Wheeler.

I'll leave the last word to Wheeler, who says that micro-moth common names 'are popular with many people and often encourage, enthuse, enlighten, amuse and occasionally anger the growing army of moth-ers in the UK. Like them or loathe them, I believe the vernacular names of micro-moths are here to stay ...'

AFTERWORD

For legal reasons, the handful of micro-moths that have either been protected or are the subject of a Biodiversity Action Plan have been given common names. Some of these, such as the Liquorice Piercer, sound quaint, even comic (though that certainly was not the intention). Others, such as the Four-dotted Pin-palp, seem unnecessarily cumbersome. The reason they were given English names is not that entomologists wished it, but because the government will apparently not provide funds for any species that lacks a familiar name.

Even so, first thoughts are not always best. A little moth hitherto known only as *Eudarsia richardsoni* was proposed for biodiversity protection, and given the name Dorset Clothes Moth. After all, it lived in Dorset and was in the Tineidae, the clothes-moth family. Only later did it occur to its would-be protectors that calling it a clothes moth was not likely to endear the species to the wider public. And so it was hastily renamed Richardson's Case-bearer. After all, its caterpillar lives inside a 'case' – and it was discovered by someone called Richardson.

A group of collectors stop for a pint in a New Forest pub in 1919. The clap net on the table belonged to a Mr Smith: it might look clumsy but the entomologist Edward Newman, collecting in the middle of the nineteenth century, would use no other. The double-handed clap-net or 'bat-fowler', originally designed to catch birds and bats, was popular among the collectors of the eighteenth and early nineteenth century, but eventually fell out of favour and was replaced by the more manageable bag-net. However, Mr Smith was obviously still keen.

73. The Cream-spot Tiger (*Chelonia villica*).

2.—The Poplar Hawk-Moth (*Smerinthus Populi*).

227. The Clouded Magpie (*Abraxas ulmata*).

Most illustrations in Book Two are taken from *An Illustrated Natural History of British Moths* (1869) and *An Illustrated Natural History of British Butterflies* (1871) by Edward Newman. Illustrations of micro-moths and some others are by Richard Lewington.

BOOK TWO
*An A to Z of weird
and wonderful names*

A

Abundance

Only one British butterfly has the word 'common' in its name: the Common Blue. It is a blue butterfly whose chief attribute was that it is common.

There are a great many 'common' moths: Common Carpet, Common Pug, Common Quaker, Common Heath, Common White Wave, Common Swift, Common Rustic, and many more. At the other end of this spectrum of abundance we get species with 'scarce' in their name. Once again we have no scarce butterflies unless you count the Scarce Swallowtail, which entered the British list by mistake, but among the moths there are the Scarce Arches, Scarce Prominent, Scarce Tissue, Scarce Vapourer and Scarce Wormwood, 22 species in all. But these are only names. Do they reflect the real status of those moths and that butterfly? Are they all actually 'common' or 'scarce'? Not always.

The Common Blue, for instance, has sadly become not-so-common in many parts of the country (though it is still the commonest blue butterfly). The Common Fanfoot is actually quite a rare and elusive fanfoot. The Scarce Footman, on the other hand, is almost as common as the Common Footman. And once electric light-traps were invented, their users soon discovered that the Scarce Prominent and Scarce Silver-lines weren't well-named either. The so-called Scarce Umber is actually a common moth. But just a bit less common than its relative, the Mottled Umber.

The Common Blue has kept its name, though it is much less common than formerly.

8ing{

There are several possible reasons for the muddle. Very likely the names reflected what was known at the time. Before the railways were built, parts of Britain, especially in the uplands, were *terra incognita* for the entomologist, hard to reach and awkward to explore. Upland species tended to be scarce in collections. The abundance of a species can also change as populations react to events. The pattern of the weather may change; it may get warmer, cooler or wetter, and, as we know from the results of recent climate change, some species can expand their range rapidly while others may die out before conservationists can catch up. Habitats also change; once widespread landscapes such as the heaths and chalk downs of southern England have been reduced to mere fragments of their former extent. Even an insect's genes may change; the Brown Argus butterfly, for example, has become more widespread as a result of a physiological change that has broadened the number of plants on which its caterpillar can feed. Some species once

considered rare have proved enduring; others that were once fairly common are seldom recorded now. Moths such as the Scarce Tissue have found an alternative habitat in gardens and are doing quite well. Others such as the Brighton Wainscot, which relied on unsprayed cornfields, have been less lucky. Life for butterflies and moths is a lottery. 'Scarce' can win the jackpot and 'common' can go bust. But they always keep the same name.

Admirals and Admirables

Why would a butterfly, even one so strikingly coloured as the Red Admiral, be named after a senior naval officer? There is admittedly a weak nautical link in that our butterfly crosses the sea on its annual migrations, but that fact wasn't known to the early naturalists. More likely 'Admiral' was an established folk name. The Red Admiral butterfly has appeared in works of art down the ages, even flitting through the borders of medieval manuscripts. Everyone seems to have known it as The Admiral, whether in England or Holland or Germany or even Sweden (where Linnaeus 'Latinised' it to 'Ammiralis').

But what does it mean? The best contemporary explanation is that of James Petiver. In one of his early pamphlets, printed in 1702, Petiver 'methodised'

Once powerful light-traps became available, the Scarce Prominent Moth turned out to be anything but.

The Red Admiral:
flying the flag for butterflies.

amid the smoke and soot. For the same reason, the butterfly had a sinister reputation, a dark butterfly in every sense with a vision of hell in its wings.

The alternate name for Admiral is 'The Admirable', and there has been much debate about which name came first. Those who favoured 'Admirable' are led by the novelist Vladimir Nabokov and the Oxford geneticist E. B. Ford, both of whom went to their graves insisting that this, and not 'Admiral', was the butterfly's proper name. It made more sense that way round, for the butterfly is indeed one to admire. The first mention of 'Admirable' is in *The English Moths and Butterflies* by Benjamin Wilkes, first published in 1749. Wilkes, too, was convinced that Red Admirable was the butterfly's true name, and later authors often followed his lead. But they are all probably wrong. Petiver's writings predate Wilkes's by nearly half a century, and he always called it The Admiral. In terms of precedent, Admiral wins.

some butterflies from Surinam in South America. For him, 'admirals' were butterflies whose brightest colour was confined to the corners of their wings, leaving the rest plain. It is a fair bet that he had borrowed the name 'admiral' from the famous Red Admiral, and used it as a generic name for other butterflies with a similar pattern. The analogy seems to have been with Admiralty flags. Whether or not by coincidence, the Union Jack was coming into use at the time when Petiver was writing – and the colours of the Red Admiral are indeed red, white and blue.

At first the name was simply 'The Admiral', as it still is in Germany. It became a Red Admiral to distinguish the species from the unrelated White Admiral (*see* Harbours). In France, by contrast, the butterfly is *Le Vulcain*, named after Vulcan, the blacksmith of the gods. Its wing pattern reminded people of flames and white-hot iron

A third name arose at about the same time, but it has long fallen into disuse. It was The Alderman, named after an official who wore formal robes of red trimmed with black. It probably helped that the name contained much the same letters as 'admirable'.

(For the scientific name of the Red Admiral *see* Vanessa.)

Arches, Architecture and Walls

Those who named our moths seem to have been well versed in architecture. Ancient building styles are represented by The Saxon and The Gothic moths. At a humbler level, we have The Wall butterfly and The Brick moth. We also have quite a number of moths named after arches. There is a Dark Arches and a Black Arches, a corresponding Light Arches, a Buff Arches and a Beautiful Arches, all moths with markings on their forewings that suggest a curved or pointed arch above a pair of columns. The Saxon moth is an 'arches' in all but name, for it too bears a rounded mark suggestive of the heavy masonry of Romanesque architecture. In the case of The Gothic moth and its fellows, the Feathered Gothic and the Bordered Gothic, the analogy is with rib vaulting and the elaborate tracery associated with Gothic architecture. The shared characteristic of these moths is a network of pale veins against a dark background. The scientific name of The Gothic is *typica*, meaning not 'typical' but 'a pattern'. In the early days they spelt it 'Gothick'.

As for The Wall butterfly, Moses Harris insisted that it was so named from its habit of settling on sunny walls. But there is surely also something brick-like in its warm-brown pattern interlaced

The Fox Moth, one of many moths named after an animal, in this case from its rich reddish-brown colour.

with dark veins of 'mortar'. Its earlier name was the Great Argus and that name survives in the Dutch name of *argusvlinder* (Argus butterfly). The Germans call it *mauerfuchs,* the wall fox.

The Scarce Brindle moth is a 'wall moth' to judge from its species name, *lateritia*, that is, 'made of brick', referring to its brick-brown forewings. There is another moth that is straightforwardly called The Brick. Look closely and you will see a pile of them near the edge of each forewing (this moth is also vaguely brick-coloured).

The Gothic moth was named after the white tracery on its wings recalling the stone ribbing of Gothic churches and cathedrals.

B

Beasts

Among the names of British moths lurks a magnificent menagerie of beasts: elephants, bears, tigers, wolves – and, at the other end of the scale, kittens and mice. We could begin with one of the oldest moth names, ·the Fox Moth, a big, hairy moth with reddish-brown 'fur' that reminded people of a fox (Benjamin Wilkes was the first to call it the 'Fox Coloured Moth'). But others see it differently. In France and Germany it is the bramble moth (*Bombyx de la Ronce*, *Brombeerspinner*), because its caterpillars were thought to feed on brambles. In Holland they know it as The Glutton (*Veelvraat*), perhaps because the female moth has a very plump abdomen.

They knew the Fox Moth's hairy caterpillar too. Country people called it 'the Devil's Gold Ring', after its distinctive yellow-orange bands. Perhaps it belonged to the Devil because handling the caterpillar can cause a rash to those with sensitive skin.

The Mouse Moth is coloured grey like a House Mouse, and it also scurries about in a vaguely mouse-like way. It is as likely to flee into a cranny as to fly away. A mouse has also visited the Dotted Footman and left a reminder. That moth's species name is *muscerda*, that is, mouse droppings. It refers to the dark, comma-shaped 'dots' on the moth's forewings, clearly left there by mini-mice.

One of the more unexpected moth-beasts is an antelope known to ancient writers as *pyrarga*, which means literally 'white rump'. The moth is *Protodeltote pyrarga*, the Marbled White Spot, and it too has a large white mark sitting neatly over its 'rump'. The usual suspect for its antlered antecedent is a kind of oryx known as the Addax, but the description better fits the Dama gazelle, which has a white patch at both ends, on its face and on its behind.

At the heavyweight end is the Elephant Hawk-moth, formerly known simply as 'The Elephant'. It is the caterpillar, not the moth, that is the elephant, for the former

The Small Elephant Hawk-moth is *porcellus* or 'the little pig', named, like its larger cousin, after its plump, snouty caterpillar.

has an extensible 'neck' recalling a trunk (though it is more probably pretending to be a little snake). I had always assumed that the moth's species name, *elpenor*, meant 'elephant' in the same way that the Small Elephant Hawk-moth is *porcellus*, the little pig. But in fact it also means 'pig'. The original Elpenor was a character in Homer's *Odyssey*, a member of the crew with Odysseus. His fate was to fall off a roof blind drunk and, according to some accounts, he was magically turned into a pig by the unforgiving Circe. (For more about hawk-moths, *see* Bees, Hawks, Monsters, Skulls and Pigs.)

In a confusion of carnivores, moth-bears (*Arctia*) are represented by the tiger-moths. The analogy is with the famous caterpillar of the Garden Tiger-moth, long known as the 'woolly bear', a once familiar hairy beast that caught people's imagination as it lumbered hairily along. In times past it was also called the 'oubit'. In much of Europe, as well as North America, they still call these moths 'bears'. But today the name 'woolly bear' has been snatched by the infinitely less prepossessing larva of the carpet beetle.

Moths named after wolves are so designated from their greyish fur that matches the coat of a northern wolf (*see* Wolves). Dogs are more sparsely represented and are so-named from markings that look like sharp teeth.

The Elephant Hawk-moth gets its name from its unusual caterpillar which appears to have an elephant's trunk.

The Dog's Tooth moth is the most obvious example, giving the impression of a pair of sharp canines along the edge of each forewing. The attractive Pyrale, *Cyneada dentalis*, has a whole row of sharp teeth that are revealed in its scientific name, which means: 'dog-form'/ (lots of) teeth'. The spiky markings form a perfect disguise when the moth is resting on a head of grass.

(For a much smaller dog, *see* Pugs. For more moth-beasts, *see* Cats, Goats, Leopards, Pigs and Tigers.)

Beauty

Ideas of beauty change. The plump, pink nudes of Rubens appeal less to us now than they presumably did to Rubens. So it is with moths. Several of those with the word 'beauty' in their name are among our least colourful moths, and their beauty is less than obvious. To understand why they were so favoured, we need to retrace our steps to the time of the Society of Aurelians. Among their leading lights were artists, embroiderers and traders in silk. They liked moths for their patterns and textures quite as much as for their colours. The moths might well have given them ideas for fabric designs. It also helped that moths such as the Satin Beauty will sit quietly with outstretched wings as if posing for a painting. And so in that light perhaps it, and the Great Oak Beauty, and the Brindled Beauty, deserve their names. Maybe we can even see beauty in the Beautiful Snout!

That pair of 'belles', the Straw Belle and the Yellow Belle, are more conventionally attractive moths, with coloured stripes and pretty feathered antennae. Perhaps they became belles rather than beauties because they are small and petite. It is harder to appreciate the very understated beauty of the July Belle, still less the Lead Belle, which take the idea of subtlety dangerously close to drab. But, as I say, the Aurelians obviously loved little grey moths.

Not so beautiful? The Mottled Beauty moth appealed to silk pattern designers.

The Camberwell Beauty doesn't live in Camberwell. Most other countries call it the Mourning Cloak.

Even more petite are the three moths named as 'pretty': the Pretty Marbled, the Pretty Pinion and the Pretty Chalk Carpet. All are dainty, charming little moths for whom the word 'pretty' certainly seems more apt than 'beautiful.'

Our single butterfly 'beauty' is by any standards a corker. To the Camberwell Beauty's gorgeousness and noble size, we can add, in Britain, the lustre of rarity. The butterfly was named after the old village of Camberwell, now buried in south London, where the first British specimen was taken. Some preferred the name The Grand Surpriz, while others managed to control their excitement and dub it The Willow Butterfly or The White-bordered. Abroad, both in Northern Europe and North America, where it is more familiar, the same butterfly is the Mourning Cloak (and in Europe too; the German name *Truermantel,* and the Dutch *rouwmantel*). Its broad wings reminded people of dark funereal garb with a contrasting white or yellow petticoat peeping out below: perhaps a woman putting on a show of mourning but wearing her party clothes underneath. The French see it in yet another way. There, the butterfly is *Morio*, from the Latin for 'fool' or 'jester'.

Bees

The Death's-head Hawk-moth entered history as the Bee Tiger Moth. Its body is striped like a bumblebee, black on yellow; and by the same token it is also striped like a tiger. Appropriately for a moth pretending to be a giant bee, it raids hives for their honey. Yet the apparent death's head on its thorax soon drove all other names away. And so this grand moth must re-enter our list under *Skulls*.

The real moth-bees are our two smallest hawk-moths, namely the Broad-bordered and Narrow-bordered Bee Hawks. Both are dead ringers for bumblebees. One could wish they were as common as bumblebees, but if they were, their secret would be out. A mimic needs to be less numerous than the original, for if predators ever worked out that bee hawk-moths are in fact sting-less and defenceless, they would be rumbled. Like bees, the moths fly by day, hence their genus *Hemaris*, which means 'of

the day'. Petiver called them 'moth drones', half bee, half moth.

The other kind of bee-moth lives inside the hive and is much less welcome. In fact the Bee Moth is a famous pest, its maggoty caterpillar feeding on whatever organic debris it can digest: old bee cells, wax, debris, dead insects, even the occasional live bee grub. Its species name, *sociella*, or 'associating together', is a reminder that you seldom find just one grub in the stricken hive; they prefer to scavenge in packs.

Another hive-raider is the Wax Moth. Its genus name, *Galleria*, derives from the larva's habit of building its own galleries in the honeycomb, though the nearest acceptable Greek word, *galeros*, means 'cheerful', which is not the likely reaction of the beekeeper! Its species name, *mellonella*, also has an ironical air: it derives from Mellona, the Roman goddess of beekeeping.

Belladonna

The Painted Lady is one of the best known, and one of the most widespread, butterflies in the world. British Painted Ladies fly up each year from the desert fringes of Morocco, usually in small to moderate numbers but occasionally in a virtual swarm, as occurred in 1996 and again in 2009. It is a flesh-coloured

The original name for the Painted Lady may have been Bella Donna.

The Bible

Scores of butterflies and moths have been named after figures in Greek or Roman mythology, yet surprisingly only one is named after a character in the Bible, and that one is very recent. It is a micro, *Monochroa moyses*, named after Moses (for whom 'Moyses' is an alternative spelling). But why Moses? Because, it seems, its caterpillar lives in bulrushes, much as the infant Moses did before his cradle was drawn forth by Pharaoh's daughter. This moth was first described and named by R. W. Uffen in 1991. It may well be that those who described and named species in times past had scruples about using the Bible as a source for names.

butterfly with dark circles in the forewings surrounding white 'eyes.' The allusion is to the cosmetics used by fashionable ladies who painted their faces with rouge, kohl and white lead, not to mention black 'beauty patches.' 'Painted Lady' does not necessarily imply women of low virtue. In France it is *La Belle Dame*, and in Spain, *bella dama o cardero*, 'the pretty lady of the thistles'. The sober Dutch dismiss the lady altogether. There it is only *distelvlinder*, the Thistle Butterfly.

It is possible that the butterfly was once known as the Bella Donna in England too. For it was 'Papilio Bella Donna dicta', noted James Petiver, 'a butterfly called Bella Donna'. That was also the name Linnaeus used half a century later. Five hundred years ago, Albrecht Dürer depicted a pair of Painted Ladies in his masterpiece, *The Adoration of the Magi*, fluttering suggestively close to the Virgin Mary. I wonder if he, too, called them Bella Donna.

A few species have names that at least allude to Bible stories. The species name of the Tortricid moth, *Eucosma campoliliana*, means 'lilies of the field', a reference to St Matthew's famous line, 'Consider the lilies of the field.' As you might expect, it is a pretty moth, pure white with dabs of black and brown. Its genus name, *Eucosma*, meaning 'well adorned', reinforces the sense of admiration.

Another possible allusion to the New Testament is *Jodis*, the genus of the Little Emerald moth. Emmet translates this as 'rusty-red', although the word appears in ancient texts as the colour of bile – that is, yellow or green. Jacob Hübner might have been thinking of the way the moth emerges in a pretty shade of pale green but soon fades to a dirty white, just as metal rusts over time. He may also have had in mind another text from Matthew: 'Lay not up for yourselves treasures upon earth, where moth and rust doth corrupt.' Hübner had a taste for verbal complexity. Linnaeus may never have seen a fresh green specimen of the Little Emerald, for he called it *lactearia*, from the colour of milk: the milk-moth.

The Seraphim moth bears the name of a band of senior angels, the ones that form a heavenly choir around the throne of God. 'Seraphim' is the plural word: one seraph, two seraphim. The allusion is clear only when the moth's wings are outstretched (John Curtis, who named it, was probably working from set specimens). According to the prophet Isaiah, a seraph has six wings. In the case of the moth, the forewings have unusual lobes that might count as extra wings. They also give the moth its genus, *Lobophora*, and its species name *halterata*, apparently from *halter*, a dumbbell used by gymnasts.

Birds

The best-known moth-bird is the Magpie Moth. Like a magpie, it is 'pied', that is, black and white. There is a similar but unrelated species, the Small Magpie moth, also with a black-and-white pattern (but a wholly different lifestyle, for this species feeds on nettles; Petiver called it the Mottled Nettle Moth).

A moth called the Bird's Wing has pinched, wavy-edged markings on the forewings which, when the moth is at rest, look a little like wings. Its genus is *Dypterygia*, meaning 'double wing', or, rather, 'wings within wings'. Of course it is only we who see such markings as wing-like. The moth hopes that no one will see it at all, relying on these inset 'wings' to disguise it as a chip of wood.

The Black Mountain Moth is *coracina*, a crow or raven. Like them it is black, but that is the limit of the comparison. And what about *scolopacina*, the Slender Brindle moth, named after *Scolopax*, the woodcock? Perhaps it was so called after the streaky pattern of its wings, resembling the streaked and mottled plumage of a woodcock. On a freshly emerged Slender Brindle you can even make out the fake feather-tips. Artists like Moses Harris and Benjamin Wilkes would have known that woodcock feathers were used to make fine paintbrushes, and you can imagine them painting this particular moth with the feathers of a real woodcock in a fusion of imagination and reality. The Feathered Brindle moth, on the other hand, has no connection with birds. Its 'feathers' are the plumed antennae of the male moth.

The Hummingbird Hawk-moth is one of the few moths to acquire nicknames.

Cepphis, the genus of the Little Thorn moth, is probably derived from the Greek word *kepphos,* a sea-bird of some kind, possibly the Storm Petrel (although *Cepphus* is the modern-day genus of the Black Guillemot). Possibly it is a pun, for *kepphos* also means 'a simpleton', or as we might say, 'a gull.' Either way the link with this undistinguished little moth is obscure.

Even more imagination is needed for the many case-bearing moths, *Coleophora,* that are named after birds. The caterpillars of these moths live inside self-spun cases of silk. The analogy, however, is not with them but with the long fringed forewings, resembling tiny feathers, of the adult moths. These mini-'feathers' are variously coloured. A moth with mottled brownish wings similar to the feathers of a kestrel is named *falconipenella.* Another, *tringipenella,* supposedly resembles the feathers of *Tringa,* a sandpiper. *Coleophora limosipenella* has the feathers of *Limosa,* a godwit. Other species of case-bearing

moth are named after a wren (*trochilella*), a bullfinch (*pyrrhulipennella*), and – this one is a stretch – a Lesser Whitethroat (*currucipenella*).

Then there are moths named after fantastical birds. Considerable imagination went into the names of The Phoenix and Small Phoenix moths. It seems that their reddish-brown wing-bars reminded someone of smoke, and the immortal bird arising from the flames with outstretched wings. The genus of the Black V moth celebrates another unlikely creature, *Arctornis,* a bear-bird – perhaps a polar-bear bird, for the ground colour of the moth is snow-white.

Last, but definitely not least, is the Hummingbird Hawk-moth, an insect that is sometimes mistaken for a real hummingbird that has somehow strayed across the Atlantic and ended up in a chilly English garden. It feeds at the hover on the nectar of flowers, and is lovely to watch as it patrols the flowerbed on warm, sunny afternoons, dipping in to sample a blossom, then darting out again. Its long tongue (proboscis) is alluded to in its genus *Macroglossum,* or 'long tongue'. Its species name, *stellatarum,* sounds starry but actually refers to the *Stellatae,* an old name for the flowers of bedstraw and wild madder on which the moth lays its eggs.

This is one of the few moths to inspire

an affectionate, if largely forgotten, nickname: 'merrylee-dance-a-pole'. In *The Book of A Naturalist*, W. H. Hudson quoted a lady who had enjoyed watching it as a child: 'We regarded it with mingled awe and joy, and followed its erratic and rapid flight with ecstasy. It was soft and brown, fluffy and golden too, and created in our infantile minds an indescribable impression of glory, brilliance, aloofness, elusiveness. We thought it a being from some other world.'

The French like it too; it is one of the few moths in France to collect a variety of local names, including *bonne nouvelle* ('good news'), *fleuze-bouquet* ('flower sniffer') and *saint-esprit* ('Holy Spirit'). Its usual name is Moro Sphinx; 'moro' is untranslatable, but perhaps carries a meaning of merriment. The Germans name it *Taubenschwanschen*, 'the pigeon's tail', as the outstretched banded 'tail' of the moth looks very like that of a wood pigeon. (*See also* Hawks, Peacocks and Swifts.)

Blood

A rush of blood to the face is the defining character of the charming Maiden's Blush, a pale moth with flushed pink 'cheeks'. To judge from its other name, *Cyclophora punctaria* ('I carry a ring ... and a dot') this maiden is engaged – although the ring is on her wing, not her finger. Closely related is another sanguinary moth, the Blood Vein, so-called from a red line that runs across both wings and joining neatly in the middle, as if an enemy had all but cut the poor moth in half.

Effusion of blood also characterises the Pearly Underwing moth, which is *saucia*, or 'wounded'. Perhaps Jacob Hübner had been impressed by the reddish tinge on the moth's forewings. This is a frisky moth that tends to scuttle about aimlessly, as if in terrible shock and pain.

A moth that actually does bleed as a defensive reaction, is the Crimson Speckled Footman, or *Utetheisa pulchella*, the 'beautiful/divine wound'. The moth's forewings are prettily sprinkled with red and black spots, like hundreds-and-thousands. Linnaeus described the effect as *nigro sanguineoque punctatis*, spotted with black and blood-red, suggesting a terrible discharge of blood and charred flesh, as if from an explosion. What he probably didn't know is that this moth can produce bubbles of actual insect blood, toxic and yellow, from behind its head whenever it is sufficiently vexed.

Blossom

The Peach Blossom is a very pretty moth with pink-spotted wings that remind me of flowery wallpaper. Peach trees were valued as much for their pink early springtime blossom as for their delicious fruit; they were often planted in walled gardens in the eighteenth century, when the moth acquired its name. The blossom on the moth's wings is not really peach but bramble. The caterpillars feed by night on the flowers of brambles and raspberry bushes, and its pink spots probably help to disguise the moth when at rest among the fallen petals. We seem to be the only nation to call it the Peach Blossom. In Europe it is usually the bramble moth (*La Batis*, after its specific name, *batis*) or, in Germany, the rose owl (*Roseneule*).

Our other blossom moth is the Blossom Underwing, a Quaker moth in all but name. Its species name, *miniosa*, means 'like red lead', a reference to the pinkish tint of some forms of the moth. The moth earned its common name because, like other early-flying Orthosia moths, it is attracted to sallow blossom. In France it is *Orthosie rougeoyante*, the glowing Orthosia, perhaps from the way the pale wings reflect moonlight or torch beam.

Peach Blossom: winged wallpaper.

The Blues

Ten species of British butterflies are coloured blue (or at least, the males are), while in Europe that number increases to eighty or more. Although our species may seem reasonably distinct, the early lepidopterists had a lot of trouble sorting out the blues. It seems they were less impressed by their brilliant colours as by the multitude of little eyed spots on the reverse of their wings, for they named them not blues but arguses (*see* Eyes).

The name 'blue' began to take over towards the end of the eighteenth century, when the Large Blue and the Small Blue first appeared under those names in William Lewin's *Papilios of Great Britain* (1795). In Victorian times, some species had alternative names. Indeed, the Adonis Blue had several: you could take your pick from the Clifden Blue, the Dartford Blue, the Turquoise Blue, the Celestial Blue and The Ultramarine, although I think the right name won in the end. *Adonis* used to be the butterfly's Latin name, alluding to the beautiful youth of myth (it is, after all, the brightest and prettiest of the British blues).

The Holly Blue has also at various times been the Azure Blue, while the Common Blue was also once the Blue Argus. In the same way, the Chalkhill Blue was also the Light Blue, and the Small Blue the Bedford Blue. In the case of the rare The

Short-tailed Blue, the alternative name of Bloxworth Blue still holds, probably because it sounds pleasantly alliterative. The names of blues had settled down by the twentieth century, but even now authors differ on how to spell 'Chalkhill'. Should it be Chalk Hill, or Chalk-hill, or Chalkhill? *Quot homines tot sententiae* (So many people, so many opinions).

Bottoms

Certain moths are noted for their colourful bottoms, or 'tails'. The Brown-tail moth was already known by that name in 1780, when its webs of stinging caterpillars caused great alarm in the London area. They stripped bushes to the bone, and anyone trying to remove the webs with his bare hands received a nasty rash for his pains. Some claimed the caterpillars had been sent as a punishment for the nation's sins, like one of the plagues of Egypt. The phenomenon was investigated by the botanist William Curtis, who concluded (correctly) that the moth would soon disappear once the weather grew cooler. His paper on the great Brown-tail scare, published in 1782 and including a beautiful plate of the moth and its life-history, was one of the first proper ecological investigations. The Brown-tail's webs are still pervasive, especially along the south coast and the Thames estuary, but they no longer cause panic.

The adult Brown-tail moth looks deceptively innocent, with its wings of pure white edged with a fringe of fluffy hair that makes it resemble a loose feather when at rest. It is named after a distinctive dark-brown anal tuft, which is especially pronounced in the female moth. This hairy bottom is celebrated twice over in the moth's euphonious scientific name, *Euproctis chrysorrhoea*, the 'good bottom' that 'flows with gold'. This name would be more appropriate for a related species, the Yellow-tail, whose species name is *similis*, that is, 'similar'. Perhaps 'flows with brown' would have given the wrong impression!

Other names guaranteed to make a schoolboy smile include *Eriogaster*, or 'woolly belly', the genus of the Small Eggar, whose bottom end is, in Linnaeus's words, 'strongly furnished with white wool'. Its purpose is not so much to keep the moth warm as to protect its eggs. After laying a batch, the mother moth

The anal tuft of the Brown-tail moth also inspired its scientific name which translates as 'the good bottom which flows with gold'!

will carefully cover them in stinging fluff detached from its rear end.

The rear end of the Pyrale *Eurhodope cirrigerella* is bright yellow. Its scientific name means 'lovely rosy-face bearing a lock of [yellow] hair', not on the moth's head but sticking out of its bottom. Not that its yellow tuft has done it any good, for 'rosy face' is no longer found in Britain.

The still common Pale Tussock moth is *pudibunda*, the shame-faced or blushing one. This is a moth that seems to have covered its genitals with a fig-leaf of hair. Another reading of its scientific name would imply the opposite, for it could also mean 'disgraceful, a shameful thing'. If so, Linnaeus may have been thinking of the moth's long hairy legs. As Colonel Emmet comments, 'No well-bred lady would flaunt her legs as this moth does.' The Germans call it *Streckfuss*, 'stretch-foot'.

Brunettes

Burnet moths are perhaps the most familiar day-flying moths, for they are brightly coloured, seeming to mock fate with their glossy, red-spotted wings. Almost as conspicuous as the adults are their squat, yellow, black-spotted caterpillars, rather like psychedelic woodlice, not to mention the highly visible papery cocoons they spin halfway up a grass stem. Their secret is cyanide,

The Six-spot Burnet has an unlikely link with the hammerhead shark.

stored from their foodplants – various species of vetch. Birds tend to give the highly toxic burnet moths a wide berth.

'Burnet' is an old name, possibly a folk name rescued by science. It meant dark, as in 'brunette', and it was also the name of a dark woollen cloth in the Middle Ages. The word is derived ultimately from the Old French *burnete*, a variation of *brunete* and a diminutive of *brun* – in other words, brown. The name has also been borrowed for wildflowers with dark bobbly heads: the Great and Salad Burnet, which, coincidently or not, often grow in places where burnet moths abound. Burnet moths also have an iridescent sheen, and so there may be some link with 'burnish', which also comes from the French word *brun*. Folk names do not need to be literal or exact.

As we have seen, *Zygaena*, the genus of all seven species of our burnet moths, is one of Fabricius's word puzzles. The name occurs twice in the natural world, for the burnets and for the original hammerhead shark! This unlikely coupling can only be explained in context. When originally set up, *Zygaena* was a catch-all genus containing all kinds of unrelated moths. Although it was subsequently whittled down to the burnet moths, it was not designed for them alone. Colonel Emmet suggests that the name was coined as a counterpoint to another kind of monster, the Sphinx, the old name for the hawk-moths; for, after all, is not the hammerhead shark a 'monstrous' fish? Or so they thought back then.

The species names of most burnet-moth species allude to their supposed foodplant, though in some cases the namers got the wrong one. The Six-spot Burnet, *filipendulae*, feeds on bird's-foot trefoil and other wild members of the pea family, not on *Filipendula*, or dropwort. Nor does the Narrow-bordered Five-spot Burnet, *lonicerae*, have the slightest interest in *Lonicera*, or honeysuckle. As for the rare Mountain Burnet, *Zygaena exulans*, it is certainly 'exiled' in Britain to some remote hills in the Highlands. But it was named for its original place of discovery, which was not Scotland but the Austrian Alps.

C

Calendar

The name originally given to the Pearl-bordered Fritillary was the April Fritillary, though there was some muddle over this, as both John Ray and James Petiver applied that same name to the later-flying Small Pearl-bordered Fritillary. The two species are very similar, but the Pearl-bordered one always emerges first. All the same, until recently it would have been unusual to see it in April. Mid- to late May, with the trees in fresh green leaf, was the peak time for Pearl Borders. The reason it was called the April Fritillary is that in those days they still used the Julian calendar, which began the year eleven days earlier, so that our 1st of May was their April 19th. The new calendar

The April Fritillary, better known today as the Pearl-bordered Fritillary.

was not adopted until 1751, having been rejected because (a) it was foreign, and (b) as it was called the 'Gregorian calendar', it was associated with the Pope, and Protestant England didn't like 'popish' practices.

With climate change upon us, the Pearl-bordered Fritillary is once again an April fritillary, at least in southern England in forward springs.

Carpets

The one thing everyone knows about moths is that they chew carpets. There is one gnawing at my carpet right now, the loathsome Case-bearing Clothes-moth. Try as I might, with hoovers and sprays and lavender bags, the moth always returns, mockingly flying around the light of the telly on warm summer nights and driving me mad. This species, plus a few more of its ghastly relatives, also enjoys nibbling woollen and fur coats, woolly jumpers, book bindings and, should you have any, tapestries. Moths are one reason why so few old tapestries survive. I knew someone whose sock drawer had been invaded by an army of Case-bearing Clothes-moths. The grubs managed to recycle the bright colours of the socks into their own silken tubes and in the end they looked as though they were all wearing Pringle knitwear. The clothes moth's habitat, the books tell us, is 'indoors'.

Only a half-dozen species of British moths are able to chew and digest woollen carpets. Nearly all the rest feed on green plants at the caterpillar stage, in most cases harmlessly. These vegetarians include species that are actually called carpet moths, not from their choice of food but because they have wing patterns that recall a carpet, which back in those days was an expensive luxury. In this sense 'carpet moth' is a compliment. The Aurelians loved their delicate, subtle colours and tints, and may have drawn ideas from them when designing fabrics. Carpets inspired the name of the moths, but they in turn might have inspired the design of a carpet. (*See* Fabrics.)

We have some fifty-four species of carpet moths. Most of them are in the Geometer family, though they are not all related. Some sound like the sort of carpet you would be happy to have in your house: the Blue-bordered Carpet, for instance, or the Silver-ground Carpet, or the Yellow-ringed Carpet – or, in another way, the Spruce Carpet. The Fortified Carpet (a rare immigrant) would surely withstand a lot of wear-and-tear, while the Scorched Carpet will need urgent restoration. The Sandy Carpet sounds as though it had suffered from bare feet in a seaside boarding house, whilst the Chalk Carpet perhaps got its dusting in a school classroom. You could imagine fairies dancing on a Wood Carpet or a Garden Carpet. And the Beautiful Carpet, as its name implies, is the pick of the bunch.

Carpet moths were named from their wing-patterns, not from their love of carpets. This is the Pretty Chalk Carpet.

Caterpillars

The life cycle of all advanced insects proceeds through four stages: tiny egg, crawling larva, immobile chrysalis or pupa, and finally the adult, which usually has wings as well as six legs. By convention, the larvae of butterflies and moths are called caterpillars, perhaps to distinguish them from less appealing kinds of larvae, such as 'grubs' and 'maggots'. Unlike the adult insect, which does not grow any further, the caterpillar begins life as a tiny being emerging from its pinhead egg, but ends up in some cases the size of a cigar. Some species are found more easily as caterpillars than as adults (at least before the invention of light traps), and hence the caterpillar was

sometimes better known than the moth. So it is not surprising that the Puss Moth, the Lobster Moth, the elephant hawk-moths, and many others, were named after their spectacular caterpillars.

An alternate word for a caterpillar, at least in learned writings, was *eruca* (or *uruca*), taken from the discourses of Pliny and other Latin authors. Whether or not by coincidence, *eruca* is also the Latin name for a cabbage plant, so perhaps the original 'eruca' was the caterpillar of the cabbage white butterfly. It has also lent us the word *eruciform*, or 'caterpillar-shaped'. Yet another common name was simply 'worm', for most caterpillars are long, thin and segmented, like earthworms. An injurious kind of caterpillar was the smooth-bodied cankerworm that digs into and damages garden vegetables. Hawk-moth caterpillars have a spike on their rear-ends that looks like a stinger and inspired the folk-name 'hoss-stengs'.

In the past, and perhaps still, caterpillars also had local names. Orkney has a unique set of names for wildlife, in which caterpillars appear as 'brottlicks'. At the other end of Great Britain, on the Isle of Wight, they are called 'mallishags'. Communal caterpillars that weave conspicuous webs in hedgerows were sometimes referred to as 'puckets'. In Scotland and northern England, a hairy caterpillar is an 'oubit', variously spelt as 'yeubit' or 'woubit', depending on how it was pronounced. Caterpillars can also be 'dogs'. Hop-pickers used to call the hairy caterpillars of the Pale Tussock moth 'hop-dogs', and sometimes called the prickly caterpillar of the Comma butterfly the same name, too. Unfortunately, you would be lucky to find a single hop-dog on today's well-sprayed crops.

Children used to give all sorts of funny names to caterpillars. I can remember 'wriggly' or 'wiggly', and 'hairy granny'; and they are also called 'shit-shooters' for obvious reasons. Do children still play games with caterpillars and make up names for them? Could be, but if they do, none of them have mentioned it to me.

Cats

The Puss Moth is famous, but which is the pussy, the moth or its fantastical caterpillar? The former is as fluffy as a white Persian cat, but perhaps it is the caterpillar that really deserves the palm with its cartoon-like 'face' (Tom in Tom and Jerry) and its angrily waving tail ('it has a forked tail springing from a blackish grape-stone,' noted Thomas Moffet with his customary inventiveness). Historically and culturally, this odd caterpillar has always received far more attention than its moth. Its species name, *vinula*, from the wine-coloured patch on

The kitten moths (this is a Poplar Kitten) are named after their frisky little caterpillars.

the caterpillar's back, like a saddle for a fairy rider, was (as we've seen) borrowed by Linnaeus from Moffet. Going with the trend, the genus name, *Cerura*, also ignores the adult moth; it means 'horn-tail', a reference to those fascinating 'tails'. Eleazar Albin had heard of another name for the Puss Moth: 'The Beau'.

The Puss Moth has kittens – three of them in Britain. Today they are named after their respective foodplants: the Alder, Poplar and Sallow Kittens. In the past they were named differently. The Poplar one was *The* Kitten; the others were The Barred Kitten and the Dark-barred Kitten. As you might expect, each kitten is like a miniature version of the Puss, with frisky little caterpillars to match. Their genus is *Furcula*, or 'fork', yet another reference to those shaking anal appendages.

The other mothy cat is a darker beast in every sense. A Pyralid moth known as 'The Large Tabby' has dark, patterned wings that recall the furry blotches and swirls of a tabby cat's coat. ('Tabby', in turn, comes from an Old French word for a striped silken fabric). Like tabby cats, the tabby moth likes people, but not in the same way. Lurking in pantries, stables and outhouses, its unlovely caterpillar, a maggoty, blackish worm inside a dirty silken tube, moves about in the dark, feeding on spilt grain, refuse and dung. It has a particular taste for old, greasy clothes of the sort you might find hanging up inside a shed or stable. Linnaeus named the species *pinguinalis*, from *pinguis* or fat (the same word that gave us penguin, a fat bird), noting that, 'It lives on fats, usually on butter etc, in houses and kitchens.' And then the Swedish master decided to shock his readers by adding, 'occasionally [found] in the human belly, the most loathsome of worms.' Leaving aside the unlikelihood of any caterpillar surviving long in our digestive tract, this bit of gossip seems to be based on folklore. Possibly this one, or a smaller moth called the Small Tabby, also known as the Grease Moth, had been found feeding on fats exuding from a rotting corpse. And why not? In nature, species like the tabby moth do a useful job in cleaning up the debris left behind by animals and birds. After we die, what are we but debris?

The first mention of a tabby moth in British history was by John Ray in the 1690s. He had managed to breed it through from a 'smooth black caterpillar' to the resulting moth. He had discovered the grub tucking into the leather bindings of his books. Instead of flattening it, he raised it with the proper care and attention of a true scientist.

Characters

Several moths have been called 'characters', not after some remarkable or eccentric person, but because of some graphic symbol visible on their wings. The Chinese Character moth, for instance, is named after a pattern delicately traced on its wing veins in silvery lines, one that looks a little like the Chinese letter 'ai'. The moth is not really trying to impress us with its knowledge of Mandarin. It is trying hard to convince a passing predator that it is nothing more than a fresh bird dropping. The glistening 'character' is part of the disguise. No other nation has seen a Chinese letter on this little

The Chinese Character has a Mandarin logogram hidden in its wings, although the British are apparently the only people to notice it.

The Hebrew Character is so named after its 'letter-mark', although Linnaeus saw it as 'Gothic'.

moth. The Dutch call it the 'white tail' and the French 'the little spike', while the Germans see the face of a tiny owl.

There is also the Hebrew Character, which has a black mark in the midst of its forewings that resembles the serif version of the Hebrew letter *nun*, the equivalent of our 'n'. Linnaeus, taking an independent line as usual, saw the mark as more Gothic in form, and so named it *gothica*. A second moth with a similar marking, this time outlined in white, is the gloriously named Setaceous Hebrew Character. 'Setaceous' means 'bearing a bristle,' and refers to the white line around the 'character' mark. A well-known Jewish moth collector, the Baron de Worms, whose thinning hair stood up in stiff tufts, was affectionately known by his fellow moth-hunters by that name. Once again, however, Linnaeus saw not a Hebrew character, but a black letter 'c', and so he named the moth *c-nigrum*, the black 'c'. (*See* Letters.)

Chastity

One of the oldest moth names is The Nun, the alternate name for the Black Arches. It transcends the barriers of language, for everyone seems to agree that this attractive black-and-white moth is a nun, whether as *nonne* in France, or as *Nonvlinder* ('nun-butterfly') in Germany and the Netherlands. Linnaeus translated the word into Latin as *monacha*, a moth dressed in a nun's habit. Perhaps the link is with the moth's white thorax, the counterpart of a nun's white headdress (just as a country name for the blue tit was 'nun', from the white fillet around its head). The moth's black markings are V-shaped and so provide it with the peculiarly English name of Black Arches. Perhaps it has something to do with the fact that we are a Protestant country.

The Black Arches is famous not only for its beauty but for the damage it can cause. On the Continent and in North America but more rarely in Britain, it is a pest of trees, particularly pines. In some years the web-living caterpillars can be abundant enough to defoliate whole boughs and so weaken the tree. The moth's genus name, *Lymantria*, refers to this dark side of The Nun: it means a 'spoiler', a 'destroyer of trees', though Hübner, who coined the name, may have been thinking primarily of the even more destructive Gypsy Moth, *Lymantria dispar.*

The Black Arches is also known as The Nun moth from its black-and-white wings over a pink body.

Two pale-coloured moths are named after the Vestal Virgins of ancient Rome. Back then, chastity was enforced on pain of death for any woman wishing to become a Vestal. The moth named The Vestal is yellow with a red stripe, which Linnaeus seems to have believed was the costume worn by the Vestal Virgins (he may have confused it with the purple-striped toga worn by senators). He named the moth *sacraria*, the female keeper of the sacred temple. A second 'vestal' is the Reed Tussock, whose pale, immaculate wings must have suggested an alternative priestly garb and so prompted the generic name *Laelia*, a Vestal Virgin who also lent her name to a genus of orchids.

Another chaste moth is The Vapourer, whose species name is *antiqua*, meaning 'ancient' or 'long ago'. A natural assumption would be that it commemorates the moth's 'antique' colour, a rich rusty-brown. But Linnaeus knew that the female Vapourer is wingless. He seems to have thought of it as a virtuous matron who stays at home and does not gad about with men. In other words, The Vapourer is an old-fashioned moth, honest and chaste – although perhaps something of a secret show-off, for its genus, *Orgyria*, means 'the span of one's outstretched arms' (the moth usually settles with its front legs well apart). (For the meaning of 'Vapourer' *see* Vapours.)

The small family Nolidae consists of five little moths, most of which are in the genus *Nola*. And what is Nola? There is a town of that name in southern Italy but without obvious relevance. More likely it comes from that well-known Latin irregular verb *nolo*, meaning 'I am unwilling', or 'I refuse' (as in Christ's admonition to Mary Magdalene, *noli me tangere*). Some of the *Nola* moths are pale-coloured, and one in particular, the Short-cloaked Moth, has wings that might remind a suitably disposed scholar of the garb of a nun. If so, then *Nola* could be yet another word indicative of purity: they are moths that say 'no', and they mean it. (For the most spectacular example of chastity among moths, the Psychidae or bagworms, *see* Dreams.)

China and Porcelain

Moths that live in wet places must be able to put up with occasional flooding. In effect, their caterpillars hold their

China-marks are aquatic moths named after the pellucid markings on some species.

breath, although they say the caterpillar of the Elephant Hawk-moth can actually swim to safety (after a fashion). But there is a select group of moth caterpillars that are perfectly at home in the water, and can breathe underwater with the help of structures resembling gills. These are the china-mark moths. The adult moths fly over water to lay their eggs on pond plants but are not otherwise aquatic. It is their caterpillars which require a pond net.

The china-marks are named from the resemblance of their wing patterns to makers' marks pressed into Chinese porcelain. These marks are most obvious on the Beautiful and the Brown China-mark moths (the others probably took their names from these two). The Beautiful China-mark is easily the prettiest species. Its generic name, *Nymphula*, was taken from the name of a water-lily, but it could also mean a water nymph or a pond spirit. In older books the moth was named *Nymphula stagnata*, a nymph of the pond, but more recently it has changed its name to *Nymphula nitidulata*, the shining nymph.

The Brown China-mark is the largest, and perhaps the commonest, species, with a caterpillar that begins life by mining into floating leaves such as water-lilies and frogbit, but which later lives like a caddisfly inside a home-spun leafy case. Its scientific name is *Elophila nymphaeata*: a nymph that 'loves a watery meadow'. It may have been named from the haunt of the adult moth before the remarkable habits of its caterpillar were known.

Cloaks and Hoods

Several moths seem to wear short 'cloaks'. Dark patches on the part of the forewing nearest the body give the impression that the moth has slipped on a cape to keep warm in the evening before venturing out. This is most obvious when the wings are closed and the moth is at rest; in flight, or on a set specimen, the two halves of the cloak are flung wide apart. The Short-cloaked moth, *Nola cucullatella*, also wears a hood, or *cucullus* in Latin. Other cloak-swathed moths, named for similar reasons, are the Cloaked Carpet, the Cloaked Minor and the Cloaked Pug.

The 'hoods' of certain other moths are formed by the shape of the crest on their thorax. This *cucullus* provides a genus name for the shark moth family, *Cucullia*, and also for the species name of

The Coxcomb Prominent has a crested thorax which reminded some of a monk's cowl and others of a jester's cap.

the Maple Prominent, *cucullina*. In the case of the pretty Royal Mantle moth, the namer, Johann Siegfried Hufnagel, evidently meant to say *cucullata* but absentmindedly left out the second 'l'. What his word *cuculata* actually means is 'cuckoo': 'the cuckoo moth'. Under the rules, this nonsensical name must stay.

For two more prominents, their thoracic crests put people in mind of different orders of monks. The Coxcomb Prominent, *capucina*, gets its scientific name from the Capuchin friars, who wore brown habits (this 'hood' is the same feature as the 'coxcomb' of the common name). The Scarce Prominent, *carmelita*, gets the Carmelite order, where they wear a dark scapular over a white habit, matching the colour of the moth's crest. They are the 'moth-monks'.

Clouds

Three butterflies, and seven species of larger moths, have cloudy names, among them Clouded Buff, Clouded Brindle, Clouded Magpie and Clouded Silver, and, of course, Clouded Yellow. What they have in common are indistinct greyish or dark markings that recall rain clouds. Often these 'clouds' suffuse or conceal other, paler colours, like a gathering thunderstorm in a summer sky. The Clouded Magpie moth, for instance, has pale greyish, blotchy markings that float on its white wings, as do the suffusions of black scales on the Clouded Silver. The unrelated Silver Cloud moth has a dark cloud relieved by a pale marking nearest the body that raises the prospect of a silver lining.

The name Clouded Yellow first surfaces in 1749 for a species formerly known as the Saffron Butterfly. It refers to the dark wing-margins and also perhaps to a greyish suffusion on the hindwings, both of which are more prominent on the female butterfly. Clouds are perhaps not the feature that would strike us today if we were naming this butterfly afresh, but where would we ever find such a perfect, poetic name? As for 'Saffron Butterfly', it is a translation of Petiver's original name, *Papilio croceus*, or the 'Crocus butterfly'. Saffron is a spice made from the deep orange stigmas of crocus flowers, and its colour is a good match for the male butterfly's wings. Fortunately, the Clouded Yellow is still classified as *croceus* after more than three hundred years.

Colours

Butterflies are the most colourful of insects, and what could be more natural than to name them after their myriad hues? Among our modest seventy-odd species almost every colour in the rainbow is represented: red, orange, yellow, green, blue and purple, as well as brown, black and white, plus the metallic colours of silver and copper. Moths, too, are often named after colours, though, as befits insects of the night that need to hide or disguise themselves by day, their names usually reflect more sombre tints: buff, clay, straw, umber, grey or chestnut. But there are brighter moths, too: greens and emeralds, silvers and golds, even reds and yellows, not to mention the eponymous Orange Moth.

Among the scientific names lurk more subtle gradations of colour. Among the moths named after shades of brown we find *brunnea* (plain brown), *baja* (bay-brown), *ferruginea* (rusty brown), *furva* (dusky brown), *hepatica* (liver-brown), *lutulenta* (muddy), *tristalis* (sad or sombre brown), *semibrunnea* (half-brown), *spadiceana* (nut-brown) and *Ceramica* (the colour of earthenware).

Some moth names refer to colour in an allusive way. Take these for example:

adusta: literally 'sun-burnt'. The Dark Brocade, you might say, has acquired a deep tan.

Agrochola: these orangey-yellow moths of early autumn are 'the colour of bile'. Their English names are kinder: Beaded Chestnut and Yellow-line Quaker.

floslactata: the 'flower of the milk' – in other words, the cream. Its English name is the Cream Wave moth.

gaunacella: from *gaunacum*, a kind of fur prepared from the skins of mice; and, yes, that fits the colour of the micro-moth, *Tischeria gaunacella*, exactly.

lutatella: a moth 'bedaubed with mud'.

What is so 'high' about the High Brown Fritillary? It's the colour: 'high brown' meant bright golden-brown, the opposite of sombre or 'sad' brown.

What colour is mud? In the case of the micro *Brachmia lutatella,* it seems to be a nondescript brownish-grey with touches of reddish-ochre.

miata: to urinate. The Autumn Green Carpet has green wings that fade to yellow.

Miltochrista: 'anointed with red earth': a suitable name for the carmine-winged Rosy Footman moth.

mulinella: 'pertaining to a mule'; in other words, mule-coloured. Like the animal, this micro-moth is grey with a dark patch running up the middle.

osseola: 'somewhat bone-coloured': an apt description of the washed-out look of the Marshmallow Moth.

pictalis: literally 'painted bright', as seen in *Pyralis pictalis,* the gaily coloured Painted Meal Moth.

porphyrana: porphyry is a kind of reddish mineral, but the moth name refers rather to an expensive dye called Tyrian purple. It is a natural dye produced from marine sea snails, and was retained for the purple line running down the robes of a senator. And yes, *porphyrana* is a pretty moth with some interesting purplish spots.

siterata: 'pertaining to corn'. The beauty of this name lies not just in the colour but a change in its hue. Just as corn ripens from green to gold, so the forewings of the Dark Marbled Carpet 'mature' from green to yellow.

suasa: 'a colour produced by dyeing', a reference to the smoky brown colour of the forewing of the Dog's Tooth moth.

thalassina: sea-coloured. The wings of the Pale-shouldered Brocade are not sea-blue but they do bear wavy markings and so could be said to be sea-like. R. D. Macleod had a more ingenious solution: the wings, he says, are reddish-brown, recalling Homer's 'wine-dark' sea.

D

Dancers

The Small Skipper butterfly is not well named. It is only a bit smaller than the Large Skipper and is bigger than several other British skippers. It is, however, a particularly skippy skipper, and is so-named, as Moses Harris explained, from 'a kind of skipping motion, which is affected by reason of their closing their wings so often in their passage'. The Small Skipper's generic name, *Thymelicus,* indicates that this skipper is also a dancer. Its lively movements, passing in a moth-like blur from one place to another, then freezing to a halt with outspread wings, reminded the learned Jacob Hübner of

The tap-dancer: the Nettle Tap.

the *Thumelikos*, a word used by Plutarch to mean 'theatrical, in a vulgar way'. Apparently the original *Thumelikos* were dancers who would hop and skip about the stage before freezing with outstretched palms, as if they were playing a game of statues. These pauses presumably came at a dramatic moment in the action when choric comment seemed to be necessary. The Thumelikos indicated their view of the proceedings not by voice but by gesture, with eloquent movements of the hands. And so, in a like manner, the Small Skipper became *Thymelicus sylvestris*, the little 'dancer of the woods' – though, in England at least, it prefers long grass in full sunshine to the shade of trees.

More little dancers are found among the micros. The genus *Choreutis* comes from another word for the chorus in Greek drama. The moths fly by day and make quick, jerky movements when they settle on a flower to feed. Their leader is the Nettle Tap, a regular tap-dancer among moths, jerking and spinning

on its nettle-leaf stage. It has a nice scientific name too: *Anthophila fabriciana*: 'Fabricius's flower-lover', which is not a long way from 'fab flower-lover'.

You might also expect to find *Morophaga choragella*, the clothes moth, whose species name means 'leader of the chorus'. This moth is quite large for a micro, bigger than its fellow nibblers, which is presumably why it is the 'leader'. Size really counts in this imaginary world.

Darts

A group of Noctuid moths with dark markings shaped like the blade of a knife. (*See* Weapons.)

Death

Doom surrounds the scientific name of the Olive Crescent moth, *Trisateles emortualis*. Quite why this little moth should carry a scientific name that means 'Thrice fruitless/pertaining to death' is a mystery. Its caterpillar feeds on dead leaves, but that was not known at the time it was named. Possibly it is a reference to the way the moth fades in collections from a pretty pale olive to a nondescript dirty yellow. Coincidentally, it is usually the last species in the field guide, right at the back just before the index. (For the Death's-head Hawk-moth, *see* Skulls.)

Different Names

Most British butterflies and moths have well-established names, but there are a few cases where we seem unable to make up our minds. Short-tailed Blue and Bloxworth Blue is one example: different names for the same butterfly. The Long-tailed Blue also has an alias. Abroad, it is often known as the Pea Blue. In North America, where they have never heard of Camberwell, the Camberwell Beauty is the Mourning Cloak.

The United States has different names for other British butterflies. When the Small White became established there, it was promptly renamed the Cabbage White (there are no Large Whites in North America to confuse matters). Our Essex Skipper, another Old World introduction, was promptly renamed the European Skipper. Our Silver-spotted Skipper is their Branded Skipper, so-named from the conspicuous black sex-brand on the forewings of the male butterfly. What we call brimstones and clouded yellows are all 'sulphurs' in America, while butterflies that look a bit like our Marsh Fritillary are 'checkerspots'. They also have a lot of Dingy Skipper lookalikes known as 'duskywings', and some relatives of the Holly Blue called 'Azures'. We say 'Apollo', they say 'Parnassian'. It's the same thing.

Doubt and Confusion

Every enthusiast knows and loves those honestly named moths The Suspected and The Confused. Each is an archetypally nondescript brown moth which is disconcertingly similar to another species, and so leaves the poor recorder in a state of doubt, if not confusion. The Confused moth, which is sometimes referred to with a disrespectful lack of the definite article as 'Confused', is a moth which closely resembles the Dusky Brocade. The Suspected has a matching Latin name, *suspecta*, which strictly speaking means 'mistrusted' rather than 'suspected'. When naming it, Jacob Hübner may have mistrusted his own judgement on whether or not the moth was really a good species. As it happens, he was right: it is. The moth knew that all the time.

The Marbled Coronet moth is named *confusa* in a different sense. There is no difficulty in recognising this pretty moth. It is its colours that are 'confused', a mishmash of black, white and brown

The Confused. But it's we that are confused, not the moth.

forming a perfect camouflage for hiding among lichen.

The moth called *anomala*, The Anomalous, is confusing not because it is hard to recognise but from its affinities. It is a Noctuid, but all the same it doesn't look like one. With its narrow, glossy-grey forewings and ample hindwings, the moth looks more like a Pyrale. It's a puzzle – in short, an anomaly.

We find more anomalies in a species that Hübner named The Doubtful Moth. His name for it, *ambiguella*, gives the game away: it is, in fact, a Tortricid moth, but Hübner thought it was a Tineid, and so gave it a name to match that family, thus ending it in *-ella* instead of *-ana*. And since you cannot change the name retrospectively, *ambiguella* it remains, an exiled *-ella* among the *-anas*.

Further areas of dubiety lurk among a quartet of micros called *dubitana*, *dubitella*, *dubitata* and *dubiella*. All are variations on the Latin word *dubius* or 'doubtful', and they are all, as you might expect, tricky little moths. More head-scratching was called for in a name coined by Jacob Hübner, *Exapate*, meaning 'gross deceit'. As Colonel Emmet explains, 'The deceit for Hübner lay in a Tineid looking like a Tortricid; in fact it is the other way round.' Confused? I certainly am.

(*See* Uncertain.)

Dreams

The ancient Greeks had a word for the soul, *psuche*, which was also their name for a butterfly, as if they were one and the same thing. It may perhaps reflect an ancient belief that the human soul is liberated from the body in the form of a white butterfly. The life cycle of butterflies and moths gave credence to this idea. It begins with a crawling earthly caterpillar (the ancients had no idea about the egg stage). Then the caterpillar seems to die and become entombed – the pupal or chrysalis stage. And finally, miraculously, a gorgeous winged being is reborn, arising from this 'tomb' and taking flight.

Artists represented the embodiment of the soul as a lovely young woman, Psyche, who sported a pair of butterfly wings, or had a butterfly fluttering permanently above her head. Psyche gave numerous artists the excuse to paint or sculpt ladies in the nude, often in combination with Cupid, who comes along to awaken in her mind the idea of love and sex, or, to state the thing more platonically, the mystic union of the spirit and the flesh.

In our day the word 'psyche' has become attached to Freudian psychology, and so has come to be associated with the subconscious and dreams. Butterflies appeal to the dreamy side of our

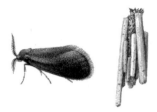

Psyche: the bagworm and its 'bag', a case built by its caterpillar.

natures. We watch them and imagine them as free or happy or feckless – a fantasy that lives on in the form of tattoos and greetings cards, and also in advertising in which real or imagined butterflies flutter around the product. The Greek god of dreams was Morpheus or Morphos, who has given us morphine as well as Morpho, the great blue jungle butterfly of South America. When I saw my first Morpho I did wonder whether I was fully awake. They are butterflies that dreams are made on.

Given the original sacred nature of *psuche*, and the inevitability of that word being used in the name of a butterfly or moth, we might expect the chosen one to be a brilliant, Morpho-like species. If so, it may come as a surprise to see what kind of creature the scientific *Psyche* actually is. It is a bagworm. A little black moth whose better-known caterpillar lives inside a self-spun bag, often with little bits of wood or lichen attached. Only the male bagworm moth has wings. The female is not only wingless

but limbless, a blind and passive lump of living matter. Its body is little more than a convenient receptacle for its eggs, and of course this helpless object represents an easy snack for any passing bird. And that is the point: the bizarre lifestyle of the bagworm makes it necessary for the lady moth to die after being grabbed and swallowed by a bird. Its eggs hatch inside the bird's guts and baby caterpillars emerge from its droppings, apparently none the worse for their ride. The wide-eyed entomologists who first studied bagworms saw this as the ultimate motherly sacrifice: dying so that the young may live. Some species of bagworm don't even mate. Their babies are produced by parthenogenesis, a seeming miracle in itself.

And that brings us back to why these moths were called *Psyche*. If the female moth refrains from sexual activity, it is, in that lonely sense, a virgin, a spiritual being. The species name of the commonest species is *casta*, or chaste. As its namer noted in wonder, the bagworm 'produces fertile eggs without having had sexual intercourse with males': the ultimate in maidenly virtue. (Actually *Psyche casta* does have functional male moths and sex, but some other species are entirely parthenogenic.)

If you think a bagworm is unworthy of the name of *Psyche*, how about the moth named after Morpheus, the god of dreams? *Caradrina morpheus* is the Mottled Rustic, a rather forgettable brownish moth. It seems that the German entomologist Johann Hufnagel, wasn't too enthusiastic either, for he described the moth as 'dirty'. It is tempting to assume he meant 'dirty dreams'. The moth's genus *Caradrina* is equally baffling. Apparently it is a reference to a river in Albania. Go figure.

Droppings

Clouded Magpie and Lime-speck Pug are surprisingly romantic names for moths that are pretending to be droppings. The former mimics the big splashy poo, moist and clammy with mucus, of pigeons. The pug imitates a smaller, drier dropping, a sparrow's perhaps. Both moths can rest confidently on a leaf, their white mottled wings fully outstretched, without fear of being eaten. Birds seem to avoid them, either because they fail to spot the moth lurking among the muck, or perhaps because they reason that a moth that looks like poo probably tastes like it too.

Most micros are too small to adopt the same strategy, but several species of Tortrix moths do their best. They are known in the trade as 'bird craps'.

Drunkards

The Drinker is a big fawn-coloured moth with a wine-bibber's nose and a monstrous hairy caterpillar. It is this caterpillar that 'drinks'; the moth seems to live solely on the accumulated fat in its plump, hairy body. The Drinker caterpillar's habit of imbibing raindrops or dew was noticed as long ago as 1662, when the Dutch naturalist Jan Goedart described its habit of 'dipping its head in the water and then lifting it up as hens do, which it repeats over and over again; for which reason it bears the name of The Drinker.' It was a true and accurate observation, and the moth has remained The Drinker ever since, not only in Britain but throughout northern Europe. It France it is *buveuse*, in Germany *Trinkerin*, although there it is also known by the charming name of *Grasglucke*, the grass-hen. In Holland it is *rietvink*, 'the reed finch'. Following

Ever since the 1670s, this big hairy moth has been called The Drinker.

an already established tradition, Linnaeus named the moth *potatoria*, or 'pertaining to drinking'. Its modern genus is *Euthrix*, 'very hairy', but in the past it was *Philudoria*, or 'loving [to drink] water' – and so it was a drinker twice over.

You would expect the moth called *Oinophila*, or 'wine-lover', to be equally fond of the bottle, but its taste (its caterpillar's taste, that is) is for the cork, not the contents. For that matter, it will happily consume any organic debris it can find in the wine cellar. In Britain it is an indoor moth exclusively, apart from the Isles of Scilly, where the weather is warm enough for the moth to creep cautiously into the open, perhaps looking for an alternative to corks.

The actual Cork Moth, *Nemapogon cloacella*, is misnamed. In Britain it is mainly found in woodland, where its caterpillar chews bracket fungus, although its species name, *cloacella*, implies that it would be at home in a sewer. A more likely species to keep *Oinophila* company in the wine cellar is the Cork Moth's relative, the Corn Moth, *Nemapogon granella*, a greedy nibbler of corks, nuts, grain, dried fruit and, perhaps more helpfully, dry rot. *Nemapogon* means 'thread-beard', from some goatee-like bristles attached to the moths' mouthparts.

Dukes

There are a number of royal or imperial moths and butterflies in Britain and Europe, but only one duke: the Duke of Burgundy. Quite why this small but feisty butterfly has been singled out for the honour is a mystery. It was something of a celebrity butterfly for John Ray, who received some specimens of the butterfly caught near Cambridge. But its ducal name first appeared, without explanation, in *The Aurelian* by Moses Harris, as the 'Duke of Burgundy Frittillaria'. Though not related to other fritillaries, the Duke shares their brown chequered pattern, and the butterfly continued to be called 'the Duke of Burgundy Fritillary' far into the twentieth century. Harris adds that it was 'commonly called The Burgundy' in his day, which suggests that the 'duke' bit might have been an afterthought. Colonel Emmet suggested that the name may have arisen from the dedication of a lost painting of the butterfly. In the eighteenth century, engraved plates of butterflies and moths were often dedicated to men and women of means, often nobles, in return for their patronage. Perhaps, then, someone had dedicated their plate of this butterfly to someone claiming to be the Duke of Burgundy. The trouble with that theory is that the title of the Duke of Burgundy has long been absorbed by the

The Duke. The Duke of Burgundy is one of the mystery names.

hindwings. It lent the butterfly its French name, *La Lucine*. In Germany it is *Perlbinde*, the pearly-band. In Holland and Sweden they know nothing of dukes or pearls. There it is the 'primrose butterfly' after the butterfly's foodplant.

E

French monarchy, although it was briefly claimed by the Hapsburgs early in the eighteenth century. Another possibility is that someone thought the butterfly resembled a much-quartered coat-of-arms, such as those worn by the Dukes of Burgundy, and named it on a whim. Or perhaps the name has more to do with the butterfly's rich brown-red colour, a match for the well matured red wines of Nuits-St-Georges or Gevrey-Chambertin. We obviously like the name because no one has thought to change it, even though no one knows what it means.

The Duke's scientific name has nothing to do with wine or dukes. *Hamearis* means 'at the same time as the spring', for this is an early butterfly, while the species name, *lucina*, refers to the goddess who brings light, probably a reference to the hand-mirror-like markings on the underside of the

Ears

Do moths have ears? Yes, in a way – or rather in two ways. Lacking mammalian earlobes, they hear via a naked tympanum or eardrum with inset receptor cells tucked into the body. Some moths have very sensitive hearing. They are tuned to high frequencies, or ultrasound, so that when they hear the

Ear Moth, with one 'ear' on each wing.

high-pitched squeaks of approaching bats they can take defensive action. The record is held by the little Wax Moth, which has hearing 150 times more sensitive than that of the human ear.

Certain moths have another, totally deaf, 'ear' in the form of a marking on their forewings known as the reniform stigma, a kidney-shaped spot. This is most obvious on a quartet of moths known as 'ears' in which the marking shines out in white, orange or gold. 'Ear' is a peculiarly English name. Where we see an ear others have seen an eye, to judge from the Latin name of the Ear Moth, *oculea*. In the eighteenth and nineteenth centuries, the same moth was known as the Golden Ear.

Anyone expecting the Feathered Ear moth to be an owl-like creature will be disappointed. Its 'ears' are wing markings and its 'feathers' are worn on its head as the antennae of the male moth. We won't see it in any case, as it seems to have died out in Britain.

Eggs

All moths lay eggs, but only one group is named after an egg, a quartet of handsome furry moths called 'eggars'. The name 'eggar' dates back to the earliest days of entomology. They are moths that would seem to have laid a monstrous egg – not the pinhead-sized one you would expect, but a big oval one up to the size of a pigeon's egg. On moors you can find these 'eggs' quite easily as hard, pale yellow balls of silk attached to sprigs of heather. They are not, of course, real eggs but the moth's cocoon, which contains its pupa. Hence, as well as eggars, these are among the very few moths to be named after their pupal stage.

The largest and most familiar species is the Oak Eggar, once known as the Great Eggar, a gorgeous moth, a harmony in warm browns and yellows. Petiver had yet another name for it, the Period Moth, after the bold white 'full stop' in the midst of its forewings. The Great Eggar has a smaller sister, the Grass Eggar, and two still smaller cousins, the Small Eggar and the Pale Eggar. Despite its accepted name of Oak Eggar, and its species name *quercus*, the moth has no particular association with oak; nor does the Grass Eggar have much to do with grass. They are

Oak Eggar, a strange and mistaken name that has stuck.

wandering caterpillars that tend to nibble on any plant they come across, although the Grass Eggar has a mild preference for clover (so they got that species name right, for *trifolii* means 'of the trefoil', that is, 'of the clover'). Is it just coincidence that the cocoon of the Oak Eggar looks a bit like an acorn?

(*See also* Bottoms.)

Emeralds

Green is such a distinctive colour that it tends to appear in the names of most of the butterflies and moths whose ground colour is green, among them the Green Hairstreak, Green Carpet, Brindled Green and Burren Green. The greenest moths of all are named after that green gem, the emerald. There is a Large and a Small Emerald, a Sussex and an Essex Emerald, a Common Emerald and a Blotched Emerald – nine British species in all. The exact shade varies from species to species, and also through age, since the pigment is unstable and tends to fade over time.

The scientific names of emerald moths invoke all kinds of subtle shades of green. Linnaeus nabbed the plain green, *viridata*, for the Small Grass Emerald, a common enough moth in Sweden, though it is scarce in Britain. The actual gemstone, which in Latin is *smaragdus*, gave us *smaragdaria*, the Essex Emerald. The Small Emerald,

A moth that looks like a green butterfly: the Large Emerald.

chrysoprasuria, commemorates a less precious gemstone, chrysoprase or green chalcedony. Taking another tack entirely, the Common Emerald is *aestivaria*, 'of the summer', that is a summer-green moth (its genus, *Hemithea*, is an even greater tribute: it means 'demigod'). The genus *Thalera*, meaning 'fresh' or 'youthful', echoes the lighter spring-green of the Sussex Emerald moth.

As any collector would tell you, these moths often lose their fresh green tints after they have been stuck on a pin and consigned to a box. The genus of the Grass Emerald, *Pseudoterpna*, hints at this posthumous transformation. It is a combination of the Greek words for falsehood and delight: delight turning to disappointment, perhaps, as the moth fades almost before your eyes. Its species name, *pruinata*, or 'hoarfrost', refers to the beautiful white frosting on its wings.

The name of the Blotched Emerald, *Comibaena bajularia*, is the exception. Instead of describing a colour, it comments on the unusual behaviour of its caterpillar. Meaning literally 'to go a bundle'/'a porter or bag-carrier,' the name refers to the caterpillar's habit of sticking scraps of leafy debris to its body to improve its disguise. Before it became the Blotched Emerald, the moth was known, rather charmingly, as 'the Maid of Honour'. Moses Harris noted that it had first been discovered on the famous oak tree named the 'Honour Oak' on top of a hill in Peckham (and still recalled in the name of the district). The moth became the tree's 'maid'. They had such charming thoughts in Georgian England.

The most resounding name belongs to the Large Emerald, *Geometra papilionaria*, surely one of the most beautiful moths on earth. *Geometra* or 'earth-measurer' was once a huge genus that included the whole of the Large Emerald's sub-family, the Geometrinae. It was raised by Linnaeus for moths whose caterpillars have a looping gait, as if they were measuring the ground inch by inch: the 'inchworms'. But gradually *Geometra* was narrowed down drastically until it now comprises only sixteen moths worldwide (and, in Britain, the Large Emerald only). Its species name, *papilionaria*, invokes a papilio or butterfly. With its butterfly-shaped wings and bright colour, the Large Emerald could easily be mistaken for one.

Emperors

The name 'emperor' is traditionally reserved for the biggest and most resplendent butterflies and moths. In Britain we have just one of each: the Purple Emperor butterfly and the Emperor Moth. Both are large and magnificent, and both, as it happens, have 'eyes' in their wings. They are all-seeing emperors.

Probably everyone will remember the first time they ever saw a Purple Emperor, for it is that kind of butterfly, rare and elusive but rewarding the patience of the watcher with its soaring flight and breathtaking flashes of royal purple. As Matthew Oates, the all-time expert on the Purple Emperor, exclaims, quoting Virgil, '*mille trahens varios adverso sole colores*'; it 'drew countless wavering colours against the sun's rays'. Purple is, of course, an imperial colour. Roman Emperors 'wore the purple'. Appropriately, only the male butterfly has purple iridescence. The larger female has a more sober brown-and-white garb.

The first Purple Emperor in English history was caught at Castle Hedingham in Essex in 1695 by a clergyman. James Petiver published a short description of it as 'Mr Dale's Purple Eye'. (The apothecary and geologist Samuel Dale, who also lived in Essex, probably supplied the specimen.) One of the butterfly's

His Imperial Highness, the Purple Emperor.

'eyes' is a reddish circle near the base of the hindwing, but there is another, bolder, eye on the underside of the forewings that comes suddenly into view when the butterfly instinctively raises its wings, presumably to shock a potential predator. By 1749, the butterfly's name had changed to 'the Purple Highflier' or 'Emperor of the Woods'. Ten years after that, Moses Harris bred it from an unknown horned caterpillar he found in a sallow bush which emerged, 'to my unspeakable Pleasure,' he said, into a 'Male Purple Emperor.' It has remained the Purple Emperor ever since. In France it is *Le Grand Mars,* the most martial and masculine of butterflies.

The Emperor's scientific name is *Apatura iris.* The 'iris' part is easy to explain. The mythological Iris is the personification of the rainbow. Iris is represented as female, yet her iridescence is found, paradoxically, only on the male butterfly. *Apatura* is a real puzzle. On the face of it, the word is meaningless, but it is probably a construct on the Greek word *apatao,* to deceive. When basking with outspread wings, the purple colour will appear and disappear according to the angle of the observer – now purple, now not. In that way, the butterfly may be said to 'deceive' us. Its author, Fabricius, seems to have enjoyed word-puzzles. He, too, might be joining in the game of deceit, leaving us to guess what he might have meant.

Our other emperor is a moth, the Emperor Moth. It is Britain's only member of the silk-moth family (there are only four species in Europe, but many hundreds more in warmer parts of the world). It has always been a well-known moth and a favourite with artists, appearing in genre paintings from the seventeenth century onwards. In some Victorian fairy-paintings, the senior fairy often wears wings modelled on the Emperor Moth, as, perhaps, did Shakespeare's fairy assistant in *A Midsummer Night's Dream*. The English name dates back to at least 1749. The scientific name, *Saturnia pavonia*, offers an alternative approach. Pavo is a peacock, while Saturnia was another name for the goddess Juno, for whom the peacock was sacred. The Emperor Moth could so easily have become the Peacock Moth, and so it is in Europe: *paon de nuit* in France; *Nachtpfauenauge*, the Night Peacock, in Germany.

Ermine

Ermine comes from the winter fur of the stoat, and is white with a black tip at the tail. It was used to trim the formal robes of royalty and the senior aristocracy, and, since it took a lot of stoats to make a cloak, an ermine robe was very expensive. Ermine was also a 'fur' or tincture of heraldry, represented by a white ground with graphic symbols to represent the little tails. Two unrelated groups of moths are named ermines because they share the same pattern of black specks on pure white wings.

The original ermine was the White Ermine, a relative of the tiger-moth. It has a very lively caterpillar, hence the Ermine's species name *lubricipeda* or 'swift-footed'. Its fellow ermines, Buff Ermine (named from its ground colour) and Water Ermine (named after its watery habitat), took their cue from the original. But in the Netherlands these moths are not ermines; they are tigers and bears (*tijger* and *beer*). Their ermines are our kitten moths.

The other, unrelated group of ermines are micros, which make up for their lack of individual size by their sometimes huge communal webs spun by countless caterpillars on bushes and small trees. In extreme cases they can cover the entire tree in a silken shroud while the caterpillars defoliate every leaf. Each species of mini-ermine takes its name from its main plant victim: Apple Ermine, Spindle Ermine, Bird-cherry Ermine, and the misnamed Orchard Ermine, which actually prefers hedgerow hawthorn and blackthorn. Their genus *Yponomeuta* refers to something else: it means, literally, 'making underground mines'. On the face of it, this seems to

Minor royalty: the White Ermine moth.

be a misnomer. Although many micro-moths do indeed 'mine' into leaves, these particular moths do not; they are web-makers, not miners. It is possible, however, that the namer, Pierre Latreille, was referring not to mines made by caterpillars but to a miner's pick-axe. Evidently he was struck by the shape of the caterpillar's mouthparts, fancifully comparing its jaws to the head of a pick.

That pretty, leopard-spotted, and, alas, nationally extinct moth, the Spotted Sulphur, is also an ermine, at least by association. Its species name is *trabealis* or 'clad in the robes of state'.

Eyes

To judge from their scientific names, two of our butterflies have lovely eyes. The genus of the Green Hairstreak is *Callophrys*, or 'beautiful eyebrows'. The ostensible eyebrows are shiny green scales, while each eye is surrounded by white, as if the butterfly were wearing spectacles. Close up, it might remind you of the extravagant eye-wear of early Elton John or Edna Everage.

The Wall butterfly, meanwhile, is *Lasiommata*, or 'hairy eyes'. It would be nice to imagine them as long-lashed and highlighted with mascara, but in fact the butterfly's dusky eyes have little downy hairs scattered all over them.

Whatever their function is, it probably isn't to look beautiful.

The most glaring, staring eyes are those on the wings of the Peacock butterfly and the Eyed Hawk-moth. There are what may be the likenesses of these two drawn on the walls of caves in France sometime in the late Paleolithic (that is, if Professor Philip Howse is right in his attribution; the scratchings were formerly thought to represent owls). Perhaps that ancient artist had felt the force of an open-eyed stare from an Eyed Hawk-moth, as if a disembodied face were penetrating his very soul – though what it is actually doing is mimicking the face of a dangerous animal, perhaps a fox. With the Peacock possibly, and the hawk-moth certainly, the purpose of these fake eyes is to startle a would-be predator. (*See* Peacocks.)

Other butterflies have fake eyes that lack that staring intensity but make up for this in sheer abundance. Some of the blue butterflies have little round eyes scattered all over their wings, especially on the undersides. The browns, too, have numerous eyes, on the front as well as the back. A hungry bird will peck at the eyes to immobilise its prey, and so it is better lose a few fake ones than a real eye. You often see Meadow Browns with a beak-shaped tear in their wing where the butterfly has survived a

Eyes that stare into your soul: the Eyed Hawk-moth.

confrontation with a bird.

Early entomologists called these eyed butterflies 'arguses' or argus-eyes, named after Argus, the mythological shepherd who had eyes scattered all over his head. This made him a very effective guardian of flocks, especially since he could keep some of his eyes open while others were closed in sleep. In times past The Wall butterfly was known as the Great Argus (it still is in Holland, as *argusvlinder*), and the Speckled Wood, the Wood Argus. Today the name survives in just five British species: the Scotch Argus, the unrelated Brown Argus and the Northern Brown Argus, and, in their scientific names, the Silver-studded Blue, *Plebejus argus*, and the Adonis Blue, *Polyommatus bellargus* or 'beautiful argus'.

Turning to moths, The Spectacle moth wears a pretty convincing pair of white goggles, as if it were about to take a spin in a Tiger Moth (in France its name is *La Lunette*). The goggles are not of course the moth's real eyes, but are perched above the head as part of an elaborate thoracic crest. Meanwhile the little white moths in the genus *Opostega*, or 'roof-face', wear 'shades' in the form of a pair of caps that cover their eyes like sun-shields.

The Silver Cloud moth has an allusive name, *conspicillaris*, meaning 'a place to look out from'. This is a Linnaean name, and fortunately Linnaeus explained it for us. The moth's wings bear two large 'eyes' without pupils, which means they must

The Sprawler Moth has a 'star-gazing' caterpillar named after the great Italian astronomer Cassini.

be closed as if in sleep. But, Linnaeus went on, whether open or closed, eyes are indeed 'places to look out from'. The Dutch like this interpretation, and there the moth is *brildrager,* 'the spectacles-wearer'. The moth shares its name with a bird, the Spectacled Warbler, *Sylvia conspicillata,* whose real eyes are circled with white, like a pair of glasses.

The former name of the Sprawler moth, *Cassinia,* involves less circumlocution. The moth was named after the astronomer Cassini because it has a caterpillar whose defence is to rear backwards as if to gaze up at the stars. Cassini was only thirty years in his grave when the moth was named. Its new genus, *Asteroscopus,* carries the same meaning: to take a telescope to the stars, to gaze at the heavens.

Finally there is that amusing name-pairing of moths, the Bright-line Brown-Eye and the Brown-line Bright-eye. The names say it all: one moth has a brown 'eye' and the other a white one; one moth bears a white line and the other a brown one. The Bright-line Brown-eye is a very common moth that can be a pest of vegetable gardens on the European mainland. There it has been given less affectionate names: *Potagère* and *Gemüseeule,* both meaning 'the vegetable moth'.

F

Fabrics

It is funny how often fabrics turn up in the names of moths. There are moths with silky sheens called satins. There are delicately patterned moths named after muslin or lace. Others with richly decorated wings are called brocades. While butterflies tend to be named after colours, moths often take their names from textures of various kinds. You might say that they have the same aesthetic appeal as a length of fine cloth or a handmade piece of lace.

Of course it is the moths themselves that produce the raw material for one fabric: silk. It is probably no coincidence that some of those who first admired moths were connected with the silk trade. The Elizabethan Thomas Moffet wrote a treatise on silkworms. Among the leading lights of the Society of Aurelians were the silk-pattern designer Joseph Dandridge, the silk trader Charles Dubois, and James Leman, who combined both roles. There was also Peter Collinson, a trader in flax, hemp and silk. It is not hard to imagine them drawing inspiration from the subtle shades and patterns in the wings of moths. As one of their younger friends, the artist Benjamin Wilkes, said, it was impossible not to be impressed by 'Nature's admirable Skill in the Deposition, Arrangement and contrasting of Colours'. Nature, in other words, had good taste. And so the fashionable world of satins, silks, brocades and lace became infused with the vocabulary of moth names.

John Keats wrote of the 'stains and splendid dyes' of the tiger-moth's 'deep-damask'd wings'. Damask is a richly decorated silken fabric, worn by wealthy ladies, and for which these beautiful moths formed a natural pattern-book. 'Brocades' are heavily-scaled, elaborately patterned moths ranging in size from the Great Brocade to the more middle-range Light Brocade, Pale-shouldered Brocade and Beautiful Brocade. Their wing patterns reminded people of contemporary shuttle-woven fabrics adorned with figures and flowers. The Beautiful Brocade even seems to wear precious stones: a moth in sequins.

Satins range over several moth families: the Satin Lutestring in the Thyatiridae, the White Satin in the Lymantriidae, the Satin Beauty and the Satin Wave in the Geometridae. What they share is a glossy sheen. In the case of the White Satin moth it is wings of the purest white, hence its generic name *Leucoma*, or 'white hair'. As for the Satin Lutestring, the latter word might have originated in a corruption of 'lustrine', a glossy silk or satin-weave fabric, rather than a musical instrument. If so, it is a satin moth twice over.

Silk is represented by the Silky Wave and the Silky Wainscot, and, in Latin, by *bombyx*, the old name for a silk-moth. The species name of the Pale Shining Brown is *bombycina*, or 'silken'. Like the satin moths, these species have glossy wings reminiscent of silken fabrics. Among the true silk-moths, those which spin threads of silk to make their large and elaborate cocoons, Britain has only one species, the Emperor Moth (*see* Emperors). At the other end of the scale is a little greyish moth called *Metaxmeste phrygialis*, whose name translates as 'filled with raw silk [as if] embroidered by the Phrygians'. The Phrygians, it seems, were the needlework champions of the ancient world, although it is

Nights in white satin:
the White Satin moth.

hard to see this particular moth as a shining example of their handiwork.

Muslin is represented by the Muslin Moth, the Muslin Footman and the Muslin Wave, the last two with a delicate tracery of greyish scales over semi-transparent wings. Lace is suggested by the web-like patterns of the Brussels Lace and the beautiful Lace Border moth, both reminiscent of fine linen or cotton lacework. Two more moths with delicate and intricate patterns are The Tissue moth and its rarer relative, the Scarce Tissue. In the eighteenth century, when these names were coined, 'tissue' was semi-transparent woven gauze, often embroidered with a silky sheen, and worn as a veil.

Some moths were named after fabrics in general. The pebble moths belong to the genus *Evergestis* or 'well-wrought garments'. Some of the prettier Tortricids are *Eana*, or wearers of 'fine robes'. The 'flounce' in the Flounced Rustic moth is not a sulk but a reference to the margin of the moth's wings, suggesting a strip of attached material.

One of the forgotten moth names is Petiver's 'furbelow', which refers to the plaited or furred fringe of a skirt or petticoat. He found it a useful name for moths with notched or scallop-edged wings, including those we know today as 'thorns' (qv). The name survived well into the nineteenth century in the Flame Furbelow, a flattering name for what is now the Common Rustic moth.

Flames

One of the things everyone knows about moths is that they are helplessly attracted to light. In the days when rooms were lit by candles, moths would circle round and round the flame – 'like the moons of Jupiter', suggested Vladimir Nabokov – edging nearer and nearer until finally they became stuck in the grease and, with a sizzle, were quickly converted to carbon. The moth is not heading into the flame in the hope of a treat. For them an artificial light is a false beacon, like the lamps used by wreckers to lure a ship onto the rocks. No one yet really knows why moths approach a bright light, although some think they mistake it for a moonbeam. At any rate the light seems to disturb the moth's usual navigation process. They become disoriented, even blinded, and so fly helplessly round and round the light source until they crash into it. It is this weakness in the moth's physiology that makes light traps so effective.

A group of pretty little Pyralid moths in the genus *Pyrausta* are named after a Greek word meaning 'to kindle or burn'. According to Pliny, the original *Pyrausta*

Pyrausta: a genus of day-flying moths which share their name with a mythical fire-breathing dragon…the size of an insect.

was a wonderful insect that actually lived in fire. Curiously, the modern Pyrausta moth flies by day like a tiny butterfly. But some species are blackish, as though singed by a flame, and that is probably the reason for the name. The same word is found in the name of a blackish micro, *Ethmia pyrausta*, and it, too, looks as if it had just emerged from a bonfire. (It also has a bright orange bottom, as if flames were shooting out of its rear end like a rocket!)

Another moth that seems to have wandered too close to the candle is the Scorched Wing, a Geometrid moth with distorted wings coloured like singed parchment. It first appears as 'the Scorch'd-Wing Moth'. Its species name offers a different analogy. It is *dolabraria*, a moth that looks like the head of a double axe – which it does, if you spot it at rest and imagine the long handle.

A moth's helpless attraction to light is recalled in the species name of the Northern Rustic: *lucernea*, or 'lamp'. According to Linnaeus, this species

was particularly prone to flying into candles: '*frequenter candelis involans*'. The related Southern Rustic shares the same unfortunate trait. It is *lucipeta*, one that 'seeks the light'.

There are also moths that, as it were, carry the flame in their wings. The species called The Flame has pale wiggly markings that might have suggested fire to some imaginative beholder, although their real purpose is to assist the moth in its disguise as a chip of wood. The Flame Shoulder moth has a slightly more impressive flame in the form of a pinkish suffusion on the leading edge of its wings, like a dying ember. Other moths with glints of fire in their wings are the Flame Brocade, the Flame Carpet, the Flame Wainscot and the Fiery Clearwing. Extend that to foreign names and we can add the Swallow Prominent, 'the firebrand', and the Buff Arches or 'flint' in the sense of 'firelighter', clearly responsible for the moth's flaming 'arches'.

The well-known Angle Shades is yet another fire-moth. It is *Phlogophora*: one that carries a flame, a rather feeble one in its case, indicated by the orange bands on the freshly emerged moth.

There is also a flaming butterfly, at least in French. There the Scarce Swallowtail (which in southern France is anything but scarce) is *Le Flambé*.

Angle Shades, sometimes misspelt as 'angel-shades'.

There is a glowing red mark near the tails which draws the eye. In Dutch it has a more distinguished name: *koningspage* – literally king-page, but in the sense of 'the king of wings'.

Flight

Certain moths and butterflies have a flight distinctive enough to suggest their name. Their up-and-down 'skipping' flight inspired Moses Harris to rename the butterflies hitherto known as 'hogs' as 'skippers'. The unfortunately named Dingy Skipper (for it is really quite attractive when fresh) earned its scientific name, *Erynnis tages*, from its habit of flying up from the ground. To the romantic German entomologist Franz Schrank, its restless behaviour suggested the terrifying *Erynyes*, better known as the Furies. These vengeful hags would hound wrongdoers from place to place until they were driven mad. Schrank raised the genus *Erynnis* for several of the skippers, but it is now limited in Britain to the Dingy Skipper, and luckily this is the species the name best fits. Its other name, *tages*, preserves the same meaning. The original Tages was a boy with the wisdom of an old man who 'suddenly rose from the ground' to instruct the ancient Etruscans in the art of divining the future.

The Wall is another butterfly that likes to warm up with outspread wings on bare ground, often on a beaten path. It will fly up on the approach of a walker and come to rest again a little distance away. This, too, suggested the Furies. And so The Wall was named *megera*, after one of the Furies named Megaera, the one who specialised in pursuing adulterers.

The Large Skipper displays a still more focussed mode of flight. It is fun to watch the male butterfly guarding its territory, darting out like a flycatcher, circling round with a flash of golden wings, and returning to perch on the same leaf. Burly and fearless, it will tackle intruders as large as a bee. That gave Jacob Hübner his cue. The Large Skipper became *Ochlodes*, meaning unruly or turbulent, while its species name was (until very recently) *venata*, from venery, or the art of the chase (it is now *Ochlodes sylvanus*). Appropriately for a hunter, it is a woodland butterfly.

Finally there is the Grayling, a name still spelt in the eighteenth-century manner, and meaning 'the little grey one'. In the early days such names were perhaps more often spoken than read so that, in 1749, Benjamin Wilkes could transcribe it as 'Grayline' or 'Grailing'. The species name of the Grayling is *semele*, named after a nymph made famous by George Frederick Handel's opera *Semele*. It may just be coincidence, but the best-known air from that opera is 'Where e'er you walk', and the Grayling is indeed another butterfly that likes to settle on paths. Poor Semele perished by getting too close to her hot lover Zeus and going up in smoke. Again, maybe it is only coincidence, but the male Grayling does often have a dusky appearance as though it had just flown through a smouldering bonfire.

Among the moths we have a trio of Highfliers: the May, the July and the Ruddy. Moths with variable mottled wings, they often fly at dusk and can be disturbed by day, and so could be glimpsed flying high around bushes and trees. Their scientific names make nothing of this, however. Their genus is *Hydriomena*, 'a water pot', and presumably reflects their liking for watery places where the moths lay on alder and sallow. The Ruddy Highflyer sounds like a moth with ambitions.

The Grayling, whose species name links the butterfly with the heroine of Handel's opera, Semele.

Food I

With a few exceptions, the caterpillars of butterflies and moths feed on green plants. Some are not too fussy and accept a wide range of foodplants; these tend to be caterpillars that wander about, nibbling as they go. Others specialise in just one or two plant species, and sometimes even particular parts of a plant, such as the Orange-tip caterpillar, which feeds on the nutritious seed-pods of Lady's Smock and Hedge Garlic, or the pug moths, which are as likely to eat flowers or seeds as green leaves. These specialist caterpillars tend to stay put; they remain on the plant their mother has chosen until it is time to pupate.

It was natural enough to name species after their foodplant, since collectors would seek out and examine those plants for caterpillars. A fair number of the hawk-moths, for instance, were named after what their caterpillars eat: Poplar Hawk, Privet Hawk, Convolvulus Hawk, Pine Hawk, Bedstraw Hawk, Spurge Hawk. (It's the same in Europe: *Sphinx du Liseron*, the Bindweed Sphinx; *Liguster-Schwarmer*, the Privet Hawk, etc.) Since the Lime Hawk-moth is greenish, you might think it was named after the colour, but, no, the caterpillar feeds on the leaves of lime trees.

In some cases the moth takes its entire name from a plant. This often happens when the foodplant is an unusual choice. For example, we have the Broom Moth, which is one of the few species to feed on broom (the other is the Broomtip moth). Others include The Mullein, The Butterbur and The Campion, whose caterpillar feeds on the seeds of the very plant its mother helped to pollinate.

A full list of plants appearing in the names of moths and butterflies would be very long. Among them are: Antirrhinum, Balsam, Bedstraw, Barberry, Bilberry, Buttercup (as 'Ranunculus'), Campanula, Catchfly (as 'Lychnis'), Chamomile, Clover, Cudweed, Currant, Figwort (as 'Water Betony'), Flax, Foxglove, Goldenrod, Goosefoot, Knot-grass, Mallow, Marsh Mallow, Orache, 'Pimpinel', Raspberry, Rest Harrow, Saxifrage, Sheep's-bit (as 'Jasione'), Spurge, Star-wort, Sweet Gale, Tansy, Thrift, Thyme, Toadflax, Valerian, Viper's Bugloss, Wood Sage, Wormwood and Yarrow. Even this long list is not complete. Several moths are named after grasses, sedges and rushes, including The Sword-grass ('sword-grass' is an old name for sedge), the Bulrush Wainscot, the Lyme Grass Moth, and the Reed Dagger.

Before the advent of light-traps, many species were found more easily as caterpillars than adults. Rearing them in cages or inside sleeves of muslin allowed the collector to obtain perfect specimens, and in the process you got to know the species pretty well. Anyone attempting to rear, say, the Marsh Mallow moth needed to find a source of Marsh Mallows and then grow them on in the garden. Hence collectors became gardeners as well as entomologists. Gardening and rearing went hand in hand: and is another reason why so many moths are named after their foodplants.

But it is as well to remember that names do not always fit the facts (even our own species, *Homo sapiens*, is not always sapient). The Viper's Bugloss moth, for instance, was first found resting on that spiky plant, but in fact it lays only on Spanish Catchfly (a bad strategy, incidentally, for when that already rare plant declined, the unfortunate moth died out). Personally, I think mistakes are part of the charm of moth names. Long live the Viper's Bugloss moth, a name that must have set generations of non-botanists wondering why a moth should be named after a serpent and a trumpet!

Food II

Not all moths feed on healthy green vegetation. 'Tinea' is one of the oldest moth names. It appears in ancient writings to mean a gnawing 'worm', a grub which attacks figs and other fruits, and, interestingly, also as 'a little

The Tapestry Moth, once a serious annoyance in great houses, now virtually extinct.

scorpion that eats books'. But in time Tinea became synonymous with a particular insect: the clothes moth. Hence Linnaeus chose that name for his tribe of cloth-nibblers, and it also became their family, the Tineidae. The caterpillars of the Tineids have digestive systems that are capable of coping with a wide assortment of animal products, including hair, wool, dung, feathers, and detritus generally. They are the clean-up merchants of the natural world, doing a useful job of recycling nutrients – until, that is, we came along with our furs and our woollen carpets and clothes, and tempted them indoors.

Those who first studied the Tineids were struck by their habits, and tended to name new species after their favourite food, or what was thought to be their food. Here is a sample:

columbariella: a moth that lives on dung and debris in a pigeon coop.

Morophaga: a moth that supposedly lives luxuriously on morel fungi (it is more often found feeding on bracket fungus).

Myrmecozela: a moth that lives dangerously,

lurking among the debris of wood ants' nests, chewing whatever organic material it can find. The name means 'ant zeal'. It is enthusiastic about ants.

Niditinea: a moth that lives in birds' nests, cleaning up droppings and rotting feathers. The name means 'bird's-nest worm'.

parasitella: another species that gnaws 'parasitic' bracket fungi.

tapetzella: the Tapestry Moth. Once a notorious scourge of indoor furnishings, it is unable to cope with central heating. For it, the wheel of fortune has turned from marauding pest to endangered species.

Although it is in a different family, we should also include the common White-shouldered House-moth here. Linnaeus named it (in error) *sarcitrella* – or 'flesh-eating'. There are, in fact, a few carnivorous caterpillars (which develop into innocent-looking moths), but this is not one of them. If Linnaeus found its caterpillars on a corpse, they were devouring fur, wool or feathers, not flesh.

The real flesh-eater is the caterpillar of the Dun-bar moth. It preys on other caterpillars (the moth has nothing to do with the Scottish town of Dunbar; it has a wing bar which is normally of a darker 'dun' colour). You would never suspect that this very ordinary-looking green caterpillar had such an appetite. Nonetheless, the Dutch know about it and call it 'the hyena'.

Foresters

Medieval foresters used to wear uniforms of green – the famous 'Lincoln Green' of the Robin Hood stories. Hence a trio of day-flying moths with bright, metallic green wings have long been known as 'foresters', despite the fact that they live not in woods but in open places such as meadows, downs and limestone dales. They don't work with trees, but they wear the uniform.

There is also a roundabout link with forests in their former generic name, *Procris*. The original Procris was a female huntress who was accidentally killed by her husband with a magic spear. Hunting took place in 'forests' reserved for the king and his cronies. And forests were looked after by foresters.

The French name is *Le Procris de l'Oseille*, The Huntress of the Sorrel (sorrel being the moth's foodplant). Confusingly, Procris is also the French name for the Small Heath butterfly.

The Forester, a moth wearing the green tunic of medieval foresters.

Fritillaries

Which came first, the Fritillary flower or the fritillary butterfly – the vegetable or the animal? The plant is a well-known garden lily that appears in *Gerard's Herbal*, which was written in the 1590s, and is also found wild in wet meadows. 'Fritillary' as the name of a butterfly surfaces only a century later, in 1699, and without explanation, as 'April Fritillary', James Petiver's name for the Pearl-bordered Fritillary. So it is possible that the lily came first and the butterfly was named later, perhaps because its wings share the same chequered pattern.

All the same, our fritillary butterflies have been known and admired for a long time. They were much commoner and hence more familiar in the past. Thomas Moffet illustrated several kinds in the 1590s. He did not name them, but then he did not name any butterfly. To my mind, it is quite possible that people knew them as fritillaries even then, and that the names of the butterfly and the flower evolved independently. 'Fritillary' does also seem a poetically apt name for these most graceful of butterflies, with its suggestion of light flitting and airy dalliance.

The ultimate origin of the word lies in ancient Rome. 'Fritillus' is mentioned in one of the epigrams of the poet Martial as the name of a chequered gaming board – in effect a chess board. Evidently it was also the name of a dice-box with a similar chequered pattern, which would certainly be a good match for the box-shaped flowers of *Fritillaria meleagris*.

Some of the individual names of fritillary butterflies are easily misunderstood. The High Brown Fritillary is not named from any high-flying habits but rather because its ground colour happens to be a rich brown, that is, brown 'to a high degree'. Nor is the Dark Green Fritillary actually 'dark green'. It is both dark and green: dark on the topside, especially in the female, and green underneath. The point was that it is both darker and greener than the otherwise similar High Brown Fritillary.

The Small Pearl-bordered Fritillary is another misnomer, for it is not noticeably smaller than its relative, the Pearl-bordered Fritillary. And the name of the Heath Fritillary is at best ambiguous. It is not named after heathland habitat, but because its caterpillars were, unusually, found on heather in Tottenham Woods in 1745, when it was bred through for the first time. All these names date from the mid-eighteenth century. The Marsh Fritillary, which came a little later, is yet another that gives a false impression, since it is by no means confined to wet places and is quite as much at home on chalk downs. Its earlier name, the Greasy or Dishclout Fritillary, might have been unkind but was more accurate, for the underside of the forewings do have a distinctly 'greasy' appearance. (For the scientific names of fritillaries, *see* Nets and The Three Graces).

The name of the Silver-washed Fritillary, on the other hand, is surely as appropriate as it is beautiful. It so perfectly describes those runnels and flashes of silver overrunning the green hindwings that it must surely have been coined by an artist. In Germany it has a still grander name: *Kaisermantel* (Emperor's mantle).

Fruit

A minority of moths are named after fruit and berries, usually because they make a nuisance of themselves in orchards and gardens. Until quite recently one of the best-known – and one of the prettiest – garden pests was the day-flying Magpie Moth, also known in England as the Currant Moth (and abroad as The Harlequin). I am old enough to remember confetti-like clouds of Magpie Moths flying over my grandfather's currant bushes, but such scenes are rarer today. In much the same

places lurked the inconspicuous Currant Clearwing, a moth that is a passable imitation of a small wasp. Chemical pesticides have done for them both.

A few micros with accepted English names are pests in gardens and orchards. The best known is the Codling Moth, the archetypal maggot in the apple. The name dates back three hundred years to a time when apples were commonly known as 'codlins' or 'codlings' (a few old varieties still are). Among other species that fruit-growers would be happier without are the Raspberry Moth, the Apple Fruit Moth, the Apple Leaf Miner, the Pear Leaf Blister Moth, the Apple-and-Plum Case-bearer and the Apple Leaf Skeletoniser, all names that neatly encapsulate the nature of the nuisance.

The Citron Plume, on the other hand, is completely innocent. This feathery moth owes its name to its lemony-yellow wings. Its caterpillar feeds harmlessly on a wild plant called Ploughman's Spikenard.

The Codling Moth, one of the oldest names for a micro. A 'codlin' is an apple.

G

Glanville

The Glanville Fritillary was, until recently, the only British butterfly to take its name from a real person (the only other one is Berger's Clouded Yellow, a name that replaced 'New Clouded Yellow' in the 1970s; the Belgian Berger described the new species for the first time). Eleanor Glanville (c.1654–1709) was one of the first English naturalists to study insects in the field. Taking an interest in butterflies might have been socially acceptable for an eccentric country vicar or physician, but was seen as improper for a respectable woman, especially the owner of an estate with a position to maintain in local society. Women were expected to conform to domestic virtues, to home and family, and not to dabble in philosophical matters. As a result, but also because of a falling-out among her family, Eleanor Glanville's will was disputed after her death on the grounds that she must have lost her wits. The case went to court at the Wells Assizes, and evidence was offered by nosy neighbours on the nature of her 'mad' pursuits. She had, for instance, been spotted beating the hedges for a 'package of worms', and witnessed running around with a butterfly net 'without all necessary cloathes'. According to legend, all this was put right by the last-minute appearance of John Ray, who testified to the great advances in entomology made by Eleanor Glanville and the esteem in which she was held in learned circles. But Ray predeceased her, and the relatives seem in fact to have won their case and succeeded in having her will disregarded. Nonetheless, 'Madam' Glanville was held in respect and affection by James Petiver and his circle, and her story was long remembered, even if they did get the details wrong.

Eleanor Glanville's best remembered achievement was the discovery of a new and attractive butterfly which she caught on a visit to Lincoln. It was named the Lincoln Fritillary, naturally enough, by Petiver, though he changed his mind later on, when the butterfly was found

The Glanville Fritillary is the only resident British butterfly named after a person.

near Dulwich, upon which he promptly renamed it the Dulwich Fritillary. By 1750, when a beautiful engraving of the butterfly and its life stages was printed and sold by the artist James Dutfield, it was already known as the Glanville Fritillary. The other names would have become unsuitable in any case. The butterfly is no longer to be found anywhere near Lincoln or Dulwich, and has in fact retreated all the way to the Isle of Wight, where it hangs on by a whisker.

Petiver named a number of moths after Eleanor Glanville, too, though these were soon forgotten. Among them were 'Glanvile's (sic) orange girdled moth' (probably the Orange Sallow), 'Glanvile's copper spotted moth' (the Gold Spot), and 'Glanvile's tipt furbelow' (the Purple Thorn). They were probably species from Eleanor Glanville's own collection which, as Petiver ruefully commented, 'does shame us all.'

Glory

The Kentish Glory is indeed a glorious moth. It can be seen on Highland moors in the spring, flying by day with a rapid, tumbling motion, a blur of reddish-brown wings. Unfortunately, it is now Kentish only in name. The moth was first discovered 'flying in a Wood near Cookham, by Westram [Westerham], in Kent' in 1741, but today it is confined to the eastern half of the Scottish Highlands. It has vanished not only from Kent but from the whole of England.

Several other moths were named 'glory', including some that might not seem all that glorious. Such a one was 'Ealing's Glory', which, as P. B. M. Allan observed, suggests that they were easily impressed in Ealing. It is now called the Green-brindled Crescent (and is certainly a pretty moth, if not gloriously so).

Unlikely glory among the micros is represented by the large genus *Cydia*. Its Greek root is *kudos,* a word which has entered the English language to mean 'prestige', or 'glory for a great achievement'. Kudos to the *Cydia* moths, then – although glory is in the eye of the beholder. I doubt, for instance, whether it is the first word to come to mind on finding *Cydia pomonella*, the Codling Moth, in your apple, or *Cydia nigricana*, the Pea Moth, blackening your pea pods.

Goats

There is only one Goat Moth and it is splendid, a big fat moth with wings that look as if they were etched on parchment by a master craftsman. However, it is not the moth but the caterpillar that

The Goat Moth, named not from its physical
resemblance but from its musky smell.

is the goat. Its most unusual feature is a musty odour produced by this large, reddish grub, somewhat like the smell of a billy goat (though others have suggested leather or wine corks). It has strong jaws that enable it to burrow into the soft wood of mature trees, especially old willows. But since wood is less nutritious than green leaves, the caterpillar can take two years or more to complete its life cycle.

'Goat Moth' is a name that dates back more than three centuries, but its memorable scientific name, *cossus*, is even older. According to Pliny and other Roman authors, the original 'cossus' was a fat grub that lived in the wood of old trees and could be eaten as a delicacy. Linnaeus jumped to the conclusion that this was the Goat Moth, though it is more likely that Pliny's cossus was a

beetle grub. Fabricius named the moth *Cossus ligniperda*, the wood-destroyer, but, under the rules, Linnaeus's species name, *cossus*, had priority, and so we have ended up with a double name, *Cossus cossus*. As it happens, there is a rare Greek word, *kossos*, that means 'a clip round the ear'. Take that, Linnaeus!

Gone

In *The Moth Requiem*, premiered at the BBC Proms in 2013, the composer Harrison Birtwistle lamented the passing of certain British moths with the help of three harps, a flute and a chorus of female voices. Merely intoning their names, he found, creates a sense of sadness. Like the newly closed railway stations in 'The Slow Train' by Flanders and Swan, these lost, forgotten moths float over the music: Lewes Wave, Frosted Yellow, Dusky Clearwing, Scarce Dagger, Union Rustic... all gone, and not coming back (unless, of course, we decide to reintroduce them). Birtwistle's piece also includes a poem, 'A Literalist,' by Robert Blazer, which describes an eerie moment when a piano began to play on its own in the middle of the night as the result of an imprisoned moth vibrating its strings in its efforts to escape. *The Moth Requiem* is a meditation on the theme of transience and loss, and also of the composer's looming mortality. It is in the spirit of John Donne: 'Never send to know for whom the bell tolls ...'

No one knows why, or even exactly when, a particular species of moth fell off the radar. All we know is that moth enthusiasts were no longer finding it in its old localities. Unlike the fuss we make of the loss of a pretty butterfly such as the Large Blue, few lamented our lost moths, although there are far more of them; no one waved goodbye to the Lewes Wave. Extinction can seem very random: why this moth and not that? We don't know. Their names carried no sense of impending doom. Look at the cheerful names of some of our more recently departed moths: Brighton Wainscot, Orange Upperwing, Stout Dart, Essex Emerald...

H

Hair

A select group of moths have unusually long mouthparts that look a bit like comic noses, and so are known as 'snouts'. You could also see them as moustaches, as their generic name suggests. *Hypena* is Greek for 'moustache': a Greek *'moustaki'*. Exaggeration reaches a peak with the scientific name of the Common Snout: *Hypena proboscidalis*: it seems to be a moustache on an elephant's trunk!

At least two genera of moths have 'beards': the spotted *Nemapogon* moths and the bright, day-flying *Nematopogon* moths with their amazingly long antennae. Both names mean 'thread-beard'. The 'threads' are the antennae, below which they have notably hairy mouthparts: their beards.

The micro *Opogona antistacta* has a name that translates as 'angle-face forelock-Myrrh-oil'. It refers to a tuft of hairlike scales that seem to be smeared to the moth's head like a greased-up Teddy Boy, whilst its mouthparts stick up at a strange angle. Clearly there is some biological purpose to such a funny face, but perhaps that need not detain us here. Meanwhile the leaf-mining moth *Bucculatrix nigricomella* has decided on a punk haircut: a Mohawk sticking up between its eyes (*nigricomella* means 'black hair'). The moth's eyes are partly shielded, as if it were wearing sunglasses – hence the name *Bucculatrix*, originally an armoured helmet with cheek-flaps. In both cases you need a hand lens and a very cooperative moth to see all this wonderful detail.

Moths with elaborate hairdos might well need the services of another tiny moth called *Exaeretia ciniflonella*. The species name comes from the word for a Roman hair-curler, itself derived from words meaning 'ash-blow', for the hair tongs were held in ash, kept hot and glowing by a slave with bellows. The moth has a smudgy greyish appearance as if someone had indeed blown ash all over it.

Less attractively, we have *Pammene albuginana*, named from 'scurf from the head'. It has crusty, rust-coloured blotches on its mottled wings.

The moths in the genus *Pechipogo*, or fanfoots, have 'hairy forearms'. This characteristic, found only on the male moths, functions as a brush to waft away some scented scales and so attract a mate. You could call them a sexy hairbrush.

Anyone who did not know them might think that the butterflies called hairstreaks have had a perm with coloured streaks in

Hairstreaks are named after the wiggly white line running down the underside of their wings.

their hair: green, brown, purple, black and white, respectively, for the five British species. But of course the butterflies were named not by hairdressers but by artists. The 'hair' in question is a streak of colour seemingly painted onto their underside hindwings – the side you see when the butterfly is feeding or at rest, which is nearly always. Its function is probably to mimic a butterfly's antenna (in some species it is joined to a little 'eye' at the bottom). Hairstreaks twitch their wings in a way that suggests the motions of a real head, no doubt confusing predators.

Oddly enough, the original hairstreak was one of the less common species: the White-letter Hairstreak, whose white hairline wiggles into a jagged W-shape. Its first appearance in print as 'The

Hairstreak' was in 1703, accompanied by the Purple Hairstreak, then known simply as 'The Streak'. Only gradually did the three other species become hairstreaks, too. To my ear the word has a pleasing vibrancy, suggesting a flicker, a shiver of lightning, a white line streaking down the wings to end in a letter, like a dashed-off initial. Surely James Petiver had observed the living butterfly, and seen how it rubs its tailed hindwings together and makes that entrancing white 'W' jiggle up and down.

While Britain has only five hairstreak species, and the rest of Europe but fifteen, in North America there are no fewer than 75 of them, subdivided into ministreaks and scrub-hairstreaks, as well as plain hairstreaks. The European names are disappointing. No hairstreaks for them; the Germans call them 'tip butterflies' (*Felfalter*), after their little tails, the French *Thecla*, after their old genus name. In the Netherlands the Green Hairstreak is *Groentje*, simply 'the green one', or 'the rookie'.

Harbours

The White Admiral used to have a very strange scientific name. It was *Limenitis camilla* (it has since been changed to *Ladoga camilla*; *Ladoga* is the name of a lake near St Petersburg, without

The White Admiral: sharing its title with Nelson (Admiral of the White).

obvious relevance). The '*camilla*' bit is straightforward: the original Camilla was a warrior maiden, a name probably chosen to match the similarly militant Atalanta, the species name of the Red Admiral. *Limenitis* comes from the Greek *limen*, meaning 'harbour'. The sense is of a harbour-keeper, perhaps a guardian deity watching over the safe passage of ships. But the White Admiral is a woodland butterfly! What would it be doing in a harbour? For an explanation, we need to go back to the time when it was first described and illustrated. It seems that Petiver's specimens were taken not from an English oakwood but from a place near the Italian port city of Livorno, then known to English mariners as Leghorn. Petiver decided to call the butterfly *Papilio livornicus*, the Leghorn White Admiral. Perhaps he thought that an admiral butterfly should have a suitably naval association. Later on, 'Leghorn' was quietly dropped.

This association with water continues in the German name for the White Admiral, *Kleiner Eisvogel*. An *Eisvogel* or 'ice-bird' is the European kingfisher, and the name invokes the flash of blue you see when sunlight strikes the ice. Why the butterfly is also an *Eisvogel* is harder to explain. There are little flashes of pale blue on its under-wings, and silver flashes on its elegant chrysalis. Or perhaps it is something to do with the white bands on the butterfly's dark wings. If so, we could see it as 'the ice butterfly': dollops of vanilla ice cream melting on dark wings.

Hawks

Hawk-moths are the grandest of moths, with their elegant narrow wings, mouse-like bodies and great beady eyes. They have been known, reared and loved for centuries. The greatest thrill for any young moth catcher is to find a mighty Privet Hawk-moth in the trap: a moth the size of a small bat. One of my cherished moth memories is of watching a Convolvulus Hawk-moth feeding at the hover one summer night in the light of the window, its long tongue piercing the white trumpet of a tobacco flower. I used to love watching the Elephant Hawk-moth live up to its generic name *Deilephilus*, 'evening-loving', as it was drawn to the heady breath of honeysuckle on the wall by my cottage door (they were not just any old moths; they were *my* moths). And the Hummingbird Hawk-moth brings joy on its blurry fawn wings every time it patrols the garden border on dreamy summer afternoons.

'Hawk-moth' is an old name. Eleazar Albin painted the life stages of the Poplar, Privet and Eyed Hawk-moths under those very names before 1720. The caterpillars of these moths were well known, perhaps partly because they made enticing fishing bait (Izaak Walton, author of *The Compleat Angler*, mentions fishing with the caterpillars of Privet Hawk-moths). But why were they called hawk-moths, and what kind of hawk was it? Although no one thought it necessary to explain, I suspect the bird they had in mind was the kestrel (all right, a kestrel's a falcon, not a hawk in the strict sense, but back then they were all 'hawks'). Kestrels hover; so do some hawk-moths. They have long narrow wings; so do most hawk-moths. Narrow wings are built for speed, and many hawk-moths, including the largest, are fast-flying, long-distance migrants. Of course, unlike hawks, hawk-moths are vegetarians. But all the same there is surely something faintly belligerent about their bold, arrowhead shape and muscle-bound, torpedo-like bodies.

That other hovering hawk, the Convolvulus Hawk-moth, was once better known as the Unicorn Hawk, from its long extended proboscis with which it probes the nectaries of long, tubular flowers. This 'horn' is visible on the moth's pupa, too; it looks like a curly handle. And yet this lovely moth carries, like most hawk-moths, a dull name that simply borrows from the scientific name *Convolvuli*, for it lays its eggs on Convolvulus, or bindweed. In similar fashion we have the Privet Hawk-moth, Poplar Hawk-moth and Spurge Hawk-moth. It is much the same across the Channel, where the Poplar Hawk-moth is simply *Le Sphinx du Peuplier*, or, in Germany, *Pappel-Schwarmer*. (For the meaning of Sphinx, *see* Monsters). A few species are named more imaginatively. The Eyed Hawk-moth is *Le Sphinx demi-paon*, the half-peacock, and in Germany the Pine Hawk-moth is *Tannenpfeil*, the pine-arrow, after its bold, arrowhead shape when at rest. And the Convolvulus Hawk-moth is *Winden-Schwarmer*, the great grey moth that comes with the warm winds of the south.

In the north of England moths in general were called 'buzzards' or 'buzzerts', not because they looked like a buzzard but because they buzzed. The wings of the larger moths are linked by a little hook attachment enabling them to fly with rapid wingbeats like a bee. Vibrations in the air create the low, loud buzz of a big moth as it blunders through the open window and round the living-room light.

Unlikely as it may seem, a tiny micro called *Epinotia nisella* is an honorary hawk-moth in the sense that its name also celebrates a hawk. Its tiny wings share the same warm shades of grey and reddish-brown as a male sparrowhawk's. The sparrowhawk is *Accipiter nisus*, and so this pretty moth has become *nisella*, the 'little sparrowhawk'.

(For the Hummingbird Hawk-moth, *see* Birds. For the bee hawk-moths, *see* Bees. And for the wonderful Death's-head Hawk-moth, *see* Skulls).

Heraldry

Among the most poetic names of moths are those drawn from heraldry, as if the butterfly or moth had become a living coat-of-arms. Their leader, so to speak, is The Herald, described by Eleazar Albin as 'a most beautiful Scallop-winged Moth'. When at rest the moth's broad, indented wings recall the flaring skirts of a herald's traditional costume, known as a tabard, on which his master's coat-of-arms was emblazoned. Since it flies late in the season, the moth could also be said to herald the coming winter, just

Finishing flag: the Argent and Sable.

as the Spring Usher moth 'ushers in' the growing season. The Herald's scientific name, *libatrix*, hints at an alternative interpretation. In classical times a *libatrix* was one who made a libation, a ritual offering of wine to the gods. And so the moth could also be seen as a Roman priestess dressed in her fine robes. In Holland, that is what they call it: *Roesje*, The Robe. Stuff and nonsense, insist the Germans. There the moth is known simply as the Pink Owl (*Zackeneule*).

The Argent and Sable is a beautifully chequered, day-flying moth, its name derived from its heraldic colours of silver and black. It is a moth that resembles a chequered shield, or flag, of the kind that finishes a car race. Another moth bearing a heraldic device is The Chevron, whose most obvious character is the orange V-shaped band on its forewings. Its genus, *Eulithis*, means 'pretty stone'.

'Ingrailed' (or 'engrailed') is a heraldic word meaning 'indented', usually in the form of a decorative border. The Ingrailed Clay moth displays this in the form of linear markings, but the unrelated Engrailed moth is indented with ripple-like patterns. Most of these heraldic names first surface in *The Aurelian* by Moses Harris, and it is tempting to think that they were coined by him, although Harris might have been using names that were already in use. All we can say for sure is that these moths have borne their coats of arms proudly for at least two hundred and fifty years.

Hermits

The Scarce Chocolate-tip moth has a caterpillar that prefers to be alone. The species is *anachoreta*, the anchorite, 'one that has withdrawn from the world', opting to spend his days in religious contemplation inside a bare, uncomfortable cell, in this case a homemade one of a bundle of leaves spun together with silk. The chocolate-tip moth genus, *Clostera*, means a 'spindle', referring to the shape of the moth's body, which narrows into a little tuft so that its rear end sticks up through its folded wings. Perhaps this helps to camouflage the moth by breaking up its outline. As for 'chocolate-tip', the wings of all three British species end in a square of chocolate-brown suggesting the end of a broken twig. Sleeping moths need all the camouflage they can get.

The Dusky Sallow is another mothy

hermit whose genus, *Eremobia*, means 'solitary' or 'deserted', possibly a reference to the moth's habitat: bare, windswept downs and heaths. Other lonely moths include *eremita* ('hermit'), the Brindled Green, and *Philereme* ('fond of solitude'), the Brown Scallop moth. Both have caterpillars that live alone inside a leafy tent. Among the more unsocial micros we find *Adela*, a group of glossy, day-flying moths with grotesquely long antennae. *Adela* means 'unseen', which hardly describes the flamboyant moths, and so probably refers to their caterpillars, each one shrouded from the world inside a veil of shredded leaf.

Homes and Habitats

All species have a place they call home. The Greek word for home is *oikos,* from which we get ecology ('home knowledge') and economics ('home law'). Home for many caterpillars, especially the smaller ones, is often a circumscribed space, a mine within a leaf, or a spinning in which a leaf is curled round to make a tube. Other caterpillars live gregariously inside a web.

The broader kind of home is the insect's environment, the surroundings in which it interacts with its world. This kind of home, generally known as a habitat, is reflected in names such as the

Chalkhill Blue butterfly or the Heath Rustic moth. Among the common names of British butterflies we find meadow, marsh, heath (three times), wood (twice) and hedge, each one broadly descriptive of their habitats.

When it comes to moths, references to habitats are still more numerous, especially among the Noctuids and Geometers. A random sample includes Wood Tiger, Coast Dart, Fen Square Spot, Chalk Carpet, Heath Rivulet, Grey Mountain Carpet and Marsh Moth. Among the species names, too, we find references to woodland (*sylvestris*), woodland glades (*nemoralis*), open landscapes (*agestis*, 'of the field'), wetlands (*palustris*, 'of the marsh'), and even arable fields (*segetum*, 'of the cornfield'). Not all these names are strictly accurate, at least in a British context. The Wood Tiger, for instance,

The misnamed Wood Tiger.
Heath Leopard would be better.

is a moth of open downs and moors more than of woods. A micro named *alpinella* actually prefers to live at low elevations in Britain!

Some allusions to homes and habitats are quite poetic: *Epiblema rosaecolana*, for example, is a moth that supposedly 'lives in a rose'. Actually the caterpillar lives in a spinning on the shoots rather than in the flower, but at least it seems to prefer roses that have a pleasant scent.

Epinotia nemorivaga has a species name that means 'wandering through the glades' – though in Britain, it doesn't. It's a moorland moth.

Aristotle wrote of a terrible bird he called the *phoyx*, noting that it 'eats the eyes of its prey'. When it came to a name for the Ringed China-mark moth, a species with an aquatic caterpillar, Jacob Hübner assumed that the *phoyx* was a heron, and so came up with *Parapoynx* or 'beside the heron', which is a roundabout way of saying that the moth lives in water.

Loosely translated, the genus of the Willow Beauty moth, *Peribatodes*, means 'around the thorn thicket', a reference to the moth's bosky habitat. *Stigmella tityrella* is named after Tityrus, a mythical shepherd who sang songs under a beech tree while tending his sheep. And, yes, as you'd expect, it's a moth that lives in a beech tree.

Limnaecia phragmitella is a 'dweller in the marshy lake/feeds on reeds'. It's a lovely name, and it's a shame that the moth isn't interested in *Phragmites* or common reeds. Instead, the caterpillar makes a warm, snug home inside the clubs of reed-mace, known to everyone except botanists as bulrush.

Hooks

It's easy to spot a hook-tip moth. Their broad, butterfly-like forewings, which are spread flat when the moth is at rest, narrow into a curved point that recalls a sickle. Their family name is Drepanidae, from the Greek word for a 'reaping hook', which has also given us *drepaniform* ('shaped like a sickle'), usually used to describe the flight profile of a swift. In 1748, Benjamin Wilkes called these moths the 'Hooked Tipped Moths'. That had morphed into 'hook-tips' by the time Moses Harris penned his *Aurelian's Pocket Companion* in 1775, and hook-tips they remain.

Britain has only seven species out of about four hundred worldwide. Their common names refer either to their wing pattern – the pale, stony Pebble Hook-tip, the wavy-edged Scalloped Hook-tip – or to their foodplant, as in Oak Hook-tip. Their scientific names, on the other hand, continue the hook idea: *Drepana*, the reaping hook; *Falcaria*, a sickle;

Hook-tip moths were named after sickles and ploughs.

cultraria, a 'culter' or plough-share. The Dusky Hook-tip, a rare visitor to Britain, is *curvatula*, or 'little curve', while the Scarce Hook-tip is *harpagula*, the little grappling hook. The odd one out is the Scalloped Hook-tip, which was named in a different way because Linnaeus didn't realise it was a hook-tip and placed it among the Geometers, which, in his classification, have names that end in *-aria*. He named it *lacertinaria*, the lizard, because the caterpillar reminded him of some scaly brown reptile from a desert region.

There is also an unrelated Beautiful Hook-tip and a Silver Hook moth, both back-of-the-book Noctuids that now have a family of their own, the Erebidae. The former, whose beauty is very much in the eye of the beholder, is *flexula*, or 'bent-wing', yet another reference to a wing that ends in a hook. The Silver Hook, on the other hand, contains its little silver fish-hook within its forewings. It is *uncula*, or 'little hook'.

Horse Chestnut

The Horse Chestnut is a beautiful flowering tree with a mysterious name. It is not a proper chestnut (you can't eat conkers), nor does it have much to do with horses, unless you count its hoof-shaped leaf scars. By the same token, a moth named after the tree and called The Horse Chestnut, *hippocastanaria*, has nothing to do with Horse Chestnuts either. Someone had blundered. Its caterpillar feeds on heather.

Few moths, in fact, showed much interest in Horse Chestnuts until the Horse Chestnut Leaf Miner came along. This is the one whose caterpillars now riddle the large fivefold leaves with unsightly blotches and can turn the foliage brown by late summer. It was unknown in Britain until 2002, but has since then spread rapidly through town and country alike, perhaps with the help of buses and lorries with infected leaves stuck in their radiators. Its species name is *ohridella*. That does not mean 'orrid, though perhaps it should. Instead it commemorates the town of Ohrid in Macedonia where the Horse Chestnut tree grows wild on surrounding rocky hillsides (and where, it seems, the moth behaves itself).

Humble Occupations

Among the funny names of moths are a wide variety of workers that read like a version of *The Canterbury Tales*. There is, for example, a Miller, a species with a powdering of white scales, as if the moth were coated in flour. Its colouring – white on a darker background with blue-grey tints – reminded Linnaeus of the Mountain Hare, common in his native Sweden, and so he named the moth *leporina*. He may also have been thinking of this moth-miller's caterpillar, which has a coat of long white bristles. That is the reason for the moth's Dutch name, *schaapje*, or 'little sheep', and its German name of *Wolleule*, 'woolly owl'.

Every wealthy household in Georgian England had its footmen, and a whole sub-family of moths share that name. We have a presumably old Hoary Footman, a red-cheeked Rosy Footman, a smart Buff Footman, a scruffy Dingy Footman, a Large Footman and a Pigmy Footman, a prize-winning Feathered Footman, and a possibly potty-mouthed Four-dotted Footman. To which we can add the Crimson-speckled Footman, who will be off sick with the measles, and the angry, bigoted Red-necked Footman (whose black wings supply its contrasting French name of *La Veuve*, the widow). Footman moths have narrow wings that either rest stiffly across their long, slim bodies, or are

rolled about them like a coat. With their beady-eyed little heads, the moths seem to stand stiffly to attention, like little toy soldiers. You would never know at a glance that they are related to the tiger-moths, whose species names are often the footmen's female domestic counterparts: housekeepers and matrons (*see* Tigers).

Another name for a liveried servant was a lackey. Two moths bear that name: The Lackey and the Ground Lackey. Since the reason for it isn't obvious, Moses Harris explained it for us. Both moths have caterpillars with coloured stripes running down the length of their

A fluffy white moth: The Miller aka the woolly owl aka the little sheep.

The Lackey, whose caterpillar wears
the 'livery lace' of footmen.

bodies. This reminded some imaginative Aurelian of the livery lace then worn by domestic servants, that is, the strips of material that decorated the cuffs and buttonholes of their uniforms. The French had the same idea. There The Lackey moth is *Livrée*, or the livery moth. In Holland it is *ringelrups*, a ring-shaped crawler, from the caterpillar's habit of curling up into a circle.

In general, where a moth is named after its caterpillar, the latter is easier to find, and so more familiar, than the adult moth. You can hardly miss a nest of lackeys, a caterpillar web in which the individual larvae can be found curling in such a way that might recall the frogging of livery lace. As for the Ground Lackey, the name is a carryover from the time when the commoner species was sometimes called the Tree Lackey. One feeds on low plants, the other in bushes and trees. Though common and widespread enough in mainland Europe, in Britain the Ground Lackey is restricted to low-lying salt marshes.

Every old house needed its chimneys swept regularly, and there are several moths lined up for the job, all of them suitably small and sooty. 'Sweeps' (or 'chimney-sweeps') was one of the old names given to the bagworms (Psychidae), which had one particularly small species called the 'Chimney Sweeper's Boy'. Today there is only one true Chimney Sweeper moth, *Odezia atrata*, a name that translates as 'a black moth sitting on the road' (from its habit of settling on damp bare ground). This is a common and familiar day-flying moth of meadows and downs whose sooty wings are prettily offset by a delicate white margin. Perhaps its wings were pure white before it took up chimney-sweeping.

I

In the Shed

A number of moths are named after the sort of things you keep in the shed: shears, for instance. Moths called 'shears' possess a pair of curved marks that resemble old-fashioned shears of the kind that clipped sheep or pruned hedges. The commonest species is simply called The Shears, but we also have the Tawny Shears (shears gone rusty?), Glaucous Shears with a greyish-green bloom, and Dingy Shears – all tools that need replacing, perhaps.

The Garden Pebble moth has a marking on its wings that, depending on how you interpret its species name, *forficalis*, could be a pair of shears or scissors. Either way it refers to the manner in which the moth folds its wings: they close neatly on a single plane to form a triangle. Perhaps that also helps explain its genus name, *Evergestis*, 'a well made garment', a goodly coat.

A useful device for drilling is a *terebra*, an auger, which was borrowed for the micro *Assara terebrella*, a moth whose caterpillars bore holes in spruce cones to feed on the seeds. Somewhere at the back of the shed may be a broken sundial, whose gnomon – the bit that casts a shadow – gave us the name of the Tortricid *Paramesia gnomana*, a moth with a mark on its wings that might be able to tell us the time, if only once a day.

Finally, and most regrettably, there is a small moth called *Mirificarma* or 'wonderful tool'. It is named not from some useful gadget but after the male moth's member, originally described as 'very long, in a tube, with an accompanying and very long filamental prong'.

Indoors

Butterflies live out of doors. So do most moths, apart from those that nibble our woollens or dry stores. But an increasing number of species native in warmer climes than ours are finding new homes in cellars, hearths, cupboards and kitchens – anywhere that is sufficiently warm and humid, and where there is something to eat (the moths themselves rarely feed; it is their caterpillars that need fattening up). Most of these indoors moths are micros. Those in the genus *Ephestia* (Pyralidae) are small, scurrying moths that live on stored products. *Ephestia* means 'beside the hearth', a place where you used to find crumbs from toasted muffins. Nowadays you are more likely to find the moth in a warehouse or a neglected cupboard than around the fireplace.

Some moths are named after their favourite food, such as the Raisin Moth, the Dried Fruit Moth and the Cacao Moth (the latter has a depraved taste for tobacco and coffee as well as chocolate). Allied to them is the Stored Nut Moth, whose species name *gularis* is taken from the Latin word for throat, *gula*, and means 'glutton'. By implication it is an exceptionally greedy moth.

My favourite, because of its name, is the Mung Moth, a pest of mung beans. Around the world, it has other names, too, depending on what it happens to be eating at the time: Soybean Pod Borer, for instance, or the Murica Pod Borer.

Insults

Where they are not neutral in tone, many names of butterflies and moths were coined in a spirit of admiration. Even when a moth is called a 'clay' or a 'rustic' or a 'drab', that name was, I think, intended to be descriptive rather than a slight. Here I'm interested in a handful of cases where, for whatever reason, the insult seems intentional, as if the poor creature were scorned by whomever described it.

The rare moth called The Silurian is curiously named after the rock strata underlying its moorland habitat. But to judge from its Latin name, *Eriopygodes imbecilla*, it is also a moth of unusually low intelligence. The original meaning of *imbecilla* or 'imbecile' was broader than today's, and could mean feeble rather than stupid. Probably the namer was thinking of the female Silurian

The Silurian, a moth named after a rock formation.

moth, which is fat of body and short of wing, and was once considered too feeble to fly. In fact it *can* fly, though perhaps not very far. Thus we can regard *imbecilla* as a sexist name as well as a calumny. Two species were seen as 'degenerate': the Sallow Nycteoline (*Nycteola degenerana*) and the Portland Ribbon Wave (*Idaea degeneraria*). Degenerate in this sense does not mean 'of low moral fibre', but harks back to the word's original meaning, 'departing from its kind'. The Sallow Nycteoline is a Noctuid that looks more like a Tortrix. It departs from the usual pattern. But that does not seem to apply to the Portland Ribbon Wave, so perhaps this one just 'departed' by going off to live on the rocky isle of Portland.

The Smoky Wainscot is dirty (*impura*), while the Rustic Shoulder Knot is *sordens* (defiled) – both undeserved insults for what, when viewed with sympathy, are not unhandsome moths. The Small Ranunculus, meanwhile, is *dysodea,* or evil-smelling. Since neither it nor its caterpillar has any detectable smell, this insult seems unmerited. But the moth can be bred on lettuce, which can pong a bit when it goes off inside a Tupperware container.

The seemingly unkind name given to The Flame moth, *putris* (putrid or rotten) is not what it seems. It is really

Bad luck with the name. This is The Dismal moth aka the Dingy Shears.

J–K

a credit to the moth's camouflage, a rotting wood chip. All the same, the French take things a step further in calling it *la Noctuelle putride*, the rotten little owl.

Among the micros, insults are surprisingly sparse when you consider that they include all kinds of pests. A moth called *Adoxophyes* or 'ignoble growth' perhaps deserves its name, for it is the Summer Fruit Tortrix, a violator of fruit trees. But you have to feel sorry for the harmless *Psoricoptera* or 'mangy-wing'. It has markings and little tufts that reminded somebody of an eruptive skin disease.

Perhaps the most undeserved insult was aimed at an admittedly nondescript but unexceptional grey moth which past generations knew as 'The Dismal'. That name survived for most of the nineteenth century. Today we have been kinder, but only slightly. It is now called the Dingy Shears.

Jesters

Momus was the Greek god of mockery. He was an unusually sharp-tongued god, the original critic and personification of satire, and he appears in that guise in two of Aesop's *Fables*. Later on, he seems to have mellowed a bit, and appeared in comedies as a jester dressed in motley, a patchwork garb of many colours. He was the effective precursor of the witty, intelligent Harlequin in the Commedia dell' Arte. The latter form of theatre was of recent memory when a colourful moth was named after Momus. *Moma alpium*, the Scarce Merveille du Jour, is a strikingly beautiful green moth patterned with black that becomes almost invisible when resting on a lichen-smothered branch. The moth

The joker: the Scarce Merveille du Jour.

may not know any jokes, but it wears a jester's costume. So does the very variable Tortricid moth *Acleris maccana* (from *maccus*, a buffoon), which can do some fairly convincing impersonations of other moths.

Jewels

Given the brilliant iridescent colours of many butterflies, it is perhaps surprising that more of them were not named after precious gems. Only one British species has a name taken from the jewel box: the Mazarine Blue. A mazarine is a deep-blue cut stone named after the Duchess of Mazarin, a mistress of Charles II and niece of Cardinal Mazarin, the seventeenth-century French statesman. Later the word was used for any brilliant-cut gem, though today it has fallen out of use. The name 'Mazarine Blue' was first given to what is now the Large Blue by Edward Donovan in 1797, but a few years later Adrian Haworth took it away and bestowed it instead on a now extinct British butterfly, *Cyaniris semiargus*, today's Mazarine Blue. *Cyaniris* means 'violet-blue/iridescent': a description of both the stone and the butterfly.

There are moths, too, that carry the names of jewels, but anyone expecting a treasure chest of glittering, gemlike moths will be disappointed. The species

Named from a blue gem:
the Mazarine Blue.

actually called The Gem is a good example of how tastes have changed. A dark, reddish-brown moth, its only gemlike attribute is some diamond-bright spots on the wings of some individuals. Perhaps it was named in the sense of 'what a lovely moth, a real gem!'

The species name of the moth *Grapholita* (formerly *Cydia*) *gemmiferana* means 'to carry a gem', though you might have trouble locating the stone in question. The name seems to refer to some silvery markings on the edge of the moth's wings. Equally unconvincing as a gem-carrier is the well known Diamond-back Moth, a notorious pest of cabbage crops the world over. While its markings may be diamond-shaped, they do not sparkle. Its genus, *Plutella* (family Plutellidae), also alludes to the 'diamonds', for Plutus was the Greek god of wealth.

The Ruby Tiger at least has the right ruby-red colour, especially on its body. And yet its species name, *fuliginosa*, suggests the opposite: it means 'sooty', and refers to the dusky forewings of some forms of the moth.

At least two moths are named after the pearl known as margarita. The Pale Emerald, for example, is *margaritaria*, in honour of the pearly freshness of the newly emerged moth. The day-flying grass-moth, *Catoptria margaritella*, has a name which means 'mirror/pearl' from a pearly white stripe on its forewing. (*See also* Emeralds.)

Joke

The cruellest joke in entomology was played on Ottmar Hofmann, a blameless nineteenth-century German physician and an authority on very small moths. Other notable entomologists have been honoured by colourful, boldly marked, feisty species. Hofmann got the Brown House-moth, a scurrying nuisance of

The despised Brown House-moth whose scientific name translates as 'loving Hofmann'.

less-than-clean places. Worse, they named it *Hofmannophila*, or 'I like Hofmann,' which is dangerously close to 'I am like Hofmann.' Its species name is *pseudospretella*, or 'false and despised'. Poor old Hofmann.

Knights

When Linnaeus came to the butterflies, he dubbed the largest and most glamorous species, swallowtails and birdwings, the knights: his Equites. For species names he drew on Greek and Trojan heroes in Homer's *Iliad,* which is why we see exotic butterflies from the far side of the world carrying the names of Hector, Priam and Helen. Linnaeus named two European swallowtails from physicians and healers in Homer's Greek army: Machaon, whose name was given to The Swallowtail (that is, our Swallowtail), while his brother Podalirius became the species name of the Scarce Swallowtail. Machaon was the leader of a faction of the Greek army and an authority on healing herbs. He was slain by an arrow in the tenth year of the siege, but Podalirius was said to be one of those who hid inside the Wooden Horse, and so helped to bring the war to an end. There is no obvious reason why Linnaeus chose those particular names except that they fitted his general scheme. But, since, unlike the birdwings and tropical swallowtails, he would have seen these beautiful butterflies on the wing, he might have felt they merited the names of these mythical proto-scientists. The swallowtails also bear the proud name of *Papilio*, meaning, simply, 'butterfly'.

Of all moths, it was the unexciting Small Angle Shades that Moses Harris chose as his 'Chevalier', or little knight. Maybe he just liked the colour.

L

Lappets

The Lappet is a splendid moth, deep russet in colour with scalloped wings, furry legs, and a notably large 'nose'. The female of the species is one of our plumpest, heaviest moths. It has a caterpillar to match: a hairy, greyish monster the size of a cigar with flecks of orange, white and dark blue. It is this caterpillar that has 'lappets'. As Eleazar Albin noted back in 1720, there are 'Flaps or Lappets on every Joint, which makes him appear to have so many feet.' These fleshy 'false feet' help to disguise

the caterpillar when it is sitting on a twig by eliminating any chinks of light showing between its legs. Despite its size, the caterpillar is difficult to locate even when you know it is there. Lappets were a familiar form of headgear in eighteenth-century England. They took the form of flaps attached to a hat or bonnet which protected the ears, while other forms had decorative ribbons that hung down in front. The proper name of the moth is The Lappet. To call it simply 'Lappet', as field guides do, is a discourtesy to a noble moth. In Germany they have an equally charming name: *Kupfer-Glucke*, the Copper Hen.

Compliments cease when it comes to The Lappet's scientific name, *Gastropacha quercifolia*, or 'fat belly oak-leaf'. The species name refers to the resting moth's uncanny resemblance to a bunch of withered oak leaves still attached to a twig (the Dutch call it *eikenblad*, oak-leaf, on that account). But the caterpillar feeds not on oak but on scrubby hawthorn and blackthorn bushes.

There are two lesser kinds of lappet. The Small Lappet, which was found on bilberry moors in the nineteenth century, seems to have died out in Britain. Like its big brother, its scientific name, *Phyllodesma ilicifolia*, 'leaf-bond holm-oak leaf', indicates that it, too, pretends to be a bunch of dead leaves (in

The Lappet moth, named at a time when lappets were a familiar form of headgear.

Dutch it is *hulstblad*, 'holly-leaf'). The Pine Lappet, on the other hand, is a Continental species that was discovered recently in Scotland. Its scientific name, *Dendrolimus pini*, means 'hunger for pine trees', and it suggests no great affection for the moth. In other countries the moth can defoliate the trees and so it is regarded as a pest. The low level of genetic variation found in the Scottish population so far might suggest a recent colonisation, but it may turn out to be an overlooked native colony, as some dare to hope.

Leopards

Our tiger-moths were once leopard-moths. The Garden Tiger-moth is one of the best known and best loved of all moths, thanks to its bold colours and its wandering 'woolly bear' caterpillar. Yet while its image often appeared in art, the moth had to wait for James Petiver to provide it with a name, and he called it not a tiger but a leopard: the Scarlet Royal Leopard. More moth-leopards followed with the Yellow Royal Leopard (now the Cream-spot Tiger-moth) and the Cambridge Royal Leopard (now the Scarlet Tiger-moth). For these two species, at least, 'leopard' is arguably the better name, because the moths are spotted, not striped. Indeed, the only British tiger-moth to bear tiger-like, black-and-yellow stripes is the Jersey Tiger-moth, which is a relative newcomer to Britain. Nonetheless, by the time Benjamin Wilkes was writing in the mid-eighteenth century, Petiver's leopards had already turned into tigers, and so they remain to this day.

We still have a Leopard Moth, whose wings were described by Moses Harris

Polka dots: the Leopard Moth.

as 'full of round dark spots like small shot'. It is also known as the Wood Leopard, 'wood' because the caterpillar lives inside a tree, not because it occurs in woodland. The moth was well known as a pest of fruit trees. There is another, much less familiar moth-leopard, the Speckled Yellow, whose scientific name, *Pseudopanthera maculata*, means 'false spotted leopard'. But across the Channel it turns into a true leopard as *Le Panthère*.

Letters

No moth is easier to spot than the Silver Y, *Autographa gamma*. As a migrant it comes to Britain in summer, often in vast numbers, flying partly by day in a blur of greyish wings, and often visiting gardens. Its most obvious feature is a little silver mark on the forewing that resembles a 'y'. (Its earlier name was in fact 'the Y Moth'.) But Linnaeus and his followers named species in Latin derived from Greek, and hence, for them, it was not a 'y' but the Greek letter gamma. The fun really starts, however, with Hübner's generic name for the Silver Y and its relatives, *Autographa*. It means 'written in one's own hand'. In other words the mark, whether you see it as a 'y' or as a gamma, is supposedly the moth's own autograph! Like someone sewing a name-label onto a shirt collar, the Silver Y has written its name on its wings.

Two more species of *Autographa* have seemingly written their mark, only this time it is in gold: the Beautiful Golden Y and Plain Golden Y. For the latter species, Linnaeus saw the sign as shaped more like a question mark. But since he had already used up *interrogationis* for another species, he settled for a dotted 'i'

The Silver Y carries its name on its wings.

instead: *iota* (or *jota*), or to give the moth its full name, *Autographa jota Linn.*

Another letter lurking in the wings of moths is 'L', or the Greek equivalent, lambda. The L-album Wainscot has a pair of distinct white Ls on its forewings formed from a streak and a dot. Its English name simply repeats its Latin one, *Mythimna L-album* or *L-mark. Mythimna* seems to be the old name for a town on Lesbos, without obvious relevance.

There is another 'L', a black one, on the otherwise pure white wings of the lovely moth called *Arctornis l-album*, but where some might see an 'L' others have seen a 'V' – hence its English name, the Black V Moth. Yet another L (or lambda) lurks in the wings of the Nonconformist moth, *Lithophane lamda*, ('shining stone bearing a lambda mark' – *see* Lithophanes), but the English name seems the more intriguing. How does a moth become a nonconformist – a word usually attached to religious radicalism? It seems that it was named in whimsical contrast with a related moth called The Conformist. That moth isn't religious either; the English name is taken from its former Latin name, *conformis*, and it referred to taxonomic conformity, not to religious preference. How disappointing.

At least two more moths have an obvious 'V' mark on their wings. The V-Moth bears a fine pair of Victory

V for Victory: the V-Moth.

Vs. Its species name, *wauaria*, alludes to this doubling of Vs (so perhaps it should really be called the W-Moth?). Since there is no 'V' or 'W' in Greek, Linnaeus invented the letter 'wau' to mean 'W'. Moses Harris saw it, equally legitimately, as an 'L': the 'L-Moth'. Benjamin Wilkes gave up and called it the Gooseberry Moth.

The second species is the V-Pug, whose scientific name, *Chloroclysta v-ata*, means 'pale green V-mark.' The freshly emerged moth is bright green, not pale green, but the colour soon fades. No doubt the namer was working from an elderly specimen.

Finally there is the Grey Chi, *Antitype chi*, a moth with an obvious 'X' (the Greek letter chi) in its wings, though in some cases it looks more like a little bar with a pair of 'V's at either end. It is a lovely moth whose camouflage works well when it rests on limestone walls.

To complete the alphabet we should perhaps include the Tortricid moth *Acleris literana*, for *literana* means a letter, any letter. It is a variable moth, and so the exact letter is likely to change from moth to moth. This species, one of the best-known micros, was beautifully figured by John Curtis as long ago as 1824, and it seems ridiculous that it still lacks an accepted English name. Two have been suggested: Lichen Button and Sprinkled Rough-wing; both need a little more work, I think.

Lithophanes

A lithophane is a piece of artwork that is etched or moulded onto a thin, translucent sheet of porcelain in such a way that you can see the image only when it is held against the light. Such pieces were fashionable in the 1820s, at exactly the time Jacob Hübner was sorting out the Noctuid moths. He borrowed the word for a group of moths whose wing patterns seem to have been etched onto a plain background. Lithophane might have become their common name, too, but for the fact that some of these moths had common names already: Tawny and Pale Pinion, and the Grey Shoulder-knot, all named after distinctive dark markings, the former pair like the flight feathers of a bird, the latter like a strip of ribbon where the forewings join the body (*see* True Knots and Shoulder-knots).

M

Manchester

Two moths are named after the city of Manchester, home to an active group of nineteenth-century moth hunters. The one called the Manchester Moth is a micro, *Euclemensia woodiella*, whose name commemorates a local entomologist called Wood. It owes its modicum of fame not so much to its pretty brown-and-yellow wings as to the mystery surrounding the moth's discovery and subsequent loss. It was first found on a rotting alder tree near Salford in 1829, and its existence today rests on just three specimens taken at that time, plus a painting made the same year by John Curtis, in which the little moth flies around a dead-nettle. Its discoverer was a Manchester collector, Robert Cribb, who gave a specimen to a friend called Wood, who in turn sent it to Curtis for identification. Curtis realised that this was a new and unknown species, and, assuming that Wood was the discoverer, named it after him (this Wood is otherwise unknown to history; we don't even know his full name). To make things worse, its true discoverer,

The Manchester Treble Bar, one of several moths with names that sound like drinking dens.

poor old Robert Cribb, was suspected of passing off a foreign species as British. He was so upset at this attack on his honour that he gave up collecting altogether. He left his moth collection with his landlady as security for a debt. She made a bonfire of it. What a sad story.

The other Manchester moth is a rather pretty upland species called the Manchester Treble-bar. It sounds like the name of a local pub, but no, the moth has three bars on each wing, and it was first discovered on the moors near Manchester. Later it turned out to be quite widespread on boggy moors, but no longer occurs near Manchester.

Markings

Like the Manchester Treble-bar, many moths of all shapes and sizes are named from distinctive marks on their wings. Indeed, these marks are often the best way of identifying them. To consider every kind of marking would take many pages, but I have dispersed many of them in these pages as 'weapons' (daggers and darts), 'knots', 'arches', 'letters' and so on. This leaves us with a smaller, more

manageable collection of miscellaneous markings to mention here.

Several moths have 'pinion' in their name. The White-spotted Pinion and its two relatives, the Lesser-spotted and Lunar-spotted Pinions, bear triangular marks along the trailing edge of their wings that recall the pinion gears of Victorian technology. They are attractive moths in the genus *Cosmia*, a complimentary word meaning well-ordered or 'becoming' (the same Greek name is found in a small family of pretty micros, the Cosmopterigidae or 'cosmets'). Similar markings are found on the Pinion-spotted Pug and the Pinion-streaked Snout.

It is hard to see such marks on those other, unrelated pinions, the Tawny and Pale Pinion moths, and I wonder in their case whether the name might refer to a different kind of pinion, the flight feathers of a bird, indicated by the

The White-spotted Pinion has gear-wheel markings on its wings.

moths' vaguely feathery markings.

Moths with 'brindle' in their name, such as the Brindled Green and the Clouded Brindle, usually have a brownish ground colour with stripes or streaks of another, contrasting colour, often in an attractive pattern. The name is used today mainly in certain breeds of domestic animal, especially dogs and cats, that are vaguely 'tiger-striped'. The Clouded Brindle has an 'L' shaped mark where its wings join the body, hence its species name, *epomidion* or 'on the shoulder'.

More straightforwardly is The Antler Moth: it bears a very bold mark in the form of cast-off 'antler', of a roebuck perhaps, in the midst of its forewing. Similarly obvious markings can be found on the Double Kidney, Double Line, Double Lobed and Double Square Spot, all of them defining features of those species. The doubling is on the same wing; if you count both wings it would be a quadrupling. But Quadruple Square Spot is not, perhaps, such a good name.

Meaningless?

Do names have to mean something? There are quite a few scientific names among the moths, particularly among genera, that defy translation and seem to be invented words. Colonel Emmet called them 'meaningless neologisms'. *Bena*, the

genus of the very pretty Green Silverlines moth, is one. So is *Tyta*, the genus of the Four-spotted moth. Interestingly, both names were raised by the same person, the Swedish entomologist Gustav Johan Billberg. His English counterpart is Francis Walker, who seemed to enjoy coining names for his own amusement. Among the gems of the Walker imagination are *Maruca*, *Daraba*, *Assara* and *Archanara*, the latter being the genus of several reedbed-dwelling moths including *Archanara geminipuncta*, the Twin-spotted Wainscot. For a more recent example, take *Dafa*, which, as its author R. W. Hodges readily admitted, is meaningless, just a fun word. He gave it to a pretty micro, *Dafa formosella*, whose genus name has since been changed to *Epicallima*. The species name *formosella* can be translated as 'little beauty'. Like Hodges, Walker, Billberg and their fellow pranksters were probably indulging in a private joke. Or maybe they just liked the sound of *Bena*, *Tyta* and *Daraba*. There doesn't seem to be a law against it.

Metal

Eleazar Albin illustrated a still unnamed moth with shiny gilded wings that reminded him of 'burnished Brass'. Maybe that became the cue for the name, because within a generation that moth had become the Burnished Brass, and has remained so ever since. The Germans agree: there it is the *Messingeule* or brass owl. But the Dutch see it as resembling copper, the *Kopernil,* while the French, noting the green tints in some lights, call it *La Plusie vert-doré.*

Many other moths have reflecting wing-scales that take on a shiny, metallic lustre. In some, such as the forester moths, this covers the entire wing, but in most it is confined to specks and splashes here and there. The best known metallic moths are the Silver Y and its relatives in the Plusiinae sub-family, which is derived from the Greek word *plousios,* meaning 'rich'. Among them are the Gold Spot, the Gold Spangle and the Golden Plusia, all species with bling on their wing. Second prize goes to the silver moths. Apart from the Silver Y there is also the self-explanatory Silver Hook and the Silver Barred moths, not to mention the Silvery Arches, which looks as though its wings have been freshly polished. Other moths carry baser metals. Copper is represented by two copper underwings, fine moths with hindwings as bright as the copper bottom of a saucepan. Lead is reserved for moths with a duller sheen: the Lead Belle, the Lead-coloured Drab and the Lead-coloured Pug, all dressed in the same sober dark grey.

Metal moth: the Burnished Brass.

When it comes to iron, the analogy is not with bright metal but with rust. The Iron Prominent seems to rust before our eyes, its dark-grey wings edged with flecks of red-brown. The Brown Rustic moth, *ferruginea,* is completely rusted through, 'the colour of iron rust'.

Mimics

Among the most intriguing moths are those which do their best to resemble some other insect, generally a more dangerous one. We have already met the bee hawk-moths (*see* Bees). Here we can conveniently place another group of equally adept mimics known as the clearwings, so-named because the wings of these moths are thinly scaled and almost transparent. In fact, with their long, thin bodies and gawky antennae and legs, they hardly look like moths at all. The clearwings are a close-knit family. We have resident species, plus one recent colonist, out of more than a thousand worldwide. The two largest are convincing mimics of the hornet, while the others pretend to be various kinds of small wasps. Their scientific names suggest a wide range of impersonations (though it is well to remember that they are just names, and not necessarily facts). They include *apiformis* ('like a bee'), *muscaeformis* ('like a house fly'), *tabaniformis* ('like a Tabanus or gadfly'), *tipuliformis* ('like a daddy-longlegs'), *andrenaeformis* ('like Andrena, a mining bee'), *scoliaeformis* ('like a Scolia or dagger wasp'), *formicaeformis* ('like a red ant') and *culiciformis* ('like a Culex or mosquito'). Perhaps impressed by its flashes of red, Moses Harris named one species, the Large Red-belted Clearwing, 'The Bishop'. In Germany they have a similar name: *Glasflüger*, that is, 'glass-wings'. In America the clearwings are often 'wasp moths' or 'borers', the latter referring to their tunnelling larvae rather than to a lack of interest.

As far as Latin names go, the odd one out is the Six-belted Clearwing, *Bembecia scopigera*, for the species name means a broom, a reference to a brush-like structure at the moth's rear end. But it, too, is a mimic. Its generic name derives from *Bembex*, a sand-wasp.

Though they are day-flying, the clearwings are among the most elusive of moths. Despairing of finding them in their adult state, collectors used to search instead for the telltale holes in living wood made by their caterpillars, or for the galls they created on other plants. Today, via an entirely different, man-made form of mimicry, they have become more accessible. Many species can be attracted to pheromone-lures that mimic the scent of the female moth.

Monarchs

The Monarch is a large and beautiful North American butterfly, a famous long-distance migrant that visits Britain now and again but will never settle here, since we lack its foodplant, milkweed. Monarch is an American name. The butterfly is said to have been named back in colonial times after King William III, or William of Orange, partly because it was one of the largest and most colourful of the butterflies of New England, and partly because its ground colour happens to be orange. If so, it would be the second butterfly to be named after that king, for here in England the Swallowtail, too, was once known as the Royal William. In Britain the Monarch was more commonly known as The Milkweed or the Black-veined Brown, while in other parts of the world it has been named the Common Tiger. The Monarch is a toxic butterfly. A non-related, non-toxic butterfly that mimics the Monarch has been given the appropriate name of

Viceroy: 'not quite a monarch'.

The Monarch is the best-known member of a mainly tropical family, the Danaidae. Its scientific name is *Danaus plexippus*, and, appropriately, the original Danaus was a mythical monarch, noted for siring fifty daughters and for founding the city of Argos. The species name, *plexippus*, derives from the name of a nephew of the king who married one of the fifty daughters, and was subsequently murdered by her. They say you can make out the fatal stabbing blade in the wings of the butterfly if you look hard enough.

Monsters

The alternative name for a hawk-moth is a sphinx. In fact nearly everybody except the British use that name. The original Sphinx was not the eroded creature that sits quietly next to the Pyramids of Giza but a fabulous monster with the head and breasts of a woman and the body of a lion. In art, the Sphinx was usually shown with her female part more or less upright and her leonine body in a prone position. This, as someone must have noticed, was reminiscent of the defensive posture of the Privet Hawk-moth caterpillar, which raises the front part of its body while its rear part clings to the twig. The name was already old when Linnaeus borrowed it

for his group name for the hawk-moths: Sphinges, which later became the family Sphingidae.

Given the association of hawk-moths with a terrible monster, it seemed consistent to scatter a few more monsters among them. The genus of the large Convolvulus Hawk-moth, *Agrius*, recalls a mighty giant of that name, one of the original inhabitants of the world, who was clubbed to death in a great battle with the Olympian Gods. The original Hyles, the genus of the Spurge Hawk-moth and its relatives, was a centaur whose misbehaviour at a wedding feast resulted in a pitched battle. The analogy of horse-men with hawk-moths was similar to that of the Sphinx: it was not the moth so much as its rearing, multi-legged caterpillar that sent the imagination racing.

Strangely enough, it is the smallest of the hawk-moths, the Narrow-bordered Bee-hawk, which carries the

Named after a terrible giant: the quiet, unassuming Narrow-bordered Bee Hawk-moth.

name of the most terrifying monster. It is *tityus*, named after the giant Tityos. As an unborn baby, Tityos split his mother's womb. When full grown, his mighty body covered a full nine acres. Like Prometheus, the God who brought the gift of fire to mankind, Tityos was punished in hell for various misdemeanours by a pair of vultures pecking everlastingly at his liver. Naming a small harmless moth after a giant might seem like a joke, but there might have been method in the mirth. In Linnaeus's original order, the name *tityus* was preceded by Tantalus and followed by Ixion, both mythological characters who suffered similarly gruesome and imaginative punishments in hell.

The species name of the Cistus Forester moth (Cistus is the former name of its foodplant, the rockrose) is *geryon*, a hellish beast with three heads and monstrous wings (although in the *Inferno* it was friendly enough and willing to give Dante and Virgil a lift down to the lower levels). Possibly the reason why this pretty green moth was named after Geryon is because Linnaeus thought the foresters and burnets were distant relations of the hawk-moths (which, if unlikely, is at least one better than Petiver and Ray, who considered them to be butterflies). As such, the Cistus Forester would have merited a monstrous name, though that did not apply to our other two species of forester, which are named after plants.

Several species of micro were named by Bryan Beirne (1918–98), who turned to the Irish legends of his native country for inspiration. His genus *Fomoria*, a group of tiny leaf-mining moths, commemorates a race of ferocious beings that were supposed to have ruled Ireland in the remote past. Perhaps the name reflected the trouble Beirne himself experienced when sorting out these moths. There is also a micro species named after Beirne, *beirnei*, though there is no reason to suppose that he wasn't a perfectly nice man.

Moods

We like to attribute human feelings to forces of nature and inanimate objects. The wind rages, the leaves dance, the clouds weep. In literature this is known as the pathetic fallacy, and in poetry no one finds anything wrong with joyous larks or chattering sparrows or laughing hyenas. What is more surprising is that the pathetic fallacy sometimes finds its way into science. Among the names of butterflies and moths are references to laughter and crying, gentleness and fear, happiness and misery. It is another reminder that those who named our

Lepidoptera, whether in England or Germany or Sweden, had often received a classical education. They knew their myths, and some of them also possessed a poetic imagination. And it seems they had a sense of fun.

Let's begin with the 'sad' butterflies. Colourful butterflies were seen as 'happy' (appearing as nymphs, for instance); dark ones were sad. What we would now call a sombre brown was formerly known as 'sad brown'. The butterflies that match this sorrowful shade – the Scotch Argus, the Mountain Ringlet and the Meadow Brown – are all named after sad things. The first two are in the large genus *Erebia*, named after Erebus, the region of darkness beneath the earth where the souls of the dead wander through all eternity. The Meadow Brown is *Maniola*, after Manes, the spirit of the departed, but in this case it is a small ghost, indicated by the diminutive suffix *-iola*, signifying a soul the size of a butterfly, perhaps. As for species names, the Mountain Ringlet is *epiphron*, 'thoughtful' but in a melancholy way. The Ringlet, equally dark, is equally cast down. In France its name is *Le Tristan*, the sorrowful one.

A group of dark little micro-moths share the genus name *Scythris*, meaning 'sullen'. They are miserable because they are dull, just as grey clouds are sullen. The Four-spotted moth, *luctuosa*, is

Named after departed spirits: the Meadow Brown.

'mournful'. Its mourning weeds are black wings relieved by spots of white, similar to the black clothes and white lace worn by Victorian mourners. Perhaps the most miserable of the lot is the micro called *Lampronia morosa*: morose and gloomy, as well it might be, to judge by its leaden wings.

The Frosted Green moth, on the other hand, is laughing. Its species name, *ridens*, means laughter of a mocking, jeering kind. Although Johan Fabricius gave no reason for this odd name, he might have been referring to the distinctive zigzag lines on the moth's forewings, which suggest laugh-lines on a grimacing face. Stare at the moth for a while and you begin to see it.

A laughing moth: the Frosted Green.

The Scarce Umber has a fierce name too: *Agriops*. The name seems to refer to the rough scales on the moth's frons (or forehead), which put someone in mind of the unkempt bristly face of a man who has spent too long in the outback. The little Hawthorn Moth, *Scythropia*, has an 'angry face'. It seems to have something to do with the moth's head-down attitude, as if he is about to dispute some point. But it is also likely that the moth's namer, Jacob Hübner, had in mind a contrast with the next genus, *Prays*, nice, well-behaved little moths that are 'gentle and tame'.

Finally, we reach the cowardly moths. The Red-necked Footman is *Atolmis*, meaning 'want of courage'. Despite its red neck, it was seen as a timid moth, for its caterpillar hides in crevices by day, creeping out at dusk to munch on lichen. The Great Prominent is another fearful moth despite its large size and handsome appearance. Its scientific name, *anceps*, means 'very timid' or 'doubtful'. James Stephens, who named it, noted that, when touched, its big green caterpillar

'trembles as if in fear'. Perhaps it appears doubtful, too, as if uncertain how to proceed. Its old name, *trepida*, describes the same trait. It means 'alarmed.' We frighten the poor beast by poking it.

Another trembler is the Angle Shades, whose name is *meticulosa* or 'afraid'. This time it seems to be the moth that is frightened, or so we must suppose from the unusual way it crinkles its wings, as if drawing in on itself. On the face of it, the Swallow Prominent sounds like another quaking moth, for its name is *tremula*. But that name is taken from the moth's foodplant, *Populus tremula* or aspen, whose leaves quake in the slightest breeze.

Agreement is the word when it comes to the Small Clouded Brindle moth. Its species name, *unanimis*, means unanimous, 'of one mind'. Unfortunately, no one thought to state what they were unanimous about.

Moons

As befits winged creatures of the night, certain moths carry a moon in their wings. It often takes the form of a dark crescent, as in the forewings of the Lunar Marbled Brown or the hindwings of the Lunar Underwing. But scientific names can often indicate another way of looking at the same thing. The Lunar Underwing,

The Lunar Underwing: moon
or belly-button?

shining half-moon has two little sub-moons, mere points of light on either side of the main body. It reminds me not so much of our moon as the moons of Jupiter seen through a small telescope.

Mourning

In times past, mourning for a loved one took place in stages, and each stage had its own dress code. For the funeral and its immediate aftermath, a fully veiled, lugubrious black was called for, but after that would come a period of 'half-mourning' in which white lace could be worn, so that the survivor wore a mixture of black and white. That provided the early entomologists with a name for what is now the Marbled White butterfly: the Half-mourner, for it wore a chequer-pattern dress of black and white. It retained that name well into the nineteenth century, and indeed it is still called that in France (*Le Demi-Deuil*), while in Germany it is The Chessboard (*Schachbrett*). The similarly coloured, though unrelated, Bath White was also once a half-mourner, distinguished as Vernon's Half-mourner after a William Vernon, who discovered the butterfly near Cambridge and brought it to the attention of the waiting world.

for example, is *Omphaloscetis*, the 'navel in the middle', indicating that the round marking is not a moon but a belly button. For moths in the genus *Pammene*, a full moon shines forth in the form of a single large round white spot, made when the wings are closed over the moth's body. It shines especially brightly in the species called *Pammene splendidulana*.

A different kind of moon-moth has half-moons cut into its wings as if with a tiny pastry cutter. The Lunar Thorn, *Selenia lunalaria* (both these names mean 'moon') has a deeply indented half-moon on its hindwings. The Waved Umber has several, creating an attractive scalloping along the margin of the hindwings which, along with a fringe of hair (*cilia*), creates its inventive name, *Menophra*, or 'moon eyebrow'.

The best moth-moon is on the tawny wings of The Satellite moth. Here the

More mourning appears in the American name for our Camberwell

Beauty, the Mourning Cloak. It is a dark butterfly with coloured fringes, as if a pretty dress were peeping beneath the dark cloak of the mourner. Perhaps she is on the way to a party after the funeral.

The scientific name of the pretty Pyralid moth *Anania funebris* means, rather intriguingly, 'without pain/a funeral'. Presumably Jacob Hübner meant, with a twinkle in his eye, that he could look on this black-and-white moth without pain, or, in other words, with pleasure, even though its species name invokes death. It is surprising that so lovely a moth lacks an accepted English name (though some have started calling it the 'White-spotted Sable'), but such is the historic divide between the popular 'macros' and the experts-only micros.

Muses

The Muses were the inspirational goddesses of ancient Greece. The name comes from *mousa*, meaning 'music' or 'song', and art was embodied by this trio of graceful and inspirational figures. How ironic it is, then, that the species that carries the name of the Muses is the most despised butterfly on the planet: the Large White, popularly known as the cabbage white. It happened in a roundabout way. When the German entomologist Franz von Paula Schrank

came to divide butterflies into families, he created the name Pieris to embrace the swallowtails and the whites. Pieris was one of the Muses who lived on Mount Pierus in northern Greece, close to the gods on Olympus. He presumably chose the name to honour the beautiful Apollo butterfly, for the lyre-playing god, Apollo, was patron of the Muses. Unfortunately, that butterfly, along with the swallowtails, was soon removed to another family, leaving Pieris alone with the whites. Little by little, the number of butterflies in that genus was whittled down until we were left with the Large White and its closest relatives. And so we have *Pieris brassicae*, the Muse of the cabbage patch. Quite a-musing, you might say. (*See also* The Three Graces.)

Musical Instruments

Moths are voiceless and, if you discount their buzzing, also silent (although the Death's-head Hawk-moth can make us all jump with its rasping squeak). Moths are acutely sensitive to the high-pitched sound of hunting bats, but their sense

A musical moth: the Satin Lutestring.

of hearing is purely utilitarian. There is no point in playing a violin to a moth. All the same, a select group of moths are named after a musical instrument, or at least part of one: the strings of a lute. On their wings are parallel lines known as fasciae that vaguely recall the strings of an instrument, even though they look slack and in need of tuning. But, as I have suggested under Fabrics, the name lutestring may in fact have originated as a corruption of 'lustrine', a silken fabric much in use at the time. All the same, 'lutestring' is an old moth name dating back to the mid-eighteenth century.

N

Nets

Three species of moths, all in the Geometer family, take their names from nets: the Netted Carpet, the Netted Pug and the Netted Mountain Moth. The allusion is to their wing pattern, a tracery of white vein-like markings that link up in a way that reminds us of a fishing net – or perhaps even a butterfly net. The scientific name of the Netted Carpet, *Eustroma reticulatum*, sees the pattern in two ways. *Reticulatum* means a net, sure enough, but Hübner's name *Eustroma* is more allusive. The Greek word *stroma* describes something spread, but it seems that Hübner had in mind a bed-frame, a net-like support for a mattress, or perhaps a hammock. If so, it translates as 'pretty hammock'.

The Netted Pug is *venosata*, 'marked with veins', which link up to form a net-like pattern (though the pattern does not coincide with the moth's real wing-veins). Like the Netted Carpet, it is a pretty moth, certainly one of the most attractive and easily recognised pugs.

For other similarly 'netted' moths, different words were found for them. The Latticed Heath has a network of dark cross-lines for which Linnaeus chose the word *clathrata*, 'furnished with a grate' or lattice. Moths in the Noctuid family that share a similar pattern of white tracery are more likely to be called 'gothics' (*see* Architecture). For The Map butterfly, a Continental species that was introduced to Britain but failed to settle, a similar network of white veins conjured up the idea of a spider's web, hence its genus name *Araschnia*, the spider's home.

There are more netted butterflies among the fritillaries. The Pearl-bordered and Small Pearl-bordered Fritillaries are now in the genus *Boloria*, which is based on the Greek word *bolos*, meaning 'a fishing net'. The reference is to their reticulate wing-pattern, admittedly one they share with other fritillaries. Formerly they were in the larger genus *Argynnis*, named after a lady beloved of Agamemnon; Fabricius probably had in mind a pun with *arguros*, or silver, from the pearly patches on the butterflies' underwings.

Nonpareil

By definition there is only one nonpareil. The moth 'without compare' is the Clifden Nonpareil, also known as Blue Underwing, a huge grey moth with hidden hindwing bands of a bright, shimmering blue, like watered silk (in Germany they call the moth the *Blaues Ordensband*, the Blue Ribbon). Blue is a rare colour in moths. The 'Clifden' part is a nod to the moth's discovery at what is now Cliveden House, by the Thames near Maidenhead. According to Benjamin Wilkes, it was found by a 'Mr Davenport sticking against the Body of a Ash Tree near Cleifden.' That is probably why Linnaeus named the moth *fraxini* after the ash, even though the moth lays not on that tree but on aspen. In another version of the story, recounted by Moses Harris, the moth was taken 'hanging against the pedestal of a statue', a more appropriate location, perhaps, for a very grand moth. This moth has long been a grail, as well as a nonpareil, for enthusiasts. The writer and journalist Michael McCarthy once travelled all the way from London to Dorset to see one caught the previous night, and found it 'hard to write without hyperbole... It was as big as a bat, a bat of sensational colours.' For 'the Old Moth Hunter', P. B. M. Allan, this was the

Without compare: the Clifden Nonpareil or Blue Underwing.

moth that put all others in the shade. 'I verily believe,' he wrote, 'that the sight of *fraxini* flying around my bedroom would make me leap from my death-bed.'

Benjamin Wilkes also mentions two other moths once associated with the Clifden Nonpareil, which he called the Cliefden Beauty and the Cliefden Carpet Moth. Judging from his engravings, they would seem to correspond to today's Pretty Chalk Carpet and The Phoenix.

Noses

Moths do not have noses, but some species have long 'palps' that stick out like one, and it was not long before they were given a name to match: the Snouts. The various snouts were distinguished by appropriate adjectives: Buttoned Snout, Bloxworth Snout, Beautiful Snout. I have always felt a little sorry for the snouts, shunted as they always are to the back of the book, along with the even dimmer fanfoots.

Another memorable nose belongs to *palpina*, the Pale Prominent; this bears moustache-like palps, which, in Allan's words, are 'as noble as the Kaiser's'. Its French name is *Museau*, the Muzzle. The Germans have the same idea: *Snuitvlinder*, the snout-moth.

Why do these moths have such long 'noses', or palps? I asked my friend Mark Young, the authority on all things moth:

Mark: For the same reason that the Pyralids [a large family of micros] have long palps.

Me: All right then, why do Pyralids have long palps?

Mark: If I knew the answer to that, I would know why snout moths have long palps!

So there we have it. No one knows.

Numbers

On the thirteenth plate of his *Natural History of English Insects*, published in 1720, Eleazar Albin illustrated a little moth 'with a double Spot of a Yellowish White like a Figure of Eight'. At some later point, that tag was shortened into the name it bears to this day: the Figure of Eight. So prominent is the '8' number on the forewing that it looks as if the moth had been numbered for a race. All the same, Linnaeus found more to interest him in the strangely coloured head of its caterpillar, and so named the species *caeruleocephala*, blue-head. Its genus name, too, takes a slightly different tack. The moth is *Diloba*, not so much '8' as 'double-lobed', one on top of the other.

Several moths are named, rather as ladybirds are, by the number of spots on their wings. There is, for example,

A moth in a football shirt:
the Figure of Eight.

the Four-spotted Moth with big white spots in the centre of each of its dark wings. There is a Twin-spotted Quaker and a Twin-spotted Wainscot, where the spots are little more than dots. On the Four-spotted Footman it is the female moth that possesses the quartet of big black spots, unlike the Four-dotted Footman, where both sexes have them, two per wing. Spots come in threes on the Triple-spotted Clay and the Triple-spotted Pug. Moving on, there is a Five-spot and a Six-spot Burnet, not to mention a Six-striped Rustic (a translation of its species name *sexstrigata*) and a Six-belted Clearwing, the 'belts' being the waspy stripes on the moth's slender body.

The highest number on the wing of a moth is on the Figure of Eighty moth, with that number delicately outlined in white on each forewing. But, once again, Linnaeus demurred. He named the species *ocularis*, 'pertaining to the eyes', seeing the figure not as '80' but as 'oo' – that is, like a pair of eyeballs (admittedly the marking does vary from

moth to moth). Its genus is *Tethea*, a sea-nymph, suggested by the moth's wavy markings. And that brings us neatly to the next section, which is:

Nymphs and Shepherds

Folklore had long seen butterflies as airy spirits or 'nymphs', and so it was natural for Linnaeus to place some of the more graceful and boldly coloured species in his Nymphales (now the family Nymphalidae). Their species names often invoke famous nymphs and other female characters from Greek or Roman mythology. For example, we have *Io* for The Peacock, a lady who was abducted by Zeus and turned into a cow, and *Antiopa* for the Camberwell Beauty, who bore two sons by the same lascivious god. Nymphs were associated with mountain springs or sacred groves

The Chalkhill Blue. Or should that be
'Chalk-hill'? Or 'Chalk Hill'?

which, as Colonel Emmet points out, make good habitats for butterflies.

There are also a few mythical shepherds about. We have already met Argus (originally Argos), the shepherd with a hundred watchful eyes. The species name of the Chalkhill Blue, *coridon*, is a stock name for a shepherd. Coridon appears in poetry down the ages as an innocent rustic fond of verse and song. In *The Compleat Angler*, Izaak Walton imagined him as the perfect companion for a day's fishing. The classic setting for shepherds like him was the chalk downs of southern England, where Chalkhill Blues would have kept them company as they tended their flocks.

The Gatekeeper, also called the Hedge Brown.

O

Old

Here is the sad story of Tithonus, a boy who wanted to be immortal. Fortunately his father, Eos, was able to help by calling in a favour with Zeus. All right, said Zeus, I'll make your boy live forever. Just don't ask me again. And so Tithonus had his wish. Unfortunately his father had forgotten one thing. He

should have asked Zeus to give his son eternal youth. As it was, poor Tithonus aged like anyone else, and it was in that decrepit, shrivelled state that he lived throughout eternity. The moral to this tale is *nihil est ab omni parte beatum*: nothing and nobody is wholly fortunate.

Why did Linnaeus name the Gatekeeper or Hedge Brown after the unfortunate Tithonus? Probably because the butterfly is one of the browns, and brown (as we have seen under Moods) is the colour of melancholy and disappointment. Several other brown butterflies were named after beings who

The Old Lady. Elderly widows used to wear black, as they still do in Greece.

came to unhappy ends, such as Semele (the species name of the Grayling), the one who burst into flames after stepping too close to Zeus.

There are several 'old' moths. The list is headed by the lovely Old Lady, a living embodiment of what Moses Harris called the 'grave brocade'. It is a big, dusky moth that lives in dark, shadowy places, and has been known to hide in window pelmets and sheds. Its delicately patterned wings resemble the kind of black lace favoured by Queen Victoria in her widowhood, and which was associated with elderly women generally – though the name is of eighteenth-century origin; that is, much older than Victoria. The moth has a species name to match: *maura*, a Moor, a dark-skinned person, like Othello the Moor. The genus name is unkind: *Mormo* is a hideous she-monster. When children misbehaved in ancient Greece, they were told that Mormo would come and bite them. The Dutch disagree that this moth

is a lady. There it is *Zwart weeskind*, a black orphan.

Other 'old' moths are naturally thin-scaled and often seem a bit bashed about even when quite fresh. Thus the semi-transparent Muslin Footman is *senex*, or senile, as well as *Nudaria*, or bald. Another oldie is the Obscure Wainscot, which lacks distinct markings and so is *obsoleta*, a moth that is prematurely aged and worn-out. Among the micros we find *Epiblema grandaevana*, or 'of great age', an appropriately grey and thinly marked moth, but also one that is bigger than most micros. I like the implied idea that moths get bigger as they age, like crocodiles. Which, of course, they don't.

Another venerable moth is the Brown Scallop, *vetulata*, from *vetulus*, meaning 'old-ish'. A thinly scaled moth that looks old before its time, it also has wavy lines on its wings that one moment seem to resemble the crinkled edge of a scallop shell and the next, wrinkles.

Owls

In his initial sorting of the moths, Linnaeus placed a whole 'regiment' of stout-bodied, night-flying species together in the Noctuae, from the Latin word *noctis*, which means both 'owl' and 'night'. With suitable rearrangements, it became the Noctuidae, the biggest family of larger moths with nearly four hundred British species. Linnaeus was buying into folklore. Throughout northern Europe, night-flying moths were known as 'owls' or 'owlets', and in Germany and the Netherlands they still are, as *Eule* and *uil*, respectively. Like owls, moths are winged creatures of the night. They are also broadly owl-coloured, greyish or brownish, and their bodies are also vaguely owl-shaped. And, like owls, big, buzzing moths were faintly scary. They flew in from the darkness, from no one knew where, and circled the lamps in an alarming way. By candlelight their eyes glowed like hot coals.

The once large genus *Noctua* is now confined to the Large Yellow Underwing and its relatives. Appropriately, the Large Yellow Underwing is the commonest large moth; almost the archetypal big, buzzing moth. Dozens may turn up at the light on a warm summer night, and when at rest they conceal their bright yellow-banded underwings beneath

Owl or housekeeper? – the Large Yellow Underwing.

brown forewings like the folds of a coat. In France this moth is *Le Hibou*, the owl, but in Germany and Holland it is *Hausmutter*, the housewife. Linnaeus took a similar female line by naming it *pronuba*, the bridesmaid. For him, moths with gaily coloured hindwings were 'female', and so took on appropriate domestic roles of home, family and, especially, betrothal and weddings (*see* Wedding Night).

Two related moths are named in

the same spirit. The Lunar Yellow Underwing is *orbona*, named after the goddess of parents who have lost their children. The Lesser Yellow Underwing is *comes*, a companion, no doubt the lady companion of *pronuba* (though Colonel Emmet suggests a marital context even here, as *comes*, the common-law wife).

A very modest peacock: the Peacock Moth.

P

Peacocks

Thomas Moffet greatly admired the Peacock butterfly. *Omnium Regina dici potest*, he wrote in his best Latin: 'It may be called the Queen or chief of all.' In the manner of a Tudor field guide, he described how bright diamonds set in a brooch of amethyst sparkled from its four wings, while about them were rainbow-coloured flashes: 'By these marks it is to be known.' As usual Moffet had no name to offer, but a hundred years later, by 1700, the butterfly was known as the Peacock's Eye, or, as Linnaeus translated, *Oculus Pavonis*. The butterfly does indeed have a peacock-like 'eye' set in each of its wings, albeit in somewhat smudged form on the forewing. By

the 1740s, however, the 'Eye' had been quietly dropped, and the butterfly has been known as The Peacock ever since, not only here but practically everywhere (though in North America they have several more 'peacock' butterflies in the genus *Anartia*).

Linnaeus found a species name to match in *io*, a beautiful nymph whom Zeus transformed into a heifer to save her from the jealousy of Hera, his wife. The original Io was placed under the care of the shepherd Argus, who had as many eyes on his head as a peacock had in its tail. The Peacock's genus, *Inachis*, is also associated with Io: King Inachis was her father, and the whole business about the heifer seems to have been his fault.

The Peacock Moth, by comparison, is a disappointment. It is a plain little white moth with a smudgy black eye in the middle of its forewings but without a drop of proper peacock colour. Linnaeus saw no connection with peacocks at all, and instead named it *notata*, meaning, simply, 'a mark'. Other nations agree that there is nothing of the peacock in it. The Dutch, for instance, see that mark as *klaverblaadje*, the cloverleaf. The Peacock Moth has two relations, Sharp-angled Peacock and Dusky Peacock, both equally disappointing.

Pearls

Real pearls come from mussels and oysters, but certain circular, silvery markings in the wings of butterflies also have a pearly lustre, changing as the light catches them, as if the insect were wearing jewellery. The best-known examples are the Pearl-bordered and the Small Pearl-bordered Fritillaries. Both have beautiful half-circles of pearly spots along the borders of their hindwings as well as more jagged ones within the wing. The High Brown and Dark Green Fritillaries have pearly spots too, but they were named after other colours, perhaps to help distinguish them (*see* Fritillaries). A less well-known name is the Pearl Skipper, an old name for the Silver-spotted Skipper, although the

The Mother of Pearl moth shimmers with a pearly luminescence.

white flecks on its underwings suggest a broken pearl rather than a whole one.

The pearly king of moths is the Mother of Pearl, a large Pyrale often found in confetti-like profusion wherever there are nettle beds. Its whole wing is suffused with a pearly sheen but, surprisingly, its scientific name makes nothing of this. *Pleuroptya ruralis* means literally 'rib-wing of the countryside'. Some of its pearly relatives take their names from the 'Mother', and hence we also have a Bordered Pearl and a Rusty-dot Pearl, even though the latter lacks any obvious pearliness.

People's Names

It is bad manners to name a species after yourself. But it is quite all right for a friend to do it for you, especially if you were the discoverer, or have made some other meritorious contribution to the study of butterflies and moths. Many moths have species names that commemorate entomologists. But it seems to be a peculiarly British custom for the common name to celebrate a living person, generally the person who first recorded the species in Britain. In my own lifetime we have seen, among others, Dewick's Plusia, named after A. J. Dewick, who kept detailed records of moths over a lifetime from his native

The Bath White, named after a piece of needlework by a lady who happened to live in Bath.

one on the Isle of Man in 1861. It is a south European species that visits Britain only occasionally on a favouring wind. He was also the discoverer of the Black-banded moth and The Grey moth (dull names, these), also found on the Isle of Man. Gregson was one of those characters who inspire stories. A straight-talking Lancastrian, he turned his professional skills as a ship's painter into a tidy business and was able to spend his leisure time chasing moths. He went to enormous lengths to obtain scarce and obscure species, in one instance having several trees felled and sent on to him by rail in case they contained the larvae of the Welsh Clearwing moth. Once, while out rabbiting, he spotted a rare butterfly. With no net to hand, he grabbed his gun and shot it. With his eyesight failing, Gregson sold his collection of 28,000 specimens. Then, his eyesight recovering, he decided to start again from scratch. He had bagged another 5,500 specimens before his death at the age of 82.

Bradford-on-Sea in Essex; and Clancy's Rustic, named after Sean Clancy, author of *Moths of Great Britain and Ireland;* and Langmaid's Yellow Underwing, first recorded by John Langmaid at Southsea, Hampshire.

Among the more memorable Victorian entomologists was Charles Stuart Gregson (1817–99), who is remembered in the name of Gregson's Dart, new to Britain when he caught

Until recently, only one British butterfly was named after a person: the Glanville Fritillary (*see* Glanville). But in 1970, what had then been known as the New Clouded Yellow was renamed Berger's Clouded Yellow after its Belgian discoverer, L. A. Berger (its species name, *alfacariensis*, commemorates Alfacar in Spain, where the original specimens

The Portland Moth: named after the Duchess of Portland – who lived in Buckinghamshire.

were taken). More recently still, in 2001, a second species of Wood White was found in Ireland; it was thought at first to be the Continental Réal's wood white, *Leptidea reali*. More recent genetic analysis suggests that is wrong, and that the butterfly is in fact a new species, *Leptidea juvernica*, or the Cryptic wood white. *Leptidea* comes from Greek words meaning 'thin-form', a reference to the narrow body and delicate wings of the Wood White and its relatives. 'Juverna' is a variant of Hyberna or Ireland, and so *juvernica* means 'belonging to Ireland', though in fact the butterfly has since been found right across Europe.

Pigs

The hyperactive butterflies now known as skippers were once little flying pigs. Called 'hogs', they originally consisted of the Golden Hog, or Small Skipper, and the Chequered Hog or Large Skipper (though James Petiver later changed his mind about Chequered Hog and chose Cloudy Hog instead). In addition, there was Handley's brown Hog Butterfly (sic), which eventually turned into the Dingy Skipper. To see the analogy you need to peer closely at their tubby brown bodies and bright, beady little eyes. Skippers do indeed resemble hairy piglets, the precursors of today's short-haired farmyard pigs. In the Netherlands, however, skippers are *dikkopje*, which literally means 'tadpole', but can perhaps be more loosely translated as 'bigheads'.

The Small Elephant Hawk-moth is another pig. Its scientific name, which dates back at least five hundred years, is *porcellus*, the piglet. Its caterpillar has a short pig-like snout but there is also something undeniably porcine about the moth too, with its stubby pink body: a plump little flying pig visiting a flower. Its full scientific name, *Deilephila porcellus*, is unintentionally poetic: the 'evening-loving little pig'. Equally poetic is its French name, *Le petit sphinx de la vigne*, 'the little sphinx of the vineyard'.

Places

Many butterflies and moths are named after localities, generally the places where they were first found (and so the places where collectors hared off to

The Rannoch Sprawler is named after a lonely railway halt on Rannoch Moor in the Scottish Highlands, near where it was first collected.

get their specimens). In the case of the Camberwell Beauty, there is no longer any connection between the butterfly and that former village, now swallowed up by south London. Nor are you likely to find the Bath White in that beautiful town; it was named from a piece of needlework by a lady who just happened to live in Bath. On the other hand, the Lulworth Skipper still flies near Lulworth.

The winner among mothy place-names is Rannoch in the Scottish Highlands, which has lent its name to three northern species: the Rannoch Sprawler, the Rannoch Looper and the Rannoch Brindled Beauty. They commemorate the lonely railway halt on Rannoch Moor where collectors would stop off to try their luck. The white-painted fence posts on the station platform were always worth a search for the Rannoch Brindled Beauty, whilst the other two species inhabited the birch and pine woods nearby.

Devon has two species, Devon Carpet and Devonshire Wainscot – or three if you count the Paignton Snout. Essex has the Essex Emerald and the Essex Skipper, a pairing of moth and butterfly with contrasting fates. While Essex Skipper has spread all over England since its discovery in 1888, the Essex Emerald, a speciality of the Essex coastal marshes, seems to have died out.

Kent has two moths: Kent Black Arches and the Kentish Glory, although the Glory has long since departed the county, while the Kent Black Arches has increased and can now be found from Dorset to Norfolk. Brighton in Sussex has the Brighton Wainscot, though its main colonies were in Wiltshire and Hampshire, while the town of Lewes had the Lewes Wave. Two moths are named after islands: the Isle of Wight Wave (yet another lost moth) and the Arran Carpet. Hampshire has (or rather had) the New Forest Burnet; it has, however, long since deserted those parts and is now found only at a single site far away in western Scotland.

Scotland has the Scotch Argus, the Scotch Annulet and the Scotch Burnet. It is worth noting that 'Scotch' was the usual adjective in the nineteenth century, when these species were named. Today of course we would say 'Scottish', but political correctness has so far left the

Lepidoptera alone. Scotland's capital has the Edinburgh Pug. Wales has two special moths, the Welsh Wave and the Welsh Clearwing, though neither is confined to the Principality. Ireland has only the recently discovered Irish Annulet, although the Burren Green moth is resident among the limestone hills of that name, south of Galway Bay.

At least two names are not what they seem. The pretty, speckled Portland Moth was named not after the headland in Dorset but a person: the Duchess of Portland, a renowned naturalist of the eighteenth century, who discovered the species in Britain and bred it for the first time. And Brussels Lace was named after the lace, not the place.

Plain

Moths can be more attractive than their names suggest. Take the Plain Clay. You might expect it to be the last word in mothy beige, but it really is quite handsome, adorned with all kinds of pleasing bands and freckles and spots. You could say the same of the Clouded Drab, a variable moth in fifty shades of grey, and even the Lead-coloured Drab is a perfectly presentable mottled moth. The Plain Wave, on the other hand, is about as plain as plain can be, and the Plain Pug is even plainer, though you could argue that it is no more drab than its confrères in the neighbouring kennels.

Plebs

As we have seen, when Linnaeus began to sort out the butterflies and moths, he set them in a kind of social order, with knights at the top and commoners or 'plebs' at the bottom. At a time when 'pleb' has become an emotionally charged word, it is as well to recognise that no insult was intended. In ancient Rome, which Linnaeus used as his model, plebs or plebeians were the free citizens; that is, pretty well everybody who wasn't a slave or a patrician. The word comes from the Greek *plethos*, meaning 'crowd'.

Linnaeus's butterfly plebs were the smaller butterflies, more numerous than his knights or Muses or nymphs. Later on the genus *Plebejus*, meaning 'belonging to the plebs', was erected for some of the blues, but most species have since been removed to other genera, leaving a sole British example, the Silver-studded Blue, *Plebejus argus* – a lonely pleb that nonetheless seems to be in the money, to

A pleb made good? The Silver-studded Blue.

185

judge from the flash silver jewels on its hindwings. There are also plebs among the larger moths, such as *Hada plebeja* (formerly *Hada nana*), whose common name is The Shears. It is evidently a dead pleb and already in the underworld, for *Hada* derives from Hades. The moth is dark and plain, but all the same 'a pleb of Hell' seems a bit harsh.

The Latin word for the great unwashed was *vulgus*. It originally meant 'the common people', but this has since been distorted into 'vulgar', that is, unrefined, coarse-mannered and lacking good taste. Compared with plants, where *vulgaris* is often a name for ubiquitous, weedy species, there are surprisingly few 'vulgar' moths (and no butterflies). One of them is the Common Pug, *Eupithecia vulgana*. An undistinguished little moth, it is also 'common'.

Plumes

Like the burnets and clearwings, plume moths look quite unlike any other kind of moth; in fact they do not look much like moths at all. With their skinny bodies, long legs and feather-like wings sticking out at right angles, they seem to be more like miniature versions of a daddy-longlegs. Their apartness was recognised as early as 1762, when the genus *Pterophorus*, 'feather-wing', was

A plume moth whose wings seem to have turned into feathers.

raised to contain all the species then known, a name later borrowed for their family name, the Pterophoridae.

There are now 44 species of 'plumes' in Britain, and, unusually for micros, they all have accepted English names. This innovation is quite recent. In the first popular book on plumes, *British Pyralid and Plume Moths* (1953), the author, Bryan Beirne, had no common names to offer. But in 2011, for his book *British Plume Moths*, Colin Hart found names for them all, and his lead has been followed in the new field guide to the micros by Phil Sterling and Mark Parsons. It is only by chance that the plumes are included among the micros; they could just as easily have been included among the larger moths.

It has to be said that the newly coined names of the plumes are not the most imaginative. Since many species are very choosy about what they eat, their new names are often based on their foodplants. Thus we find Mugwort

Plume, Thyme Plume, Horehound Plume, and an exceptionally brave Sundew Plume, whose caterpillar has managed to turn the tables on an insect-eating plant. The best-known species, the pale-brown Common Plume and the day-flying White Plume, have been known by those names for much longer. In times past, the latter even had a couple of folknames: the Phantom and the Skeleton. So flimsy and skeletal was its construction that it looked like the ghost of a moth.

The scientific names of plume moths also tend to run to a common formula. In most cases, each one ends in '-*dactyla*', meaning 'finger'. There is, for example, *parvidactyla* ('small finger', the Small Plume), *rhododactyla* ('rosy finger', the Rose Plume), *zophodactylus* ('gloomy finger', the Dowdy Plume), *punctidactyla* ('spotted finger' or Brindled Plume), and so on, all referring to the fingerlike lobes of the wings. The same attention to anatomical detail went into genus names such as *Amblyptila* or 'blunt wing-feather', *Platyptilia* or 'wide wing-feather' and *Leioptilus*, 'smooth or bald feather-wing'. But, as usual, there are exceptions. For the genus *Agdistis*, comprising the Cliff Plume and the Saltmarsh Plume, the namer turned to mythology for inspiration – Phrygian mythology, that is, not the usual Greek or Roman myths. The original Agdistis was a nature goddess, some say the original earth-mother, others a transgender being who chopped off his male parts, and from whose fallen testes an almond tree arose, symbolising rebirth. That seems to have nothing at all to do with two innocent little moths.

Poverty

In the eighteenth century, a poor countryman, speaking with a strong accent and dressed in humble clothes, was sometimes referred to as a rustic. Brightly coloured clothes required expensive dyes; the brighter the fabric, the more it cost. Rustics could not afford bright silks and satins, and even if they could they were forbidden to wear them under the sumptuary laws. Cheap cloth, such as hessian, was brownish, and that is also the usual ground colour of moths named rustics.

Our mothy rustics all belong to the same large family, the Noctuidae, but they are not all close relations. Unnecessary confusion is caused by different moths called the Common Rustic and The Rustic. Not all rustics are drab. The Dotted Rustic and Northern Rustic are both handsome, well-marked moths. The Light Feathered Rustic, another well-set moth, sounds like one that has come up in the world and wears a feather in its cap, which is more than you could say for the poor Neglected Rustic (sometimes known simply as The Neglected). Rustics do not have a monopoly on brown or grey. Similarly dusky, subfusc moths are found among those called Drabs, Chestnuts and Quakers (qv). Poverty in moths is defined by a want of bright colour or distinctive markings. If markings represented money, you would expect the Pauper Pug to be bankrupt. It takes its common name from *egenaria*, meaning 'poor and needy'. The Tortricid moth *pauperana* is another needy moth; an 'undeserved reproach' in the view of Colonel Emmet, though its old name of Spotted Drab did it no favours either. Yet, by contradiction, its genus, *Eucosma*, means 'graceful' or 'well-adorned'. It seems you can be poor but still have good taste.

We reach utter penury with two dissimilar moths that share the name of *mendica*, meaning 'a beggar'. Oddly, both are quite attractive. The Ingrailed Clay, *Diarsia mendica*, is sufficiently well marked to receive a heraldic common name (*see* Heraldry). The Muslin Moth, *Diophora mendica*, though a drab dark-grey in the male, is a very pretty ermine-like colour in the female (a beggar wearing ermine?). Perhaps Johan Fabricius, who named it, only knew the beggarly male of the species. But, as Colonel Emmet

reminds us, Fabricius seldom gave an explanation for his names, 'and there need not necessarily be one.'

Prominence

Moses Harris, author of *The Aurelian*, noticed that certain handsome, hairy moths share a common feature: 'a small piece projecting from the flip side of the inferior wing' (he meant the base of the forewing). When the moth is at rest, this 'piece' (in fact a tuft of scales) sticks up like a little pyramid. Its purpose is presumably to help break up the outline of the moth and add to its already convincing camouflage. Harris correctly deduced that all these moths were related and called them 'prominents', the eighteenth-century name for projections of that sort. The same feature lies behind the name of their family, the Notodontidae, which means 'tooth on the back'.

The common names of these lovely

The Swallow Prominent, probably named not after a swallow but a sallow, a broad-leaved willow.

moths often spotlight some individual peculiarity. One species, the Plumed Prominent, has huge feathery antennae (or at least the male does). Another, the Pebble Prominent (originally just The Pebble or Pebble Moth) has a round, stony mark on its forewings. Yet another has a crested thorax like a jester's cap – hence its name, the Coxcomb Prominent.

By contrast, their scientific names often focus on some aspect of their life cycle. The Pebble Prominent is *ziczac,* that is, zigzag, because its spiky caterpillar sits in a Z-shape when at rest. Back in the seventeenth century the Dutch naturalist Jan Goedart knew of this unusual caterpillar and dubbed it 'the terrible Eruca', explaining that 'the risings on the Back are a Guard to defend itself.' The Iron Prominent is another one with a strange caterpillar, this one with a pronounced hump like a camel's. Hence it became *dromedarius,* the one-humped camel. Three more species are named after the crests on the moth's thorax, which reminded people of the hoods of monks (*see* Cloaks and Hoods). The Pale Prominent is *Pterostoma* or 'feather mouth', named after its long fringed mouthparts, which project beyond the head and help the moth to look even more like a broken chip of wood than it does already.

The hardest to explain are the names of the Swallow Prominent and its relative, the Lesser Swallow Prominent. There is nothing about either to remind you of a swallow, nor are the moths about in April when the swallow returns. I suspect that the name originated as a misspelling or corruption of 'sallow', which is one of their foodplants; if so, this must have happened early, since 'The Swallow Moth' was already well known to collectors and artists by the mid-eighteenth century. It is a subtly beautiful moth. P. B. M. Allan, who had taste in these things, went into rhapsodies about the Swallow Prominent: 'He is, to me, aesthetically the perfect insect … the *summa perfectionis* of outline, of tints, of design; the perfect *tout ensemble.*' In France they call it *La Porcelaine.*

Pugs

The pug moths have given me, as I'm sure they have given many others, a hard time over the years. There are more than fifty of them, and they are not only small, the smallest of all the 'macros', but many are disconcertingly similar. To make matters worse, pug moths are often worn by the time they have finished fluttering around the moth trap. Collectors would search instead for the caterpillars and rear them on to obtain perfect specimens. But that is no mean task either, for pug larvae are very choosy, often preferring a single kind of plant, and eating the seeds or flowers rather than the leaves. There is some evidence that certain pug caterpillars will creepily stock up on protein by grabbing and chewing up other helpless insects. At least they do in Hawaii, and the same behaviour has been witnessed with at least one British species.

Nonetheless, there have been people with a soft spot for pugs. The entomological artist John Curtis was one, writing around 1820 that he thought them 'pretty moths' and so coining a suitable generic name for them: *Eupithecia* or 'pretty dwarf'. 'When alive they are characterised by the elegant attitude in which they repose, with their wings beautifully expanded, lying close to the surface on which they rest,' wrote Curtis.

The little flat-faced pug dog was popular with ladies of leisure at that time, as readers of Jane Austen will know. To call a moth after a lap dog implies affection, but what do dogs and moths have in common? Fortunately, Adrian Haworth told us. The resting posture of these little moths, with their wings outstretched and flat, is reminiscent of the head of the pug dog with its drooping jowls. Just as the

lower lip of a pug is shorter than the upper, so the hindwing of the moth is much shorter than its forewing. That is why they are called pugs.

Up until the nineteenth century, pug moths were largely ignored. In *The Aurelian* (1766), Moses Harris illustrated only one: his dainty 'Lime Speck', now the Lime-speck Pug. His contemporary Edward Donovan also illustrated just one, the equally distinctive Netted Pug, which he called 'the Pretty Widow'. The breakthrough in pug-ology had to wait until 1839, when William Wood provided decent hand-coloured illustrations of twenty-four species, making it possible for collectors to identify them. There are now around fifty species, and new ones are added to the list from time to time. The Cypress Pug was not noticed until 1959; the Sloe Pug not until 1972, while the Epping Pug became the first pug of the new century in 2002.

Many pugs are named after the plants on which the moths lay, such as the Valerian Pug, Toadflax Pug, Juniper Pug and Golden-rod Pug. Others are named after a distinctive pattern or mark, such as the Marbled Pug and White-spotted Pug. A few are named more imaginatively. The species name of the Bilberry Pug is *debiliata*, meaning 'weakened' or 'debilitated', because its original green colour fades rapidly to dull brown. The yellowish Tawny Speckled Pug is *icterata*, or 'jaundice', a word that is shared by the similarly coloured Icterine Warbler. But the prize must go to the Foxglove Pug, whose name, *Eupithecia pulchellata*, translates as 'pretty little goodly dwarf'. Adrian Haworth himself receives a mention in despatches: he gets *haworthiana*, or Haworth's Pug.

Punctuation Marks

Several butterflies and moths carry wing markings that remind us of accents or punctuation marks. From the start, a bright butterfly with raggedy wings was always known in England as The Comma because, as everyone could see, it bore a curly white comma on the dark side of its wings. Linnaeus saw the same mark as a 'c', and so named the butterfly *c-album*, the 'c-mark'. The French are more impressed with the butterfly's reddish colour and deeply notched wings, hence their name of *Robert le Diable*. In folklore the devil was a red-skinned figure, with horns like a butterfly's, while the name Robert or Robin was synonymous with red, as in Robin Redbreast or the red-flowered weed Herb Robert.

In ancient Latin or Greek, the comma mark could be straight or V-shaped as well as curly. That seems to be the reason why the Silver-spotted Skipper butterfly and the Shoulder-striped Wainscot moth both have *comma* as their species name. For the skipper, this 'comma' mark is white and V-shaped, in the middle of the hindwing's underside. For the wainscot, the 'comma' is the dark streak where the forewing meets the moth's body.

We find a full stop in the Dot Moth, a dark moth with a big white spot on each forewing. This is another old name, originally spelt 'Dott' and dating back to *The Aurelian* of Moses Harris.

The Comma carries a white 'c'-mark on its wings. The French are more impressed by its ragged wings: *Robert le Diable*.

Several other moths have a white spot in their wings, but this one is the archetype, the definitive dot. Another grammatical moth is the White Colon, which has a discreet pair of white dots in the midst of the forewings; its common name is a straight translation of its species name, *albicolon*. There used to be a semicolon moth too, a name Petiver gave to the Drinker Moth. It is a big, bold semicolon, too, outlined in white, though it is more obvious in some individuals than others.

The question mark belongs to *interrogationis*, the Scarce Silver Y, a moth of northern moors. The mark glows whitely in the midst of the dark forewing, as if the poor moth didn't know its name: 'Who am I?' it seems to ask. An exclamation mark is an alternative way of seeing the markings in the Heart and Dart moth, and it provided Linnaeus with the species name, *exclamationis* (though, being rather dingy as well as common, it is hardly a moth to invite an exclamation!). Among moths that are only occasional visitors to Britain we find a circumflex accent in *circumflexa*, the Essex Gem, while the Accent Gem, *accentifera* ('I carry an accent') has a cute little acute accent. And so it should: it's a French moth.

Q

Quakers

A number of plain brown moths are named 'Quakers' in reference to the sombre clothing traditionally worn by members of that dissenting movement. Many of the Quaker moths are in the genus *Orthosia*, meaning 'straight', a name that refers to a linear mark on the wings of some species. Some of the common names of the Quakers are as pretty as the moths. Powdered Quaker has tiny black speckles on its fawn wings, as if someone had upturned a pepper pot. The Twin-spotted Quaker has a pair of black squiggles, like quotation marks, on each forewing. In Germany they call them springtime moths (*Fruhlingseule*) or, for some reason, 'kittens' (*Katzcheneule*).

There are two more Quakers in the unrelated genus *Agrochola*, meaning 'bile-coloured field'. Unlike the *Orthosia* moths, which fly in the spring, the *Agrochola* Quakers appear in September, and their colours seem designed to blend with the turning leaves. The Red-line Quaker is distinguished by red circles and a thick red line on its

The Common Quaker is one of a number of pale-brown moths named after the sober garments worn by the early Quakers.

greyish wings. Yellow-line Quaker has a distinct yellow line on its fawn wings, though that too is faintly lined with red. This genus is a good example of the random nature of common names. As well as the two Quakers, *Agrochola* also contains three species called chestnuts, one called a pinion and another called The Brick.

Whether or not by coincidence, a number of prominent entomologists in the eighteenth and nineteenth centuries were Quakers. Peter Collinson, a cloth merchant, gardener and leading Aurelian, was one, as were Edward Newman and the Doubleday brothers, Henry and Edward. Another Quaker, William Curtis, founded the *Botanical Magazine* and made one of the first in-depth studies of a British moth, the Brown-tail, whose stinging caterpillar had caused trouble in London in the 1780s. In the United States, they had Quaker counterparts in the anti-slavery campaigner and keen entomologist Mary Townsend, and in Thomas Say, founder of the Academy

of Natural Sciences in Philadelphia. Quakers felt a natural affinity with the natural world, and were taught to respect and care for it. The growth of scientific experiment and observation also appealed to the Quaker mindset, even though they were at first excluded from British universities. As a group with great social cohesion, they enjoyed sharing knowledge. Moths were named Quakers primarily from their plain brown colours, like rustics and chestnuts, but the name also honoured a significant group of naturalists and scholars.

R

Rivers

Why should a moth be named after a waterway? Yet many are, and the reason is nearly always the same: they have wavy lines (fasciae) running down the wings that vary in width and recall anything from a winding brook to a river in full flood. Those at the brook end of things are known as rivulets, small, sandy-coloured or piebald moths in the Geometer family. Among the watery scientific names is *rivata*, the

The Rivulet, one of many small moths
named from the flowing lines in their wings.

Wood Carpet, a river indicated by pale, splashy markings running along the outer edges of its wings. *Rhyacia*, the genus of the Dotted Rustic moth, simply means 'a stream', but *Xanthorhoe*, the genus of some more of the carpet moths, is specifically a 'yellow stream', evidently a muddy one, unlike those in the genus *Cosmorhoe*, which means a 'stream in good order'. The Balsam Carpet, *biriviata* or 'two rivers', has a pair of streams running in parallel down the dark central band on its forewings. A moth called The Streamer is *derivata*, a divided stream, for its watercourses seem to have been diverted to opposite ends of the wing. Least desirable for bathing is the river of the Green Carpet moth and its relations in the genus *Colostygia*. It means 'stunted/pertaining to Styx': in other words, the waters of Hell. It seems to be a dry season in Hell, for the river has been reduced to a line of puddles which, appropriately enough, are black.

Another watery subset of moths contains the 'waves', delicate, often pretty little moths with suitably wavy markings. Their English names are basically descriptive and pertain to colour or markings: Tawny Wave, Rosy Wave, Dwarf Cream Wave, Dotted Border Wave and Small Dusty Wave. Those in the genus *Idaea* are named after Mount Ida, the sacred mountain in Crete from where the gods watched the battles of the Trojan War. *Idaea serpentata*, the Ochraceous Wave, bears a serpentine marking in the form of a wiggly band running down its wings. The Least Carpet, *I. vulpinaria*, has reddish marks reminiscent of Vulpus, the fox – though it is now *I. rusticata*, having apparently swopped its fox fur for rustic garb.

S

Seafood

The Lobster Moth is a quiet grey-brown moth with one of the world's oddest caterpillars. When newly hatched it is a long-legged object resembling an ant, but later on, after several skin changes, it puts forth long, grasping front legs and a swollen forked tail that rears up over its bloated, plasticky body.

The early entomologists mistook the caterpillar of the Lobster Moth for a beetle.

The early naturalists knew the beast but did not know what to make of it. Moffet thought it must be a kind of beetle, perhaps a relative of the Devil's Coach-horse. Eleazar Albin, though noting its similarity to what he called 'the crustaceous fish', realised it was a caterpillar, but of what he did not know. When, eventually, someone managed to rear it through to the adult moth, they must have been disappointed. Fantastic caterpillars often produce unassuming moths. The Lobster is a good-looking moth, in warm shades of grey and brown, with hairy legs sticking out at the front, but all the same it does not live up to its advance billing. The Dutch call it *eekhoorn*, the squirrel.

A group of Tortricid moths are sometimes called 'conches' from the genus *Cochylis*, meaning a 'conch' or 'shell'. The resemblance, it has to be said, is not strong, and seems to relate to the vaguely mother-of-pearl markings of some species. Other moths are named after seashells. The Scallop Shell is a delicately pretty moth with parallel wiggly lines running down its wings and, near the outer margin, a scalloped edge that does in fact recall the shape of a scallop. Its darker relative, the Brown Scallop moth, shares the same general pattern and shape. But their genus, *Rheumaptera*, denotes not scallops but ripples. It means 'stream-wing', while the Scallop Shell's species name, *undulata*, means in effect 'marked with waves', like ripple-marks in sand.

For the seaside in general, what could be better company than the Sand Dart, the Shore Wainscot and the Sandhill Rustic? These are moths you might expect to find on holiday, whilst building castles on the beach.

Sharks

A sub-family of sleek-bodied moths in the Noctuidae are called 'sharks'. Originally, that was the name of the largest, commonest species, The Shark or Shark Moth. It is suitably sleek and grey, and, viewed from above, seems to have a pointed shark-like 'nose' in the form of the moth's thoracic crest (Moses Harris added that it has 'fine streaks along the wing parallel to each other',

Pointy-nosed and sleek: The Shark moth.

though whether he thought sharks had those is uncertain). As often happens, the scientific name takes an alternative route. The Shark's pointed 'nose' could also be seen as a monk's hood or cowl. In Latin this is a *cucullus*, which lent its name to the Shark's genus, *Cucullia*, and its sub-family Cucullinae (the moth is known in Dutch as *monnik*, or 'monk'). The Shark's caterpillar is shy and hides by day, behaviour that perhaps suggested its species name, *umbratica*, 'in the shade'. Its relatives, the Chamomile Shark, The Wormwood, The Star-wort, The Water Betony, The Cudweed and The Mullein took their English names from respective larval foodplants – or what was thought to be their foodplants. Water betony is an old name for the figwort plant.

(For the unlikely association of burnet moths and the hammerhead shark, *see* Brunettes.)

Skin

High on a list of insects you wouldn't want to encounter on a dark night is the Skin Moth. Its horror, however, lies mainly in the name. In reality the Skin Moth is a kind of clothes moth whose caterpillar that can chew and digest woven wool but which will also, given the chance, feast on other things animals leave behind, such as fragments of skin, rotting feathers or droppings. No doubt the Skin Moth would not turn up the chance to nibble on a dried-up corpse either. We live artificial, twenty-first-century lives, but should we die and the Skin Moth find us, you might say that with its help we will come to re-embrace the world of nature.

The genus of the Skin Moth and its relatives is *Monopis*, or 'one-eyed', after a transparent disc in the middle of its tiny wings. One species is named *weaverella*, after Richard Weaver, a mild-mannered museum curator from Birmingham.

Skulls

The infamous moth-with-the-skull is of course the mighty Death's-head Hawk- moth. That piratical Jolly Roger on the moth's thorax has carried all before it. Across Europe the moth has become a stand-in for the figure of Death: for the Latin scholar it was *caput mortuum*; in France it is *Sphinx tête de mort*; in Germany *Totenkopfschwärmer*, in Holland *Doodshoofdvlinder*, and in Sweden *Dodskalle* – all these names mean the same thing: a death's head. The moth's scientific name, *Acherontia atropos*, continues the theme. Acherontia is a river in hell. Atropos is one of the Fates, the one who cuts the thread of life.

That we can still respond to the dark side of moths is suggested by the 1991 film *The Silence of the Lambs*, where the role of the Death's-head Hawk-moth is played by a North American relative, the Tobacco Hornworm.

What is the biological purpose of carrying an impression of a human skull on your back, like a Hell's Angel? It seems that the resemblance is accidental. Where we see bones, a bee might see a friendly face. The moth invades the nests and hives of bees to lick up the honey with its short but powerful proboscis. Its old name was the Bee Tiger, for, just as the moth robs bees, so it also has a tiger-striped (or, more to the point, bee-striped) abdomen. The skull seems to be part of the moth's defence against stings. The poor unthinking bee assumes that it is seeing (and possibly smelling) the front end of another bee entering the hive (one thinks of the similarly naive Reed Warbler faced with a huge baby cuckoo in its nest). Hence the bee leaves the great moth alone to carry on thieving.

Another, more modest-sized moth

The wonderful Death's-head Hawk-moth was seen as a harbinger of disaster.

also has a disguised skull, this time hidden in its wings. The species name of the Coronet moth, *craniophora*, means 'I carry a skull'; when the moth is at rest you can see two black spots that seem to stare at you. Fit some white markings around them and you have the skull. The name Coronet comes from a more obvious marking, like the paper crown you get inside a Christmas cracker. When, for the purposes of writing this entry, I took another look at The Coronet moth, I saw something else, and it made me jump. There in the midst of those quiet wings is the face of a fierce, snarling dog, eyes blazing. The wings of moths are full of surprises.

Skulls and crowns; these moths remind me of the famous lines from Shakespeare's *Richard II*: ' ... within the hollow crown/ That rounds the mortal temples of a king/ Keeps Death his court.'

Slugs

A large, mainly tropical or New World family of moths, the Limacodidae, takes its name from *Limax*, meaning 'a slug'. In North America these moths are known as slug-moths. The 'slugs' are the caterpillars, and are among the strangest on earth. They seem to lack feet, and appear to glide along like a slug

The stubby little Festoon belongs to a mainly New World or tropical family of 'slug moths' named from their unusual 'legless' caterpillars.

with the help of a lubricant, a kind of liquefied silk (actually they do have feet but they are tucked away out of sight). The best-known species is the North American Hag Moth or Monkey Slug, *Phobetron pithecium*, whose stinging caterpillar appears to mimic the cast skin of a tarantula. It transforms into a moth that mimics a bee, complete with fake pollen baskets. The Monkey Slug has taken an unlikely evolutionary path, but presumably its disguises help fool its predators. Members of the family have also been called cup-moths from the shape of their cocoon.

In Britain we have just two slug-moths: the Festoon and the Triangle, traditionally classed among the larger moths. The Festoon is a small, yellow-brown moth that rests in an odd posture with its rear end pointing skywards. Its scientific name, *Apoda limacodes*, means a grub 'without feet, like a slug' and of course refers to the peculiar caterpillar shaped like a woodlouse. Surprisingly, the English name predates the Latin and describes not the caterpillar but the adult moth. A festoon is a decorative tassel found on carved ceilings or fireplaces, or on the end of an old-fashioned bell-pull. The hunched posture of the moth with its short wings drawn in tight recalled such a decoration. At the time festoons were a popular design idiom that everyone would have recognised. (For The Triangle moth, *see* Triangles.)

Sorcerers

A moth called *alchymista*, The Alchemist, a rare visitor to Britain, wears dark sorcerer's robes. Its black forewings contrast with white, black-banded hindwings and reminded someone of a medieval sorcerer wearing a dark cloak over his white garment as he tries to turn base metal into gold. The Alchymist's genus is dark too. *Catephia* comes from a Greek word indicating a sorrowful, cast-down look: the dejected droop of a would-be wizard, perhaps, who had searched for the magical philosopher's stone but found nothing more than a lump of lead.

The Alchemist moth wears the sombre robes of medieval sorcerers.

A second, much smaller mothy alchemist is the micro *Caloptilia alchemiella*, or 'beautiful-wing alchemy'. Perhaps it is a more successful sorcerer, since it has flecks of gold on its wings. As its namer, Giovanni Scopoli, remarked, 'Blessed indeed would alchemists have been had they been able to doctor their metals with the full richness of this dye.'

There are also mothy soothsayers or diviners. The micro-moths of the genus *Semioscopis* are fortune-tellers with indecipherable runes scattered over their tiny wings.

Spices

'It is the colour of nutmeg,' sneered the Constable of France of the Dauphin's horse in Shakespeare's *Henry V*. The Dauphin had been bragging about his 'palfrey', and the Constable was intent on pulling him down a peg or two. For nutmeg is a colour as well as a spice, a dull smoky grey, so hardly a suitable colour for a horse bearing a Prince of France. The Nutmeg moth, too, is smudgy grey with a coarse pattern that must have reminded someone of that knobbly spice. In America the moth is known with less affection as the Clover Cut-worm. There is also a Large Nutmeg moth, slightly bigger and unrelated, but with a broadly similar greyish (or fawn) mottled pattern.

Sport

The Coast Dart moth *Euxoa cursoria* is a sprinter. The moth lives in sandy places around the coast, and is said to prefer running or jumping to flying, should you spot one in the beam of your torch. Appropriately, its species name, *cursoria*, is taken from the Latin word for a 'racetrack'. The link is with sand, once used to surface racetracks for runners (the word 'arena' comes from the Greek word for sand). Hence the name neatly combines the moth's habits with its habitat.

The genus name of the Kentish Glory, *Endromis*, means 'a tracksuit', originally a wool or fur coat that kept the athlete warm before a race. The moth's tracksuit is its own hairy body. It needs to keep warm in the uncertain springs of northern Scotland.

Spring

The Merveille du Jour is a lovely moth with wings of a bright fresh-green flecked with black. When isolated from its leafy habitat, it is extremely conspicuous, but when at rest on a lichen-covered branch it merges into near-invisibility. Its unusual English-French common name was an everyday expression in eighteenth-century England. The moth was a 'wonder of the day', a prodigy among moths. But when it came to choosing a species name for it, Linnaeus chose *aprilina*, from the month of April. That presents a puzzle, because the moth doesn't appear in April but October (and since it flies only by night, it is, strictly speaking, not a Merveille du Jour, either, but a Merveille de la Nuit!). What Linnaeus seems to have had in mind is the moth's spring-green freshness of colour, similar to tender leaves bursting from the buds. April itself comes from the Latin *aperio*, to open: the season of opening buds. And so, for this moth, 'April' represents not a season but a colour. I am not sure whether this is understood in Germany, where the moth is *Aprileule*, the April Owl. The Dutch have opted for Diana's Owl, *Diana-uil*, for this is a moth of the forest, where Diana went hunting.

Following the same channel of thought, Linnaeus named another moth with a similar colour and pattern *praecox*, meaning literally 'early in the year'. Since this is the Portland Moth, which actually flies in August, he must have been referring once again to the springlike freshness of the moth's wings (for the meaning of 'Portland', *see* People). That may also explain the name of yet another summer moth named after the spring, the Cream-bordered Green Pea, *Earias clorana*. In its case, Linnaeus seems intent on having it both ways: *Earias* means 'spring', and the species name, *clorana*, means 'bright-green' (which it is).

Several other moths are named after the early part of the year because their early appearance was the most remarkable thing about them. One, simply named The Early Moth, appears as early as January – or, in mild years, even December, when perhaps The Late Moth would be more appropriate! Its species name, *primaria*, also refers to the first part of the year. This species is soon followed by the delightfully named Spring Usher, and then the March Moth, creatures you come across on those first mild evenings as you pass the beam of your mothing torch along the hedgerow. There is no April Moth: too many species are on the wing by then. But there is a May High-flyer, a moth that flies high up around alder trees.

There are more echoes of the spring in the early-flying Orange Underwing whose genus, *Archiearis*, means 'beginning spring'. Another is the Small Quaker, *Orthosia cruda*, whose species name means 'unripe', a poetic way of saying 'early'.

Stones

The original brimstone was a crystal of sulphur, of the kind you find as bright yellow patches near hot volcanic springs (the same 'fire and brimstone' that engulfed the wicked cities of Sodom

The yellow Brimstone Moth shares its name with the better-known Brimstone butterfly.

and Gomorrah in Genesis). Yellow cakes of sulphur were used medicinally, for example in the horrible mixture of 'brimstone and treacle' that dosed the boys at Dotheboys Hall in *Nicholas Nickleby*. The word was ready-made for our one pure yellow butterfly. The male Brimstone matches the colour of sulphur perfectly, but not the female, which is a much paler yellowy-green. Brimstone is among the oldest butterfly names. It was listed under that name by Petiver in 1699 without explanation, suggesting that it was already a familiar name. No one has ever come up with a better one. It has even been suggested that the Brimstone was the original 'butter-fly'. There is also a Brimstone Moth, also yellow; in fact it was once also known as the Yellow Moth. If you've got a good name, why not share it? Though in Holland they ignore its colour; there it is simply *hagedoornvlinder*, the hawthorn moth.

The Cinnabar is another colourful, well-known moth named after a mineral. Cinnabar is mercuric oxide, a brightly

The bright, day-flying Cinnabar moth is named after a red pigment.

coloured substance used to make the pigment vermilion. The Cinnabar moth is a similar colour (when flying it looks bright-red), and no doubt entomological artists used that very pigment to paint it: a Cinnabar painted in cinnabar. The collector Robert Watson managed to breed a beautiful pure vermilion form of this moth without any of its usual dark patches. In Germany, however, they see not pigments but blood. There the moth is the *Blutfleck*, the Blood Stain. In France they see it differently again, as *L'Ecaille du senécon*, 'the tortoiseshell of ragwort'.

You might think that the pretty little moth called The Mocha would be named after coffee, but in fact it commemorates a semiprecious stone called moss agate or mocha stone (the original name for the moth was The Mocha Stone). This gem has greenish filaments within a quartz base that are recalled in the delicate wiggles and streaks on the moth's wings.

Another mineral-inspired name is *pyritoides*, the species name of the Buff Arches moth. It means 'like pyrites',

the crystal form of iron sulphide, or 'fool's gold', which appears in the fiery patches on the moth's forewings. Although these are vaguely arch-shaped, 'buff' hardly does justice to the moth's flaring orange, further adorned with artistic squiggles. In Germany it is *Achateulenspinner*, 'the agate owl'.

One of the old names for the Marbled White butterfly was The Marmoress. It sounds like a title, but in fact is in the feminised form of *marmor*, the Latin word for marble. Like some marbles, the butterfly has a black-and-white pattern. Like its alternative name, the Half-mourner, 'The Marmoress' was in common use for a century or more.

A humbler kind of mineral is found among the footman moths. Originally, many of them were placed in the same genus, *Lithosia*, meaning 'plain' – probably not because the moths seem suitably petrified but because their caterpillars feed on lichens on rocks and stone walls. A casual observer might conclude that they are chewing the stone itself.

The Blood-vein moth is mysteriously known in Germany as *Liebling*, the darling one.

Strange

Both 'peregrine' and 'pilgrim' come from the same root word, and mean the same thing: 'a wanderer', as in 'peregrination'. It became attached to the Peregrine Falcon because it was once thought to be a wandering bird, that is, a bird of passage. By the same token, there is a rare, wandering moth called The Stranger, whose original name was *peregrina* (though it is now *Lacanobia blenna*). It sets off on long migrant journeys, and when, on occasion the moth visits Britain, it comes, as it were, as a stranger in our midst.

Another mothy pilgrim is a micro, *Prays peregrina*, though unfortunately *Prays* doesn't mean 'prayers', but rather, 'gentle and mild' (why these particular moths should be seen as gentle is anyone's guess). Strictly speaking, this species is neither a foreigner nor a stranger, since it lives in London, and, so far, nowhere else. It was new to science when first found on Hampstead Heath in 2003, and has since been found elsewhere in and around the city, mainly in gardens. The supposition is that it is a foreign species accidentally introduced here with imported vegetables or nursery plants. If so, it is a stranger whose real home is still unknown.

That fine moth The Pale Shining Brown is known in France as *L'Etranger*.

But the way things are going, it may soon be a stranger here, too, since this once widespread moth is now a rarity.

The dark moth called The Exile is also something of a stranger, in the sense that it is doomed to spend its days on the farthest shores of Britain, in the Shetland Isles. It took its common name from its former scientific one, *exulis*. But our moth is now considered to be a form of the more widespread Northern Arches moth, whose species name is *zeta*, from a marking resembling the letter 'z' in the Greek alphabet. The true *exulis* is a North American moth. It is very much at home there and not an exile at all.

Sunshine

Butterflies fly in bright, warm sunshine; we see them as the very essence of carefree summer days. But only one British species has sunshine in its name, and even then solely in French and German. There they see the lovely orange orbs of the male Orange-tip butterfly as the rising sun, embodied as Aurora, the goddess of dawn, and call it *L'Aurore* or *Aurorafalter*, the daybreak butterfly. Its genus name is equally poetic: *Anthocharis*, the flower-grace. Does it mean that the butterfly has the grace of a flower, or that the butterfly lends grace to the flower on which it sits? Perhaps both.

Several day-flying moths take their names from the sun. *Heliothis*, 'of the sun', is the genus of the Bordered Straw and its relatives. The tiny moths called *Heliozela* are 'eager for sunshine' and fly around bushes on warm days in the spring. And *Heliodines* is the 'sun whirligig', a pretty little moth with a whirly flight. In the same spirit, the Tortricid moth *Philedone* is supposedly 'fond of pleasure', that is, it revels in sunshine. *Heliophobus*, the Bordered Gothic, on the other hand, 'fears the sun'. It hides by day and waits until dark to fly about (like most moths, it must be said).

Surprising Compliments

What a lovely moth! Hübner seemed to admire the Mottled Umber moth, naming it *Erannis* or 'lovely to behold'. Past notions of beauty were often inexplicable, and it is hard to see much to praise in the parched fawn wings of the typical Mottled Umber (all right, some of its other forms are prettier). Its caterpillars can be so numerous as to strip whole trees of their leaves, hence its species name, *defoliaria*.

One also wonders what Gustaf Billberg saw in the unremarkable wings of the Treble Lines moth to inspire his name *Charanycha*, or 'nightly delight'. One could say the same about an even dimmer moth, a micro called *Argyresthia dilectella* or 'silver dress choice', which the German entomologist Philipp Zeller found 'a dear little moth'. Equally baffling are the names of two more micros, *Opostega spatulella*, or 'voluptuous', and *O. salaciella*, or 'lustful'. Colonel Emmet suggests that the original specimens were caught 'in copula'; that is perhaps the kindest explanation.

There is a whole family of tiny moths known as 'cosmets', over which entomologists once went into raptures. One of their genera is *Cosmopterix*, or 'ornament-wing'; another is *Pancalia*, or 'entirely beautiful'. They remind me of a specialist I knew who saw the tiniest of micro-moths as inexpressively lovely, whilst regarding tiger-moths and their like as utterly vulgar.

Among other unlikely compliments is the micro genus *Telephila*, meaning 'faraway love'. The name owes its origin to the Greek writer Theocritus and a rather obscure passage in his *Idylls* about an unusual plant which you could clap on the underside of your arm to see whether the absent lady 'loves me or loves me not'. If the signs were good, it would stick; if not, it would wither. The appeal of the name to me is strengthened by the fact that it was coined by the renowned micro-lepidopterist Edward Meyrick, who used to live just down the road from me – though a century earlier. *Telephila* is to most eyes a rather dull little moth. But love is blind. Meyrick obviously liked it. Alas, the moth has since been moved to a new genus, unkindly named *Acompsia*, or 'unadorned'.

Perhaps the most surprising compliment of all is the German name for the moth we call the Blood-vein, from its single red line running across both pairs of wings. The Germans know it as 'Liebling', the Darling, the little loved one. Quite why, no one seems to know.

Swifts

The primitive swift moths appear at the beginning of recent field guides, and so they draw attention to themselves that way, if for no other. Moses Harris was good enough to explain why they are so-named. 'They fly low and very swift,' he noted ungrammatically. He might have added that they also have long narrow wings, like a swift. There must be many moths that can fly as fast, or faster, than swift moths, but since the latter fly at dusk we are able to watch them zooming about. Harris called the Common Swift 'the Common Evening Swift'.

The Map-winged Swift, unknown in Britain before 1801, is the prettiest of the family. In times past it was also known as the Northern or Beautiful Swift. Its species name is imaginative: *fusconebulosa* or 'dark clouds'.

The largest and best-known species is the Ghost Moth, or Ghost Swift, whose males perform an eerie late-evening seesaw dance above the grass to attract any lurking females. The males are a ghostly white. They sometimes dance together, seen from a distance as mysterious wandering lights. Until recently, it and the other four British species all belonged to the same genus, *Hepialus*, from the Greek word for 'fever'. (The name refers primarily to their 'feverish' evening flights.) The species name of the Gold Swift, *Hepialus hecta*, alludes to this ritual; its short flight is swaying and shivering, in a word, 'hectic'.

The Ghost Moth, *Hepialus humuli*, and the Common Swift, *H. lupulinus*, have species names that seem to commemorate the hop vine, *Humulus lupulinus* – but neither of them has anything to do with hops. Possibly Linnaeus was making a

The pure-white wings of the male Ghost Swift perform eerie evening flights like a pale wandering light, moving to and fro.

little joke about their 'drunken' flight, as if the moths had drunk too much hoppy beer, and most West European countries call it the 'hop-moth', as in *hopvlinder* (Dutch), *Hépiale du houblon* (French) and *Epiale del luppolo* (Italian). More likely, *lupulinus* involves a pun with *lupus*, the wolf. Another French name for a swift moth is *La Louvette*, the she-wolf – for which I must refer you to Wolves.

Swapping and Sharing

If you've got a good name, why not share it? We have a Peacock butterfly and a (disappointing) Peacock moth. We have a Swallowtail butterfly and a Swallow-tailed moth. And, as we have seen already, we also have a Brimstone butterfly and a Brimstone Moth.

In America they occasionally use the familiar English name for a different species. For example, their Checkered Skipper is not our Chequered Skipper but one more closely related to our Grizzled Skipper (where we see grizzles, they see checkers). The actual Chequered Skipper is usually known there as the Arctic Skipper.

In the past, a familiar name was sometimes attached to a different species. As we have seen, 'Small Tortoiseshell' was once the name of the Small Copper, while in France it is tiger-

moths that are the tortoiseshells. The White-letter Hairstreak was sometimes called the Black Hairstreak until a new species came along to steal that name permanently. The Clouded Yellow was once also the moniker of a little moth now known as the Barred Yellow. The name Mottled Beauty, now the name of a grey moth which few today would find particularly beautiful, was formerly attached to a much more attractive black-and-white species, until Moses Harris came along and renamed it the Argent and Sable.

T

Tame?

Micropterix, or the 'little-wings', are the most primitive of moths. Unlike all the others they have functional jaws, so they can munch solid food such as pollen grains as well as imbibing nectar. The shape of their mouthparts gives these moths heads like little birds, complete with what looks like a tiny 'beak'. They are active by day, but instead of flitting about from place to place like

The tiny *Micropterix* moths are the most primitive of the Lepidoptera.

The Three Graces

The Three Graces were the mythological daughters of Zeus and embodied the cardinal pleasures of life: beauty, mirth and good cheer. They would preside at celestial banquets and gatherings to amuse and delight the gods and their guests. The trio are present, bare-bottomed and alluring, in Antonio Canova's famous sculpture, *The Three Graces*, and are also seen dancing in a ring in Sandro Botticelli's equally renowned painting, *Primavera*. They were the pagan precursors of St Paul's Christian virtues of faith, hope and charity (though you have to admit the pagan version sounds more fun). The names of the Three Graces were: Aglaia, the eldest, who stood for splendour and elegance; then the joyful, fun-loving Euphrosyne; and finally the youngest, festive Thalia, who was fond of music and singing.

butterflies they tend to sit tight inside a flower or on a catkin, gorging on pollen. That is probably the reason why *Micropterix mansuetella* (it means 'tame little-wing') is so-named. The moth spends most of its short life clambering about on the pollen-carrying heads of sedges. They are so engrossed with feeding and mating that you can watch them through a hand lens; so long as you do not poke them with a finger or blow on them or shake the plant, they are content to ignore you. *Micropterix* moths have also been called 'golds', from their metallic wings, which flicker green, then gold.

The Dark Green Fritillary isn't 'dark green'. It's dark and green, a name that helps to distinguish it from the similar High Brown Fritillary.

If these names sound familiar, it might be because they are also the names of butterflies. Linnaeus gave Aglaia to the Dark Green Fritillary, *Argynnis aglaja,* and Euphrosyne to the Pearl-bordered Fritillary, *Boloria euphrosyne.* Clearly he loved these butterflies, which were as familiar to him in Uppsala as they were to his English contemporaries. But Linnaeus dealt an unfortunate falling from grace to Thalia, wasting her name on a South American butterfly now known as *Actinote thalia.* Some years later that error of judgement was put right by his German follower, von Rottemburg. He wanted to use that same name for another pretty fritillary, now known as the Heath Fritillary. Unfortunately, under the rules he could not use 'Thalia' again, so he settled for the next best thing, '*athalia*'. The '*a*'- prefix is meaningless; it was Thalia who was being honoured. And so, thanks to him, all three Graces have come home. All you can say is that they could not have gone to nicer butterflies.

The Marbled Minor, one of a trio of mothy 'robbers'.

furuncula, or 'small thief'. The last of the dastardly trio is the Least Minor, *captiuncula*, meaning 'taking a robbery'. We could add a fourth member of the band, the somewhat prettier Marbled Grey moth, which is *raptricula*, 'a female robber', perhaps Bonnie to the Tawny Marbled Minor's Clyde.

These moths are among the smallest Noctuids – and that may be the point. Being small and dressed in subdued colours suggests that they have stealthy and furtive habits. Three of the robbers operate by night, but the Least Minor is day-flying. As its genus, *Photedes*, or 'delighting in light', indicates, it is a daylight robber.

Thieves

A trio of robbers lurk among the innocent-looking moths known as minors. The Tawny Marbled Minor, is *latruncula*, or 'little thief'. His henchman is the Dick Turpin-like Cloaked Minor,

Thorns

A natural group of Geometrid moths are called 'thorns', not owing to any feature of the adult moths but because of a sharp projection on the back of their stick-like caterpillars. This little spike improves their camouflage, so that the caterpillars seem to melt into the undergrowth, becoming almost impossible to detect. Three species of thorn moths are named after months or seasons: Early Thorn, August Thorn and September Thorn. There is also a Lunar Thorn with a neat half-moon shape cut out of each hindwing, and another with bright yellow hair on its thorax, called the Canary-shouldered Thorn. Those in the genus *Ennomos* are delightfully (and seemingly nonsensically) named. *Ennomos* means 'within the law'. Unlike the thieving minors, these are law-abiding moths.

Tigers

Tiger-moths have always been among the best-known moths. With colours as bright as any butterfly's, they have attracted non-entomological artists both as decorative objects and also, more interestingly, as metaphors. The early Renaissance artist Piero di Cosimo (1462–1522), for instance, decided to paint a Jersey Tiger-moth perched on the knee of the semi-naked goddess in his allegorical painting *Venus, Mars and Cupid*. It seems that, like the white rabbit nuzzling Venus's thigh, he meant the brilliantly coloured moth to be a symbol of sexual excess.

The Jersey Tiger is the most tiger-like:

The Jersey Tiger is the most tiger-ish of the tiger-moths, though nowadays it could just as easily be called the Devon Tiger or the London Tiger.

it is the only species of moth in Britain to have yellow-and-black-striped wings. But other nations see it as flag-like. One of its German names is *Russische Fahne*, the Russian banner. In Holland it is the *spaanse vlag*, the Spanish flag, which shares the moth's yellow and red colours. In France they think more of tortoises: it is *L'Ecaille chine*, the heather tortoiseshell.

The folklore of tiger-moths has nothing, in fact, to do with tigers and everything to do with bears. The so-called 'woolly bear' is the caterpillar of the largest and best-known species, the Garden Tiger-moth. In Germany most of these moths are 'bears': *Schönbar*, the beautiful bear, better known to us as the Scarlet Tiger-moth, and *Brauner Bar*, the brown bear or Garden Tiger. In Sweden the Garden Tiger is *Bjornspinner*, the bear-moth.

Their scientific names, too, ignore tigers. Instead they commemorate Roman women: the Garden Tiger-moth is *caja*, the name of a Roman lady (it's the female equivalent of Caius). The Cream-spot Tiger is *villica*, a housekeeper; and the Scarlet Tiger is *dominula*, mistress of the *domus* or home (one could wish it had been named *dominatrix*, a suitable name for a scarlet lady!). The connection, which I will explore further under Wedding Night, is with bright colours. They recalled the silken costumes of wealthy ladies, and so the moths, too, must be 'female'. (For more female housekeepers, *see* Owls.)

Tinies

Many micros are so small you need a lens to make out their details. The tiniest of them all are the Nepticulids or 'Neps', a large family of moths no more than a centimetre across from wingtip to wingtip. *Nepticula* is the diminutive of *neptis*, a granddaughter, in this case a very small one. In North America they are more straightforwardly known as 'pigmy' or 'midget' moths. Specialists peering at them through a microscope have found a strange beauty in the Neps. Schrank, for instance, called them *Edelmotte*: 'noble moths'. The adult moths are hard to find (and even

harder to identify), so Nep-hunters look instead for the telltale mines in leaves and shoots made by their caterpillars. Since most Neps feed on a single species of plant, many species can be identified most easily by their foodplant. It follows that they tend to be named after plants, such as *crataegella*, which mines hawthorn leaves, or *roborella*, which prefers oak. You might imagine the species called *minimella* ('smaller than smallest') to be the tiniest of the lot, though in fact, just to be awkward, it is one of the bigger Neps.

The moths called *Phyllonorycter*, named from Greek words meaning 'leaf-digger', are also tiny. The nickname 'midgets' has been suggested, although no one seems to be using it. As their name implies, their caterpillars mine the leaves of their foodplants, living inside their self-made tunnels. On the same minimal scale are moths in the genus *Elachista*, from *elachistos*, or 'very small'; again, someone has suggested calling them 'dwarfs', although the sort of people who can identify *Phyllonorycters* are not always keen on common names.

Tortoiseshell

At the time when moths and butterflies were first acquiring names, a precious material called tortoiseshell was in fashion. It was imported from China and made from the shells of sea turtles (not tortoises), especially the Hawksbill Turtle. Used sparingly in small pieces, or in thin, translucent slices, tortoiseshell could be used as a decorative inlay for furniture, or to make expensive trinket boxes, combs and the frames of spectacles. Not only are its orangey mottled colours attractive, but the material is durable and easy to work, and feels curiously warm next to the skin. The word 'tortoiseshell' could mean a colour combination as well as a commodity, and so we have tortoiseshell cats and guinea pigs – and of course tortoiseshell butterflies. Trade in tortoiseshell was finally banned by CITES in 1973. Modern tortoiseshell is made from plastics in a factory, not from endangered turtles.

Although the ancient Romans used tortoiseshell, the material was little known in Britain until the seventeenth century. Hence it is unlikely that the name 'tortoiseshell butterfly' is much older than that. It first surfaces in print in the catalogues of James Petiver in 1699, without explanation. He knew two kinds of tortoiseshell butterflies, the Greater and the Lesser (or 'the Common'). Confusingly, there was a third unrelated species that Petiver called the 'Small Tortoiseshell', not the butterfly we know by that name but the one we know as the Small Copper. Clearly all three were named from their common colours and patterns, not from any natural relationship. In due course the 'Lesser' Tortoiseshell became the Small Tortoiseshell, while the 'Greater' became the Large Tortoiseshell. The latter species is now vanishingly rare in Britain, but must have been much commoner in the gardens and wooded lanes of Georgian England, for everyone seems to have been familiar with it.

In France, it is not butterflies but tiger-moths that are called tortoiseshells (or *écailles*). Our Small Tortoiseshell is their *La Petite Tortue*. In Germany the same species is *Kleiner Fuchs*, the little fox, sometimes translated as 'the little chestnut horse'. In Sweden and Spain they are content to call it 'the nettle butterfly'.

Trees

While legions of species are named after plants, usually their larval foodplant (or supposed foodplant), only one resident butterfly has a tree in its common name: the Holly Blue (although the Large Tortoiseshell was once also known as The Elm Butterfly). Its scientific name, too, contains a holly tree: *Celastrina argiolus*, 'holly-tree little argus-eyes'. Both English and Latin names contain only a half-truth.

The Holly Blue is double-brooded, and it is only the spring brood that chooses holly. The summer brood prefers to lay its eggs on ivy. Holly Blue is a pleasant enough name, but a comparatively late arrival. In the nineteenth century it was more commonly known as the Azure Blue, even though 'azure' is just another word for blue.

Many more trees can be found among the names of butterfly species: *rhamni* (buckthorn) for the Brimstone, for instance, and *crataegi* (hawthorn) for the Black-veined White, *pruni* (blackthorn) for the Black Hairstreak and *quercus* (oak) for the Purple Hairstreak, all of which are the usual foodplants of their caterpillars. But the Brown Hairstreak, *betulae*, is incorrectly named after birch; its caterpillar feeds on blackthorn in hedgerows and thickets. The name of the Wood White, *sinapis*, is another misnomer; *sinapis* means the cabbage family, but its caterpillar actually feeds on vetches and trefoils.

Lots of larger moths are named after trees, from the bulky Poplar Hawk-moth and Oak Eggar down to the tiny Oak-tree Pug. No fewer than fourteen common names contain the word 'oak', including the Oak Beauty, the Oak Lutestring and the Oak Tortrix. The next most frequent trees in the names of moths are 'sallow' (thirteen) and 'pine' (ten). There are also species named after apple trees (six), willow (six), poplar (four), spruce (three), larch (three), lime (two), alder (two), birch (two), maple (two), juniper (two), cherry (two), cypress (two), sloe (two), hazel or 'nut-tree' (two) and horse chestnut (two); plus one each for hawthorn, bird cherry, plum, pear, sycamore, spindle, barberry, holly, laburnum, tamarisk, azalea and Pyracantha or 'firethorn'. If you include the scientific names you can add *Arbutus*, the genus for the strawberry tree. About the only principal trees ignored in the names of moths are yew and beech (there is a Beech-green Carpet moth, but that is christened after a colour rather than the tree).

Sometimes you wish a moth had been named more imaginatively. The name Sycamore Moth was borrowed from its Latin label, *aceris*, from Acer, a maple or sycamore, but it completely overlooks the moth's amazing caterpillar (which in any case feeds on a wide variety of vegetation, not just sycamore). The moth is greyish and forgettable; but its

The Beech-green Carpet: beech-green is its colour, not its habitat.

flamboyant caterpillar with its tussocks of flaming orange resembles nothing better than a feather from the world's most colourful parrot (or perhaps a particularly extravagant punk haircut).

Triangles

The little dark-brown Triangle moth has, as you might expect, three-cornered wings. When at rest they join in geometric fashion to form a single neat triangle. But its scientific name is more interested in the moth's unusual caterpillar. It is *asella*, meaning 'a woodlouse', which it much resembles. The moth's genus, *Heterogenea*, or 'different genus', has a small but significant place in entomological history. Linnaeus divided moths into two very broad groups, the hawk-moths, and all the rest: his 'garden moths'. His pupil Fabricius noticed that The Triangle, with its weird caterpillar, was an oddball, and so he reclassified it among the primitive swift moths. His contemporary, August Wilhelm Knoch, realised that this wouldn't do either, and raised the genus *Heterogenea* for The Triangle moth alone. Hence this insignificant little moth became one of the very first departures from the system Linnaeus had set up in 1758: it's the little moth that single-handedly upset the overloaded Linnaean apple-cart.

A few more moths have triangles in their names. *Deltote*, or 'deltoid', is the genus of the attractively marked Silver Hook and Silver Barred moths, whose wings also form neat three-cornered outlines when at rest.

The old scientific name, *Euclida stolida*, given to a rare migrant moth known as The Geometrician, contains an in-joke. On the face of it, it means 'stupid Euclid'. The explanation is this. When its wings are folded, the moth forms the shape of an isosceles triangle. The ancient Greek scholar Euclid had used the mathematical attributes of the isosceles triangle as a proposition for separating the fleet-minded from the slow-witted: his famous *pons asinorum*. Linnaeus's pupil Fabricius, with his love of wordplay, borrowed this notion to link the name of the quick-witted Euclid with a complete dullard: the moth. Unfortunately, others ruined the joke by changing The Geometrician's genus to *Prodotis* ('before talent', another name indicative of slow wits). The name *Euclida* survives today as the genus of the Burnet Companion moth.

True Knots and Shoulder Knots

The True Lover's Knot is a well-marked, reddish-brown moth of heather moors that sports a little bow in each of its forewings. It is the lovers and their knot

The True Lover's Knot has a double loop in its wings, an age-old symbol of love and friendship.

that are 'true', not the moth.

Another kind of 'knot' found on certain moths is the shoulder-knot. There is, for example, a Rustic Shoulder-knot, whose species name, *sordens*, means 'dirty', and so lent the poor moth its equally unfortunate former name of 'Sordid Rustic'. As Colonel Emmet justly remarks, this is 'an unjustified description' of a decent-looking Noctuid. There is also a Grey Shoulder-knot, a Minor Shoulder-knot and Blair's Shoulder-knot, which is currently increasing its range on a diet of Leylandii hedges. What they all have in common is a dark streak close to where the wings join the thorax, resembling not so much a knot as a strip of ribbon.

'Shoulder-knots' were in fashion in the late seventeenth century, just as people were starting to take an interest in insects. They were worn on the shoulder of the coat as a set of ribbons or bows in a contrasting colour. Just a bit of decorative bling, shoulder-knots were already going out of fashion by 1700, but they were obviously remembered by the Aurelians when it came to the naming of moths.

On the other hand, the moth called The Knotgrass contains no knots. It is named after the knotgrass plant, *Polygonum*, which they supposed to be its foodplant. (In fact its colourful caterpillar feeds on a wide range of plants high and low.) Knotgrass plants have stringy stems running along the ground with 'knots' of tiny flowers.

U–V

Uncertainty

One of the moth-recorder's headaches is a bland-looking trio of Noctuids respectively called The Rustic, Vine's Rustic and The Uncertain. The last name, which always causes amusement, reminds us of those other honestly named problem moths, The Confused and The Suspected (*see* Doubt and Confusion) – although The Uncertain is arguably trickier than either to identify correctly. The species name of its near lookalike, Vine's Rustic, enlarges on the difficulty. It is *ambigua*, or 'doubtful'. Is it a species or isn't it? How can I tell? Vine's Rustic, incidentally, has nothing to do with vines or vineyards. It commemorates a Victorian entomologist called Arthur Charles Vine, who caught the first specimen near Shoreham in 1879.

Vanessa

My father knew the Latin name for only one butterfly: *Vanessa atalanta*. I heard it quite often as a small child, probably every time we saw a Red Admiral. The original Vanessa was not a mythological nymph, like the species names of most of the Red Admiral's relatives, but a real person. She was the adored pupil of the poet and satirist Jonathan Swift. Vanessa was Swift's nickname for her, based on the reversed syllables of her actual name, Esther Vanhomrigh. It may also incorporate a pun on the Greek god Phanes, or 'one that shines', whose female derivative is Phanessa. This name also gave us 'phalene', an old word for a moth, from the way they reflect the light from a torch beam or candle. We know about Esther-Vanessa because, after her premature death, Swift published a narrative poem, *Cadenus and Vanessa*, first written during the course of their romance in 1712. Cadenus was Swift himself, dressed up in classical shepherd's guise (Cadenus is an anagram

of the Latin *decanus* or 'Dean'; for Swift was Dean of St Patrick's Cathedral in Dublin). In the poem Vanessa is described as a 'nymph', a word associated with butterflies, indeed a name that recalls Nabokov's novel *Lolita*, where a similarly precocious young girl is described as a 'nymphet'.

When researching butterflies in England years later, Johan Fabricius borrowed the name *Vanessa* for his newly erected genus for the Red Admiral. He coupled it with Linnaeus's name *atalanta*, a maiden warrior and huntress from Greek mythology. Fabricius had presumably consulted *Cadenus and Vanessa*, for there is a passage in that poem that links the two words: 'When lo! Vanessa in her bloom/Advanced like Atalanta's star.' Vanessa has been a popular girl's name ever since. I wonder whether the parents of Vanessa Redgrave – 'Red Vanessa' – were keen on butterflies.

Vapours

Among the more puzzling moth names is The Vapourer. A reddish-brown moth that flies by day, it has a rapid, skittish motion suggestive of a smoke particle rising from a bonfire. But the name is in fact taken from the moth's invisible scent trail. The female Vapourer moth

The Vapourer moth is named from the invisible chemical trail followed by the males to track down the wingless female.

Vegetables

Moths named after garden produce usually have a taste for crops which, from our point of view, turns them into pests. The Cabbage Moth and the Large White butterfly are both named *brassicae*, for the cabbage family. However, the Cabbage Moth was never as notorious as the butterfly, and Moses Harris had an almost affectionate alternate name for it: The Old Gentlewoman, suggested by the moth's dark, lace-like wing pattern.

The Turnip Moth is another maligned Noctuid whose caterpillar is a 'cutworm' capable of gnawing its way into carrots, beets and cabbage stalks, not to mention the eponymous turnip (all these crops have wild counterparts in Britain, and so the moths may have moved naturally from the countryside to the crop-field or allotment).

is wingless, and more or less immobile. It attracts the winged male with a powerful pheromone, which the latter picks up from afar with its feathered antennae. Moth collectors understood this, and if they wanted some Vapourer moths they would imprison a newly emerged female in a little cage, hang it on a tree somewhere and wait for the randy males to arrive. They called the process 'assembling'. Hence this invisible 'vapour' consists of pheromones peculiar to this species. (For an equally intriguing scientific name, *antiqua*, *see* Chastity.)

The Vapourer was a well-known moth, and Moses Harris devoted a delightful plate to it, picturing The Vapourer flying round a sprig of bramble with the Lime Hawk-moth for company. He knew it as the Common Vapourer, in contrast with the Scarce Vapourer, also known by Harris as the Orange Tussock (a name that describes not the moth but its more flamboyant caterpillar).

Turning to the micros, we find a Leek Moth, a Corn Moth, a Parsnip Moth and an Alfalfa Moth, and many others that feast on orchard fruit, vines, berries and nuts. As noted before, if a micro has an accepted common name, it is odds-on to be a pest. The Pea Moth, *Cydia nigricana*, is so notorious that it has familiar names in every language: in France the pea budworm (*Tordeuse de Pois*), in the Netherlands the pea-leaf roller (*Erwtenbladroller*). Like us, the Germans call it the pea moth

(*Erbsenwickler*). The Cream-bordered Green Pea owes its strange name to its resemblance to the (unrelated) Green Oak Tortrix, *Tortrix viridana*, whose old name was the Pea Green Moth. Since they looked very similar, with forewings about the size of a pea, they shared the pea name. The Cream-bordered one is now classed as a Noctuid. Rather surprisingly, both moths were known to the first generation of entomologists. James Petiver called them Dandridge's Small Green Moth and Our Small Greenish Moth, respectively.

The potato is represented by the greatest moth of all. In the past people digging up potatoes would occasionally come across the Churchill-cigar-sized caterpillar of the Death's-head Hawk-moth. They called them 'tatur dogs'. Another, smaller, 'dog' used to turn up on hop-vines. It was the 'hop dog', the ostentatiously hairy caterpillar of the Pale Tussock moth.

Veneers

A veneer is a slim layer of fine-grained wood used by carpenters to disguise cheaper wood beneath. It made a handy name for grainy-looking moths, especially the pale, narrow-winged moths in the Crambidae family known as 'grass-moths'. (They are the ones that fly up in

clouds as you walk through tall grass on a summer's day.) Among the forgotten names are the Streaked Veneer, the Pearl Veneer and the Gigantic Veneer, the last being a giant among micros and a resident of reed-beds. The name lives on in the Water Veneer, a tiny pale-grey moth with a wingless female that swarms near the waterside on warm summer nights (when they are easily mistaken for caddisflies). In America, where this moth was introduced as a biocontrol agent, it is known as the Water-milfoil Moth. The other surviving 'veneer' is the Rush Veneer, an immigrant that arrives some years in vast numbers. All the same, it is misnamed; it feeds on clover, not rushes, and the Latin name, *Nomophila*, or 'I love pastures', is more accurate.

W

Wainscots

Some moths with pale, grainy wings reminded people of wood panelling, or wainscoting. The word comes from the German *Wagenschot*, meaning 'wall-board'. In the eighteenth century, the best rooms in upper-class brick or stone

The Common Wainscot is one of many moths of grassland and reedbeds named after pale wooden panelling.

houses were panelled in wood to make them more comfortable. Wainscoting was originally cut from slow-grown, fine-grained oak trees, producing wood that was knot-free and easy to work. By the eighteenth century, however, most panels were being made from cheaper pine, and usually confined to the lower half of the wall above the skirting board. The pale wings of the wainscot moths recall the colour and grain of pine more than oak. If we were naming them afresh, we would probably think in terms of pine tables and dressers rather than wood panelling. I can imagine them being called 'Ikeas'.

The wainscot moth's pale wings help to conceal them in their marshy habitat as they cling to a length of straw-coloured reed. Reedbed-dwelling seems to offer a large variety of evolutionary opportunities, for there are around forty species of wainscot moths arranged in two main groups within the Noctuidae. Most of them

share the same washed-out colour (I remember a friend looking at a drawer of wainscot moths and commenting that this sort of thing could give biodiversity a bad name). Fortunately many have distinctive markings that help to identify them and that often find their way into their common names, such as Shoulder-striped Wainscot, White-mantled Wainscot and the White Speck (which, just to be awkward, misses out on the word 'wainscot'). Several of the less common species are named after nineteenth- or twentieth-century entomologists: Webb's Wainscot, Mathew's Wainscot, Morris's Wainscot. Confusingly, there is a Fenn's Wainscot named after someone called Fenn, but also a Fen Wainscot, which lives in fens. The name of the Mere Wainscot sounds vaguely pejorative – a 'mere' wainscot, instead of something more interesting – but the 'mere' in question is in fact a place: the now-vanished Whittlesey Mere in the Fens, once the largest lowland lake in England. It was a magnet for entomologists, and was where this little moth was first found in Britain.

Names do not necessarily reflect biological realities. The closest relatives of the Mere Wainscot, for instance, are not its fellow wainscots but a pair of similarly pallid moths called The

Concolorous and the Small Dotted Buff. By tradition, newly discovered moths are given names that fit the existing system. And so a moth found for the first time in Britain in 1945 was named Blair's Wainscot to honour its discoverer, Kenneth Gloyne Blair – and because it was related to several other moths already called wainscots.

Wealth

Wealth is counted in gold. King Croesus of Lydia was the first monarch to issue gold coins; to be 'as rich as Croesus' has been a common expression ever since. Two small but richly coloured moths take his name. *Adela croesella* boasts a bright band like a gold bar. And the old genus *Croesia* contains several moths that look as though they are made of gold; unfortunately, the best examples are non-British.

Gold is, in fact, a fairly common colour among moths, especially among the Noctuids. We have met several of them under Metals. But only one species has its

Wearing its wealth on its wings: the Golden Plusia, a moth named after money.

entire forewing flushed with gold. This is the Golden Plusia, a once rare moth that took off in the twentieth century after we started growing delphiniums, its caterpillar's plant of choice. This is clearly a wealthy moth and its species name *moneta* acknowledges this, in a teasing, roundabout way. Moneta is an epithet for the goddess Juno, in whose temple the Roman mint was situated. It was where all the money came from.

Gold in butterflies is more often to be found on the chrysalis. The famous Society of Aurelians ('the golden ones') took their name from gilt chrysalids named *aureoli*, from *aureus*, Latin for 'golden'. Look for gold on the hanging chrysalids of the Red Admiral and Small Tortoiseshell. Their gilt or silver flashes actually seem to aid their camouflage.

Weapons

Proper pub darts began with the invention of the dartboard in 1896 (before that, they must have taken turns to have a shot at the top of a beer barrel). So when, long before that, certain moths were named 'darts', they were not thinking of pub games so much as a weapon, a short thrown arrow weighted with lead of the kind the Romans called a *plumbatum*. Moths called darts bear a suitably sharp, pointed black mark. Most

Wounded heart: the super-common
Heart and Dart moth.

of the various species of dart either take their names from their habitat, such as the Coast Dart, Sand Dart and Garden Dart, or from a distinctive marking, as in the White-line Dart and Shuttle-shaped Dart. The Archer's Dart was named from markings that could be seen as a bow and arrow. Its old Latin name was *sagittifera*: 'I carry an arrow.'

The commonest of the darts is the Heart and Dart, a brownish, well-marked moth with the heart-and-dart shape clearly laid out on its wings, along with various smudges and squiggles. It is a name that sounds like a pub, just as its relative, the Heart and Club, sounds like a gambling den. Suitably for a common and ubiquitous moth, its genus *Agrotis* means 'of the field' or (depending on how you pronounce the original Greek) 'a countryman'. The species names of several other dart moths invoke similarly distinctive markings: *obelisca* (a spit); *vestigialis* (a footprint), *clavis* (a key or club), *ipsilon*, sometimes transliterated as 'upsilon' (the Greek letter Y).

Moths also carry daggers. The Grey Dagger has wing-markings that suggest a dagger with a V-shape forming the handle at the outward end, as though the poor moth is about to stab itself. Its fellow dagger-moths are the sinister-sounding Dark Dagger and the Reed Dagger, even though the latter has no obvious weapon and looks more like a wainscot. Once again, Linnaeus saw things differently. Instead of a dagger he made out the Greek letter *psi* (Ψ) and that became the Grey Dagger's name, *Acronicta psi*. *Acronicta* means 'nightfall'; moths come out at night.

The Rustic moth defends itself with a shield, at least to judge from its genus name *Hoplodrina*, from *hoplon*, a round wooden shield carried by spear-carriers or *hoplites*. But its shield is tiny and would not be much use in battle: it is the circular stigma in the midst of its forewing.

In Dutch, the Chocolate-tip and Buff-tip moths are both *wapendrager*, literally 'weapon-carrier' or 'armour-bearers'. What they have in common is a roundish patch of colour on the tips of their forewings reminiscent of a little shield, whilst their silvery-grey ground colour suggests a breastplate.

The sword-grass moths, on the other hand, have no swords. They are named after what was supposed to be their foodplant, sword-grass or sedge, a marsh plant with sharp-edged leaves. 'I once took one of these Caterpillars feeding on the Sword-grass in the Marshes at Rotherhithe,' noted Benjamin Wilkes in 1749. The French have a nice name for it: *Bois-sec*, the moth that resembles dry wood.

Weather Forecasting

The micro-moth *Rhigognostis* is 'one who knows cold'. Several butterflies (and many more moths, especially in the Noctuid family) fly late in the year and can survive the winter in a dormant state, thus prolonging their lives by several months. Despite their diminutive size, the trio of *Rhigognostis* species, moths that resemble caddisflies, perform the same trick. Hence they 'know' all about icy weather. The Pretty Chalk Carpet, meanwhile, carries 'a storm of rain' on its wings, indicated by its species name, *procellata*. Its genus *Melanthia* means 'black blossom'. This does not mean that the moth is particularly fond of blossom, black or otherwise; it is a poetic way of describing the dark patches on its wings, of dark clouds foretelling rain.

Grass moths appear in swarms in rough grass in midsummer.

Wedding Night

The genus *Catocala* contains some of the most gorgeous moths in Europe. They all have mottled, greyish forewings but garishly coloured hindwings, like a bright dress beneath the folds of an overcoat. Britain has only four resident species compared with several dozen found in mainland Europe, and still more – nearly a hundred species – found in North America. The commonest by far is the Red Underwing, *Catocala nupta*, often seen in late summer in brief, red-flashing day-flights that soon come to rest on a wall or tree trunk. Our other three species are much rarer: the Light and Dark Crimson Underwings, and the Blue Underwing or Clifden Nonpareil, all similarly named after the colour of their hindwings.

Linnaeus composed the name *Catocala* from the Greek words *kato* and *kalos*, meaning 'behind' and 'beautiful', that is, 'beautiful hindwings'. He was also responsible for naming three of our four species: *Catocala nupta*, the Red Underwing, *C. sponsa*, the Dark Crimson Underwing, and *C. fraxini*, the Blue Underwing. The names *nupta* and *sponsa* are unusual in that they seem to have nothing to do with moths and everything to do with marriage. *Nupta* means 'a bride'; *sponsa* 'a fiancée'. The Light Crimson Underwing, discovered

The Red Underwing is the best-known of a tribe of similar moths
named after a bride or a fiancée.

a few years later, is *Catocala promissa*, one that is 'promised', or pledged, in marriage. The theme continues with some of the non-British species: *C. pacta*, for example, means 'the betrothed'. What was going through Linnaeus's mind? The obvious link is the bright underwings, usually in shades of red with black stripes and a frilly white border. The natural assumption is that eighteenth-century Swedish brides wore gaudy underwear, or naughty knickers, to tempt the groom, or at least that Linnaeus had reason to think that they did. This enjoyable speculation is made explicit in a picture by the digital artist Maggie Taylor called *The Moth House*, in which a young woman wears a grey skirt patterned in the same way as a *Catocala*, opened at the front to reveal a red-and-black striped petticoat.

This idea caught the fancy of later entomologists, who named new *Catocala* species in the same way. They include *Catocala dilecta* (the Loved One) and *C. electa* (the Elect), yet another name for a fiancée. The mothy nuptials were also given a bridesmaid, *C. nymphagoga*, or 'one who leads the bride from her house'. Perhaps reacting against all this sugar, some cynic came up with three characters that no one would want anywhere near their wedding: *C. lupina* (the she-wolf), *C. adultera* (the adultereress), and *C. elocata* ('one hired as a prostitute'). All these characters and roles are female. Needless to say, all these moths were named by men, quite possibly giggling men.

The New World has also joined in the game. There the wedding theme continues with *C. muliercula* (the Little Wife Underwing), *C. connubialis* (the Connubial Underwing), and *C. amatrix* (the Sweetheart Underwing). For other, usually dark-coloured species, we see perhaps the outcome of a broken marriage: *C. maestosa* (the Sad Underwing), *C. lacrymosa*, (the Tearful Underwing) and *C. insolabilis* (the Completely Inconsolable Underwing).

The Dutch won't have any truck with all this. There the red underwings are not brides but *weeskinderen*, or orphans.

Giving brightly coloured moths female roles became a habit. Linnaeus continued the trend with his names for tiger-moths recalling Roman matrons and housekeepers. He temporarily switched to a masculine character for the Orange Underwing as *parthenias*, the son of a concubine. But it may be that Linnaeus was confusing that word with *parthenos*, a virgin maid. The name of the related Light Orange Underwing doesn't beat about the bush: it is *notha*, the bastard.

Another orange moth, the Orange Footman, seems to be of fluid gender. In its common-name form it is clearly male, one of a whole tribe of mothy footmen standing stiffly to attention. But its species name is *sorurcula*, the little sister. In France meanwhile, it is *Le Manteau Jaune*, the yellow-coat. Unusually, this footman moth has prettily coloured hindwings. Under his yellow coat, is he wearing pinky-orange knickers?

Lathronympha is a micro-moth that avoids the limelight. Its name means 'secretly married'. Its caterpillar sits tight inside a little web on a St John's-wort stem. Are there are two of them in there? (*See also* Owls.)

Winter

There are no active butterflies in the frozen winter, but there are still a few moths about, taking advantage of those long winter nights with the help of antifreeze in their veins. The commonest – possibly the commonest moth of all in terms of numbers – is the eponymous Winter Moth, whose species name, *brumata*, or 'short', alludes to the shortest days of the year. There is also the Autumnal Moth and the November Moth, thinly scaled lookalikes that also fly towards the end of the year. More attractive is the December Moth, a relative of the eggars, whose name was hinted at as long ago as 1720, when Eleazar Albin described it as one that 'flies around the month of December.' Actually, it is easier to find in November, but that name was already taken.

The Yellow Horned moth is another cold-season species that emerges around February. Its bright yellowish-brown 'horns' (its antennae) suggested the species name, *flavicornis,* or 'yellow horns', but its genus is *Achlya*, from a word meaning 'mist and darkness': the season of long cold nights.

Witches

Moths, especially large ones, were sometimes called 'witches' or 'wicks'. Like reputed witches, they were secret flying creatures of the dark, mysterious and slightly sinister. Some said that the soul of a witch would escape the body in the form of a black moth. All this hinted that moths could be bad news, especially if they landed on you. The folklore of moth-witches is much stronger in the New World than in Europe, perhaps because there they have a big black moth the size of a bat, called, naturally enough, the Black Witch, *Ascalapha odorata*. In Jamaica, where it is also called the 'duppy' or 'duppy bat', it is seen as a malevolent spirit. It is said to bring death and misfortune, though some believe it can also bring good luck; it might depend on the circumstances. There is also a White Witch, an even larger New World moth (in fact one of the world's largest) called *Thysania agrippina*.

The original Agrippina was also bad news: she was the wicked mother of Emperor Nero.

Although any big dark moth can be a 'witch', we have only one that is named after an actual one. Her name was Mother Shipton, a perhaps mythical prophetess who lived in a cave near Knaresborough. She was said to be revoltingly ugly, with a great hooked nose and an equally projecting chin. Long after her death she became a stock character on the stage; some say she was the original panto-dame. The moth that takes her name has a profile of Mother Shipton's ugly face outlined in white on its dark wings: nose, chin, beady eye, and an ambiguous little smile. The Mother Shipton moth is common and flies by day in grassland, and so its funny face is well known and easy to see. But Linnaeus's contemporary, Carl Clerck, looked hard at the moth and saw something else: a large letter 'M' clearly marked on the underside of the hindwing. That explains its short-but-memorable species name, *mi*, a Latinised form of the Greek letter *mu*, or 'm'. It was also sometimes known as the Mask Moth: a scary mask for Halloween and other spooky occasions.

Mother Shipton. Can you see her face?

The Tineid (*Trichophaga mormopsis*, meaning 'hair-eating/ugly face') may not be a witch, but it is named after the Greek *mormo*, usually translated as 'bugbear', an object of dislike or terror. Perhaps someone saw another scary face in its wings. Or, as a moth whose caterpillar will eat fur, including fur coats, it may be that it has frightening habits.

Wolves

It must be said that moth-wolves are disappointing. The 'woolly bear' does at least remind you vaguely of a lumbering, hairy beast, and the elephant hawk-moth caterpillars do have little trunks. But *Lycia*, the Brindled Beauty, and *Luperina*, the Flounced Rustic, both named after *lupus* the wolf, have no obvious lupine qualities. The link seems to be with the moths' hairy bodies, for the Brindled Beauty's scientific name, *Lycia hirtaria*, means 'shaggy wolf'. A slightly more convincing wolf is the Common Swift, *Hepialus lupulinus*, which the French call *La Louvette*, the she-wolf. When you look closely at the moth head-on, you will see why. It has a hairy, surprisingly fierce little face with a pointed muzzle.

Words

We've already noted various letters, numbers and punctuation marks in the wings of moths and butterflies. But how about whole words? There are a few examples, though the words are short. The Poplar Lutestring has markings that seem to spell 'OR', as if they were its initials. The letters come about by a chance fusion of the two stigmata markings on the moth's wavy-lined forewing. The moth's original describers spotted it right away and named it *Tethea or*, that is, 'the sea goddess that says "or"'. Or what? It doesn't say.

The Ni Moth is named from marks that look like the Greek letter for 'N' (which is shaped more like a 'V') plus 'i'. In Monty Python fashion, it is the moth that says 'ni!' In North America the same species is known less affectionately as the Cabbage Looper. There is also a moth that says 'oo!' This is *Dicycla oo*, the Heart Moth. The name comes from a couple of round markings on each forewing (so with

The moth that says 'ni'. The Ni Moth.

The Double Dart has crazy,
unreadable runes in its wings.

wings outspread it would read 'oooo!'). Since the moth is rare as well as pretty, you can easily imagine someone saying 'ooh!' when they saw one. But the Latin is pronounced 'oo-oh', as though one had caught the moth and then lost it. Others see the mark not as letters but as a number, specifically zero. In Holland it is the *nullenuil*, the zero-owl.

The Double Dart moth has writing all over, to judge by its scientific name, *Graphiphora augur*. *Graphis* is a Roman stylus for writing on wax pads, and so the genus name means, in effect, 'I carry a stylus.' Why it does so is revealed by the species name, meaning 'an augur' or 'soothsayer' and referring to scribbles on the forewings that look a bit like runes. Unfortunately, no one can read what they say.

The same is true of the Burnet Companion moth, *Euclida glyphica*. Its species name means 'an emblem or device' and its lower wings bear black hieroglyphic markings, though no one can read them: it is a cryptic companion.

Euclida refers to the triangular shape of the moth when at rest. Euclid knew all about triangles (*see* Triangles). As for its English name, it is pleasing and poetic, as well as hallowed by age. Yet while the Burnet Companion certainly occurs in the same habitat as burnet moths you seldom see them together, for the so-called companion is usually done for by the time the Six-spot Burnet crawls from its chrysalis.

Worms

One of the earliest mentions of butterflies in the literature is by Albertus Magnus (c.1200–80) in his *De Natura Animalibus*. His rather dismissive name for them was 'flying worms' (to him, most insects were kinds of worm). Today the 'gnawing worms' *(tinea)* belong to the Tineidae, the family which includes the notorious clothes moths. The Tineids are unusual in that only a minority of their caterpillars feed on fresh green plants like other moths. The rest feed on detritus of all kinds, including fur and wool, bracket fungi and skin (*see* Food 2). With the help of a sturdy digestive system, the caterpillars can break down keratin, the fibres of protein found in animal products, so they are able to feed on natural fabrics such as wool, silk, cotton and felt. Some African species can even subsist on the horns and hooves of dead animals, while an American one specialises in the shells of dead tortoises. But even clothes moths cannot digest synthetic materials. Nylon and polyester garments are quite safe.

Apart from the Tineids, several other moths have been insulted as 'worms'. The micros include the genus *Athrips*, 'a heap of worms', so-called because the caterpillars are small, thin and gregarious. There is also *Archips*, or 'chief worm', a genus that includes certain notorious pests of vineyards and fruit trees. 'Worms' are really caterpillars in the wrong place, in much the same way that 'weeds' are wildflowers that grow where we don't want them.

Y–Z

One of the curiosities of Latin is that there is no letter 'Y'. It is usual to substitute the letter 'J' instead, pronouncing it as though it were a 'Y'. Hence a little moth named after the great English naturalist John Ray is spelt *rajella* (pronounced 'rayella').

Unlike us, the Dutch have plenty of moths whose names begin with Z, among them *zoomspanner* (our Bordered Beauty), *zilverhaak* (Silver Hook), *zomervlinder* (Large Emerald) and *zeggeboorder* (Small Quaker). I think my favourite must be *zandoogje*, the Sand Eye, the Dutch name for our Gatekeeper butterfly.

We do have a few scientific names beginning with Z, among which the most mysterious is *Zuezera*, the buzzy-sounding genus of the Leopard Moth, *Zuezera pyrina*. On the face of it the word is meaningless, but it might have been a misspelling of *Zenzura*, a gnat (early printed sources are full of typos). The moth looks nothing like a gnat, but its caterpillar does have powerful jaws for burrowing into wood. Not that gnats have jaws exactly, but they do at least bite. So maybe that is the link: in their different ways, both of them 'bite'.

Zygaena, the genus of the burnet moths is traditionally the last word in the entomological alphabet. This is the Transparent Burnet.

A plate of carpet moths from *Index Entomologicus* by William Wood.

Historical names of butterflies and moths

TABLES CHARTING THE DEVELOPMENT OF BUTTERFLY
AND MOTH NAMES FROM THE EARLIEST TIMES TO
THE TWENTIETH-CENTURY 'NAMING OF THE TINIES'

TABLE 1: PETIVER'S BUTTERFLIES

Petiver tended to change his names from time to time. Here I use those that he settled on for his *Papilionum Britanniae* of 1717. I have retained his spelling and errant use of capital letters. Note that Petiver often allocated separate names for sexes that differ markedly, whether or not he knew, or suspected, that they were the same species. Modern names are in brackets. Species not included were discovered later.

The Streaked golden Hog (Small Skipper, male)
The spotless golden Hog (Small Skipper, female)
The streakt Cloudy Hog (Large Skipper, male)
The Cloudy Hog (Large Skipper, female)
Handley's small brown Butterfly (Dingy Skipper)
The Brown Marsh Fritillary (Grizzled Skipper)
The small-spotted brown Marsh Fritillary (also the Grizzled Skipper)
The Royal William (Swallowtail)
The small white wood Butterfly (Wood White, male)
The white small tipped Butterfly (Wood White, female)
The Saffron Butterfly (Clouded Yellow, male)
The Spotted Saffron Butterfly (Clouded Yellow, female)
The Brimstone (Brimstone, male)
The Male Straw Butterfly (Brimstone, female!)
The White Butterfly with black Veins (Black-veined White)
The Greater White Cabbage-Butterfly (Large White, male)
The Great Female Cabbage Butterfly (Large White, female)
The Lesser White Unspotted Butterfly (Small White, male, probably spring brood)
The Lesser White Double-spotted Butterfly (Small White, possibly male summer brood)
The Lesser White Treble-spotted Butterfly (Small White, probably female)
The common white veined Butterfly with single spots (Green-veined White, male)
The common white veined Butterfly with double spots (Green-veined White)
The lesser, white, veined Butterfly (also the Green-veined White)
The white marbled male Butterfly (Orange-tip, male)
The white marbled female Butterfly (Orange-tip, female)
The holly butterfly (Green Hairstreak)
The brown double Streak (Brown Hairstreak, male)
The golden brown double Streak (Brown Hairstreak, female)
Mr Ray's blue Hairstreak (Purple Hairstreak, male)
Our blue Hairstreak (Purple Hairstreak, female)
The Hair-streak (White-letter Hairstreak)
The Small Tortoise-shell (Small Copper)
The Small Lead Argus (Silver-studded Blue?)
The Edg'd, brown Argus (Brown Argus)
The Blue Argus (Common Blue, male)

The Mixed Argus (Common Blue, female)
The Selvedg'd Argus (also Common Blue, female)
The pale blue argus (Chalkhill Blue)
The Blue Speckt Butterfly (Holly Blue, male)
The Blue Speckt Butterfly with black Tipps (Holly Blue, female)
Mr Vernon's Small Fritillary (Duke of Burgundy)
The White Admiral, previously the White Leghorn Admiral
Mr Dale's Purple Eye (Purple Emperor)
The Admiral (Red Admiral)
The Painted Lady
Lesser or Common Tortoiseshell (Small Tortoiseshell)
The Greater Tortoiseshell (Large Tortoiseshell)
The Peacock's Eye (Peacock)
The Silver Comma (Comma)
The Pale Comma (also a Comma)
The Jagged-wing Comma (yes, another one)
The Small Comma (and that concludes the Commas)
The April Fritillary (Small Pearl-bordered Fritillary)
The April Fritillary with few Spots (Pearl-bordered Fritillary)
The Riga Fritillary (Queen of Spain Fritillary)
The greater silver-spotted Fritillary (High Brown Fritillary)
(Described and figured by Petiver but without a name) (Dark Green Fritillary)
The Greater Silverstreakt Orange Fritillary (Silver-washed Fritillary, male)
The Greater Silverstreakt Golden Fritillary (Silver-washed Fritillary, female)
Dandridge's Midling Black Fritillary (Marsh Fritillary)
The Small Black Fritillary (also Marsh Fritillary)
The Dullidge Fritillary, previously the Lincoln Fritillary (Glanville Fritillary)
The Straw May Fritillary (Heath Fritillary)
The White May Fritillary (also Heath Fritillary, perhaps a pale aberration)
The Enfield Eye (Speckled Wood)
The London Eye (Wall, female)
The London Eye, with a black List (Wall, male)
The common half-Mourner (Marbled White)
The Tunbridge Grayling (Grayling)
The Brown Tunbridge Grayling (Grayling, male)
The Hedge Eye with double Specks (Gatekeeper)
The Brown Meadow-Eye (Meadow Brown, male)
The Golden Meadow-Eye (Meadow Brown, female)
The Brown and Eyes (Ringlet)
The Brown seven Eyes (also Ringlet)
The golden Heath Eye (Small Heath)
The selvedg'd Heath Eye (also Small Heath)

TABLE 2: THE BUTTERFLY AND MOTH NAMES OF ELEAZAR ALBIN (1720)

The Admiral Butterfly [Red Admiral]
Meadow Brown
The Hairstreak Butterfly [Brown Hairstreak]
Purple Hairstreak
Green-veined Butterfly [Green-veined White]
Privet Hawk-moth
Eyed Hawk-moth
The Elephant [Elephant Hawk-moth]
The Drinker
The Fox [Fox Moth]
Brown-tail
Yellow under Wing [Common Yellow Underwing]
Red under Wing [Red Underwing]
Wood Leopard [Leopard Moth]

TABLE 3: MOTHS KNOWN TO BENJAMIN WILKES (1742 AND 1749)

These were originally arranged in no particular order (there being no true order back then).
I have rearranged the species in rough systematic order for ease of reference. The modern
name is in brackets; where there are no brackets, Wilkes's name is still current.

The Goat-Moth
The Leopard Moth
The Small Oak-Egger-Moth [The Festoon]
The Burnet-Moth [Six-Spot Burnet]
The Forester Moth
The Lackey-Moth
The December Moth
The Small Egger-Moth [Small Eggar]
The Great Egger-Moth [Oak Eggar]
The Grass Egger-Moth [Grass Eggar]
The Fox Coloured Moth [Fox Moth]
The Drinker-Moth
The Lappit-Moth [The Lappet]
The Wild Pine-tree Lappit-Moth [Pine Lappet]
The Glory of Kent [Kentish Glory]
The Emperor-Moth
Small Ermine Moth [Orchard Ermine]
The Codling Moth

Small Green Oak Moth [Oak Tortrix]

Provence Rose Moth [Probably the Garden Rose Tortrix]

Plumb-Tree Moth [Plum Fruit Moth]

The Mother of Pearl Moth

The Crimson and Gold Moth [*Pyrausta purpuralis*]

White Spot Moth [*Anania funebris*]

Orange Underwing Moth

The Green Broom-Moth [Grass Emerald]

The Buff Argus Moth [?Maiden's Blush]

The July Arrach-Moth [Shaded Broad-bar]

The Streamer

Cliefden Beauty [Pretty Chalk Carpet]

Blue-bordered Moth [Blue-bordered Carpet]

Mottled Beauty [Argent and Sable]

Scallopshell Moth (Scallop Shell)

Treble Bar'd [Treble Bar]

The Large Magpye, Great Magpye or Curran-Moth [Magpie Moth]

The Gooseberry-Moth (V-Moth]

The Swallow-tail Moth

The Orange Moth

Scorch'd-wing Moth [Scorched Wing]

The Brimstone Moth

Speckled Yellow Moth

The October-Moth [Feathered Thorn]

The Scallop Winged Moth [Early Thorn]

The Richmond-Beauty [Lilac Beauty]

The Hawthorn Moth [Lunar Thorn]

The Brindle Beauty [Brindled Beauty]

Oak Beauty

The Spotted Elm-Moth or Pepper'd Moth [Peppered Moth]

The Mottled Umber-Moth

The Waved Umber

The Lime Moss Moth [?Brussels Lace]

The Brindle-Moth [Pale Brindled Beauty]

The Heath-Moth [Common Heath]

The Olive-Shades or Lime Hawk Moth [Lime Hawk-moth]

Poplar Hawk

Eyed Willow-Hawk Moth [Eyed Hawk-moth]

Privet Hawk

The Unicorn or Bindweed-Hawk Moth [Convolvulus Hawk-moth]

Bee Tyger or Jessamine Hawk Moth [Death's-head Hawk-moth]

The Elephant [Elephant Hawk-moth]

Small Elephant hawk Moth [Small Elephant Hawk-moth]

The Ladies Bedstraw or Elephant Moth [Elephant Hawk-moth]

The Swallow Moth [Swallow Prominent]

The Osier or Pebble Moth [Pebble Prominent]

The Puss or the Puss Moth

A Moth called the Kitten [Sallow Kitten]

The Pebble Moth [Pebble Prominent]

The Buff-Tipt Moth [Buff Tip]

Buff Arches

Peach Blossom

The Dark Tussock or Black Tussock-Moth [Dark Tussock]

The Light Tussock or Yellow Tussock-Moth [Pale Tussock]

The Black-Thorn Moth or Figure of 8 [Figure of Eight]

The Red-Spot Tussock-Moth [Vapourer]

The Orange Tussock-Moth [Scarce Vapourer]

The Yellow-Tail Moth

The White-Satin

The Gipsey Moth (sic)

Black Arches

The Yellow July Oak-Moth [Four-spotted Footman]

The Great Ermine Moth [White Ermine]

The Spotted Buff-Moth [Buff Ermine]

The Spotted Red and White Underwing Moth [Ruby Tiger]

The Small Tyger Moth [Wood Tiger]

The Great Tyger Moth [Garden Tiger]

The Cream-spot Tyger Moth

The Scarlet Tyger Moth

The Great Yellow-Underwing Moth [Large Yellow Underwing]

The Yellow Underwing [Lesser Broad-bordered Yellow Underwing]

Gothick Moth [Light Brocade]

The Dagger Moth [Grey Dagger]

The Bramble Moth [?Knot-grass]

The Sycamore Tussock-Moth [Sycamore Moth]

The Ranunculus Moth [Large Ranunculus]

The Water-Betony Moth [Mullein Moth]

The Sword-Grass Moth [Red Sword-grass]

Ealing's Glory [Green Brindled Crescent]

The Angle-Shades

The Pease-Blossom
Broom-Moth
The Sallow Moth [Orange Sallow]
The Scallop-winged Oak Moth [Heart Moth]
Small Yellow Underwing
The Green Moth with Silver Lines [Green Silver-lines]
The Nut-tree Tussock-Moth
The Gold-Spot Moth
The Golden Y Moth [Plain Golden Y]
The Silver Y Moth
The Willow Red-Underwing Moth or Great Red Underwing [Red Underwing]
The Crimson Underwing Moth [Light Crimson Underwing]
The Cliefden (sic) Nonpareil

TABLE 4: THE PRINCIPAL PUBLICATIONS OF THE GOLDEN AGE

James Petiver (1717) *Papilionum Britanniae Icones*
The first illustrated work on British butterflies.

Eleazar Albin (1720) *A Natural History of English Insects*
The first publication with coloured engravings that show the full life cycles of British butterflies and moths, and their parasites.

Benjamin Wilkes (1749) *The English Moths and Butterflies*
Much improved coloured engravings showing a wide range of moths and butterflies.

Moses Harris (1766) *The Aurelian or The Natural History of English Insects*
The best coloured engravings of moths and butterflies with many species illustrated for the first time.

Adrian Haworth (1803) *Lepidoptera Britannica*
The first thorough scientific classification of British moths and butterflies with many new species described for the first time.

TABLE 5: BUTTERFLIES AND MOTHS DESCRIBED FROM BRITISH SPECIMENS (LISTED IN ALPHABETICAL ORDER) TOGETHER WITH THEIR LOCALITIES

I leave a blank where no precise type locality is given. Only three butterflies, but, by my count, at least 58 larger moths were first described from Britain and Ireland, attesting to the great industry of eighteenth- and nineteenth-century naturalists.

Butterflies

Large Copper. Named and described as new to science by Adrian Haworth, 1803, though known long before, e.g. illustrated as *Argus Aurantius Elloensis*, 'the Orange Argus of Elloe' by the Spalding Gentleman's Society from specimens caught at Dozen's Bank, near Spalding, in 1749.

Northern Brown Argus. Named as *Hesperia artaxerxes* by Fabricius in 1793, from specimens caught on Arthur's Seat, Edinburgh, by a collector called Jones. Long considered to be a subspecies, but recognised as a distinct species, *Aricia artaxerxes*, in 1974.

Cryptic Wood White. Identified in 2011 as a new species from DNA markers from specimens formerly believed to be an Irish sub-species of Wood White, and, later Real's Wood White. Type locality: 'Ireland'.

Other butterflies, such as the Green, Brown and Purple Hairstreak may well have entered the world of science via British specimens, but their formal Linnaean descriptions were based on Continental sources.

Larger Moths

Name	Year	Describer	Type locality
(The) Anomalous	1809	Haworth	
Ashworth's Rustic	1855	Doubleday	Llangollen, N. Wales
Barrett's Marbled Coronet	1864	Doubleday	Dublin, Ireland
Beautiful Golden Y	1809	Haworth	
Black Rustic	1809	Haworth	
Black-banded	1869	Gregson	Isle of Man
Bond's Wainscot	1861	Knaggs	
Butterbur Moth	1847	Doubleday	Falkirk, Scotland
Centre-barred Sallow	1809	Haworth	
Clouded Brindle	1809	Haworth	
Crescent Dart	1824	Stephens	Whittlesea, Cambs.
Crescent Striped	1809	Haworth	
Crinan Ear	1908	Burrows	Crinan Canal, Scotland
Fenn's Wainscot	1864	Fenn	Ranworth, Norfolk
Flame Wainscot	1828	Curtis	Lewisham, Kent
The Grey moth	1866	Gregson	Isle of Man

Haworth's Minor	1829	Curtis	Whittlesea Mere
Least Minor	1855	Stainton	Darlington, Durham
Lunar Underwing	1809	Haworth	
Marbled Green	1771	Forster	'England'
Marsh Oblique-barred	1850	Doubleday	'Ireland'
Matthew's Wainscot	1896	Barrett	'Suffolk & Essex'
Middle-barred Minor	1809	Haworth	
Morris's Wainscot	1837	Dale	Charmouth, Dorset
Mountain Burnet	1872	Buchanan White	Braemar
New Forest Burnet	1888	Briggs	Stubby Copse, New Forest
Northern Arches	1847	Doubleday	Rannoch, Scotland
Northern Footman	1860	Gregson	
Northern Rustic	1839	Stephens	'Cairn Gowr', Perth
Pigmy Footman	1847	Doubleday	Deal, Kent
Pinion-streaked Snout	1834	Stephens	
Rosy Footman	1771	Forster	'England'
Rosy Marsh Moth	1821	Stephens	Yaxley Fen, Hunts.
Rosy Minor	1809	Haworth	
Sandhill Rustic	1864	Doubleday	Rhyl, N. Wales
Saltern Ear	1888	Tutt	Deal, Kent
Scotch Burnet	1872	White	Braemar, Scotland
Shore Wainscot	1827	Curtis	Christchurch, Dorset
Silver Barred	1775	Fabricius	
Six-striped Rustic	1809	Haworth	'GB'
Slender Scotch Burnet	1919	Rowland-Brown	Oban, Scotland
Small Dotted Buff	1809	Haworth	
Small Fanfoot	1775	Fabricius	
Small Rufous	1809	Haworth	
Small Wainscot	1809	Haworth	
Speckled Footman	1758	Linnaeus	
Stephen's Gem	1830	Stephens	
Svensson's Copper Underwing	1968	Fletcher	
Tawny Pinion	1809	Haworth	
Twin-spotted Wainscot	1809	Haworth	
White-speck	1809	Haworth	

TABLE 6: THE FIRST USE OF PRESENT-DAY BUTTERFLY NAMES

I list the species in systematic order beginning with the skippers. In the original context there was often a respectful 'flie' or 'butterfly' tagged on to the name, which was also usually prefixed by 'The'.

Name	First use	Authority
Chequered Skipper	1803	Haworth
Small Skipper	1766	Harris
Essex Skipper	1906	South
Lulworth Skipper	1833	Curtis
Silver-spotted Skipper	1803	Haworth
Large Skipper	1766	Harris
Grizzled Skipper (as the Grizzled Butterfly)	1748	Wilkes
Dingy Skipper	1766	Harris
Swallowtail	1766	Harris
Wood White	1766	Harris
Pale Clouded Yellow (for the female only); (otherwise Haworth, 1803)	1775	Lewin
Clouded Yellow	1742	Wilkes
Brimstone	1695	Petiver
Black-veined White	1766	Harris
Large White (as 'Large Garden White', Lewin, 1775)	1803	Haworth
Small White (as 'Small Garden White', Lewin, 1775)	1803	Haworth
Green-veined White	1795	Lewin
Bath White	1795	Lewin
Orange-tip	1749	Wilkes
Green Hairstreak	1795	Lewin
Brown Hairstreak	1710	Ray
Purple Hairstreak	1720	Albin
White-letter Hairstreak (as 'White-w Hairstreak', Morris, 1853)	1896	Kirby
Black Hairstreak	1829	Curtis
Large Copper	1795	Lewin
Small Copper	1795	Lewin
Short-tailed Blue	1906	South
Small Blue	1795	Lewin
Silver-studded Blue	1775	Harris
Brown Argus	1803	Haworth
Common Blue	1775	Harris

Chalkhill Blue	1775	Harris
Adonis Blue	1906	South
Mazarine Blue	1803	Haworth
Holly Blue	1853	Morris
Large Blue	1795	Lewin
Duke of Burgundy	1766	Harris
(as 'Duke of Burgundy Fritillaria')		
White Admiral	1717	Petiver
Purple Emperor	1766	Harris
Camberwell Beauty	1766	Harris
Red Admiral	1799	Donovan
(as 'The Admiral', Petiver, 1699)		
(as 'The Red Admirable', Wilkes, 1742)		
Painted Lady	1699	Petiver
Small Tortoiseshell	1742	Wilkes
Large Tortoiseshell	1742	Wilkes
Peacock	1742	Wilkes
Comma	1717	Petiver
Queen of Spain Fritillary	1775	Harris
Small Pearl-bordered Fritillary	1803	Haworth
(as 'Small Pearl Border Fritillary', Wilkes, 1742)		
Pearl-bordered Fritillary	1775	Harris
High Brown Fritillary	1742	Wilkes
Dark Green Fritillary	1766	Harris
(as 'Darkned (sic) Green Fritillary', Wilkes, 1742)		
Silver-washed Fritillary	1803	Haworth
(as 'Silver wash Fritillary', Harris, 1766)		
Marsh Fritillary	1795	Lewin
Glanville Fritillary (as 'Glanvil Fritillary Butterfly')	1748	Dutfield
Heath Fritillary	1748	Wilkes
Speckled Wood	1766	Harris
The Wall (as 'The Wall Flie')	1766	Harris
Mountain Ringlet	1812	Haworth
Scotch Argus	1807	Donovan
Marbled White	1766	Harris
Grayling (as 'Grayline', Harris, 1766)	1803	Haworth
Gatekeeper (as 'Large Gate Keeper', Harris, 1766)	1803	Haworth
Meadow Brown	1720	Albin
Ringlet	1766	Harris
Small Heath	1710	Petiver
Large Heath	1803	Haworth
Monarch (as 'The Milkweed', South, 1906)		

TABLE 7: IAN HESLOP'S NAMES FOR MICROS AS RE-INTERPRETED BY PORTER (2002) AND WHEELER (2017)

Common name	Genus/family
Argent	Argyresthiidae
Bagworm	Heslop called them 'smokes' and 'sweeps'; Psychidae
Bent-wing	Opostegidae, Bucculatricidae (*Phyllocnistis, Leucoptera*)
Bell	Tortricidae (*Epinotia, Eucosma, Epiblema*)
Bright	*Lampronia*
Button	Tortricidae (*Acleris*)
Carl	Tischeriidae
Case-bearer	Coleophoridae
China-mark	Pyralidae (Acentropinae)
Clothes Moth	Tineidae
Conch	Tortricidae (*Aethes, Cochylis*)
Cosmet	Cosmopterigidae, Batrachedridae
Crest	Gelechiidae (Dichomeridinae)
Diamond-back	Plutellidae
Dowd	Blastobasidae
Drill	Tortricidae (*Dichrorampha*)
Dwarf	Elachistidae
Ermel	Roeslerstammiidae, Praydidae
Ermine	Yponomeutidae
Fanner	Glyphipterigidae
Flat-body	Oecophoridae (*Depressaria, Agonopterix*)
Gold	*Micropterix*
Grass-veneer	Pyralidae (*Crambus, Agriphila, Catoptria*)
Grey	Pyralidae (Scopariinae)
Groundling	Gelechiidae (Gelechiinae)
Knot-horn	Pyralidae (Phycitinae)
Lance-wing	Epermeniidae
Leaf-cutter	Incurvariidae
Lift	Heliozelidae
Long-horn	Adelidae
Marble	Tortricidae (Oletheutinae)
Metal-mark	Choreutidae
Midget	*Phyllonorycter*

Mompha	Momphidae
Neb	Gelechiidae (Anomologinae)
Obscure	Autostichidae
Owlet	Scythrididae
Pearl	Crambidae
Piercer	Tortricidae (*Cydia, Grapholita, Pammene*)
Pigmy	Nepticulidae
Plume Moths	Pterophoridae
Purple	Eriocraniidae
Roller	Tortricidae (*Ancylis*)
Sable	Heslop's name for some of the *Pyrausta* moths
Shade	Tortricidae (*Eana, Exapate, Cnephasia*)
Shoot	Tortricidae (*Gypsonoma*)
Signal	Stathmopodidae
Slender	Gracillariidae (Gracillariinae)
Smudge	Ypsolophidae
Sober	Glechiidae (Anacampsinae)
Spear-wing	Douglasiidae
Stem-moth	*Ochsenheimeria*
Streak	Oecophoridae (*Pleurota*)
Tabby	Pyralidae (Pyralinae)
Tortrix	Tortricidae (Tortricinae)
Tubic	Oecophoridae, Chimabachidae, Lypusidae
Twist	Tortricidae (*Pandemis, Archips, Clepsis*)
Water-veneer	Pyralidae (Musotiminae)

References

Primary sources (by date)

Moffet, Thomas (1658). *The Theatre of Insects: or, Lesser living Creatures*. First printed in London by 'E. C.', 1658, as Volume 3 of *The History of Four-footed Beasts and Serpents and Insects* by Edward Topsell. Facsimile edition published by Da Capo Press, New York, edited by Willy Ley, 1967.

Petiver, James (1717). *Papilionum Britanniae icones, nomina, etc. Containing the Figures, Names, Places, Seasons etc. of above eighty English butter-flies*, by James Petiver, printed for the author in London, 1717. Facsimile by Gale ECCO print edition reproduced from the British Library.

Ray, John (1710) *Historia Insectorum*. A & J Churchill, London.

Albin, Eleazar (1720) *A Natural History of English Insects: Illustrated with a hundred copper plates, curiously engraven from life*. Printed for William Innys, London.

Wilkes, Benjamin (1741–42) *Twelve New Designs of English Butterflies*. Re-published in facsimile by E. W. Classey, 1982.

Wilkes, Benjamin (1749) *The English Moths and Butterflies: Together with the Plants, Flowers and Fruits whereon they Feed and are usually Found*. Printed for and sold by the author, London.

Harris, Moses (1766) *The Aurelian, or The Natural History of English Insects; Namely Moths and Butterflies. Together with the Plants on which they Feed*. Published by the author, London. Reprinted by Country Life Books, London, with a foreword by Robert Mays (1986).

Harris, Moses (1775) *The English Lepidopterist: or, The Aurelian's Pocket Companion*. J. Robson, London. Reprinted by E. W. Classey (1969).

Berkenhout, John (1769–73) *Outlines of the Natural History of Great Britain and Ireland*. 3 vols. Printed for P. Elmsly, London.

Lewin, William (1795) *The Papilios of Great Britain*. J. Johnson, London.

Donovan, Edward (1792–1813) *The Natural History of British Insects*. Printed for the author and for F. C. and J. Rivington, London.

Haworth, A. H. (1803) *Lepidoptera Britannica: sistens digestionem novam insectorum Lepidopterorum quae in Magna Britannia.* J. Murray, London.

Samouelle, George (1819) *The Entomologist's Useful Compendium: or An Introduction to the Knowledge of British Insects.* Thomas Boys, London.

Stephens, James Francis (1829) *A Systematic Catalogue of British Insects.* Printed for the author by Baldwin & Cradock, London.

Wood, William 1833–38) *Index Entomologicus; or, A Complete Illustrated Catalogue, consisting of 1,944 figures of the Lepidopterous Insects of Great Britain.* Printed for the author, London.

Westwood, J. O. & Humphreys, H. N. (1841) *British Butterflies and their Transformations.* William Smith, London.

Westwood, J. O. & Humphreys, H. N. (1843–45) *British Moths and their Transformations.* 2 vols, William Smith, London. Reprinted by Reink Books, 2018.

Humphreys, H. N. (undated, c. 1860) *The Genera of British Moths.* Paul Jerrard & Sons, London.

Stainton, Henry Tibbats (1867) *British Butterflies and Moths: an introduction to the study of our native Lepidoptera.* Reeve & Co., London.

Newman, Edward (1869) *An Illustrated Natural History of British Moths.* W. Tweedie, London.

Barrett, Charles Golding (1893–1907) *The Lepidoptera of the British Islands: a descriptive account of the families, genera and species indigenous to Great Britain and Ireland, their preparatory states, habits and localities.* L. Reeve, London.

Meyrick, Edward (1895) *A Handbook of British Lepidoptera.* Macmillan & Co, London.

South, Richard (1907, 1908) *The Moths of the British Isles.* 2 vols, Warne Wayside & Woodland series, London.

Heslop, I. R. P. (1964) *Revised Indexed Check-list of the British Lepidoptera.* Self-published 'Library Edition', 145pp.

Emmet, A. Maitland (1991) *The Scientific Names of the British Lepidoptera. Their history and meaning.* Harley Books, Colchester.

Bradley, J. D. (2nd edition, 2000) *Checklist of Lepidoptera recorded from the British Isles.* Privately published, D. Bradley, Fordingbridge.

Agassiz, D. J. L., Beaven, S. D., & Heckford, R. J. (2013) *A checklist of the Lepidoptera of the British Isles.* Natural History Museum, London.

Wheeler, Jim (2017) *Micro Moth Vernacular Names. A nomenclatural checklist of British Microlepidoptera.* Clifton & Wheeler, Norfolk.

Secondary sources

Allan, P. B. M. (1947) *A Moth-Hunter's Gossip*. Watkins & Doncaster, London.

Allen, David Elliston (2010) *Books and Naturalists*. Collins New Naturalist, London.

Beirne, Bryan P. (1952) *British Pyralid & Plume Moths*. Frederick Warne, London.

Brock, Jim P. & Kaufman, Kenn (2003) *Kaufman Field Guide to Butterflies of North America*. Houghton Mifflin, New York.

Dunbar, David (2010) *British Butterflies. A History in Books*. British Library, London.

Emmet, A. Maitland & Heath, John (Eds, 1989) *The Moths and Butterflies of Great Britain and Ireland*. Volume 7, Part 1. *The Butterflies*. Harley Books, Colchester.

Ford, E. B. (1945) *Butterflies*. Collins New Naturalist, London.

Ford, R. L. E. (1952) *The Observer's Book of the Larger British Moths*. Warne, London.

Gandy, Matthew (2016) *Moth*. Reaktion Books, London.

Goater, Barry (1986) *British Pyralid Moths. A guide to their identification*. Harley Books, Colchester.

Hart, Colin (2011) *British Plume Moths*. British Entomological and Natural History Society, London.

Heslop, I. R. P., Hyde, R. E. & Stockley, R. E. (1964) *Notes and Views of the Purple Emperor*. Southern Publishing Co., Brighton.

Howse, Philip (2014) *Seeing Butterflies. New perspectives on colour, pattern and mimicry*. Papadakis, Winterbourne, Berks.

Leverton, Roy (2001) *Enjoying Moths*. Poyser Natural History, London.

Marren, Peter (1998) A short history of butterfly-collecting in Britain. *British Wildlife*, 9(6), 362–370.

Marren, Peter (1998) The English names of moths. *British Wildlife*, 10(1), 29–38.

Marren, Peter (2004) The English names of butterflies. *British Wildlife*, 15(6), 401–08.

Marren, Peter (2015) *Rainbow Dust. Three centuries of delight in British butterflies*. Square Peg, London.

Marren, Peter & Mabey, Richard (2010) *Bugs Britannica*. Chatto & Windus, London.

Macleod, R. D. (1959) *Key to the Names of British Butterflies and Moths*. Pitman, London.

Mynott, Jeremy (2018) *Birds in the Ancient World*. Oxford University Press.

Newman, L. Hugh (1967) *Living with Butterflies*. John Baker, London.

Oates, Matthew (2005) Extreme butterfly-collecting: A biography of I. R. P. Heslop. *British Wildlife*, 16(3), 164–173.

Porter, Jim (1997) *The Colour Identification Guide to Caterpillars of the British Isles*. Viking, London.

Raven, Charles E. (1947) *English Naturalists from Neckam to Ray. A Study of the Making of the Modern World*. Cambridge University Press.

Raven, Charles E. (1942) *John Ray: Naturalist. His life and works*. Cambridge University Press.

Riley, Adrian M. & Prior, Gaston (2003) *British and Irish Pug Moths. A guide to their identification*. Harley Books, Colchester.

Salmon, Michael A. (2000) *The Aurelian Legacy. British butterflies and their collectors*. Harley Books, Colchester.

Skinner, Bernard (1985) *Colour Identification Guide to Moths of the British Isles*. Viking, London.

Stearns, Raymond Phineas (1953) James Petiver, Promoter of Natural Science, c.1663–1718. *Proc. American Antiquarian Society*, 243–365.

Sterling, Phil & Parsons, Mark (2012) *Field Guide to the Micro Moths of Great Britain and Ireland*. British Wildlife Publishing, Gillingham, Dorset.

Stokoe, W. (1938) *The Observer's Book of British Butterflies*. Warne, London.

Thomas, Jeremy & Lewington, Richard (2010) *The Butterflies of Britain and Ireland*. British Wildlife Publishing, Gillingham.

Waring, Paul & Townsend, Martin (2003) *Field Guide to the Moths of Great Britain and Ireland*. British Wildlife Publishing, Hook, Hampshire.

Wood, the Rev. J. G. (undated, c.1886) *Common British Moths*. George Routledge & Sons, London.

Young, Mark (1997) *The Natural History of Moths*. Poyser Natural History, London.

Index to Scientific Names

Most of these names have stories behind them. I have omitted the many references to genus or species names since they will not mean much to the non-specialist and would only prolong the already lengthy index.

Index

Acknowledgements

My mentor and guide on the scientific names of butterflies and moths is a man I had never met: Colonel Maitland Emmet. His *Scientific Names of the British Lepidoptera* is an all-time entomological classic, and it left few stones unturned when elucidating the names of Linnaeus and his followers. Without Emmet at my elbow I would probably have had to restrict this book to English names only.

The full text was read by Jeremy Mynott, who, like Maitland Emmet, is at once a fine naturalist and a leading scholar of Latin and Greek, and the author of *Birds of the Ancient World*. The text was also read with an entomologist's eye by my old friend, Dr Mark Young, a leading expert on the Lepidoptera. Despite his loathing of common names for micromoths, he was, like Jeremy, both helpful and encouraging. I am grateful to both friends for so generously sharing their wisdom and insights.

I have also, at various times, and perhaps unrealised by them, benefited from the knowledge and thoughts of other friends, notably the late Basil Harley, Professor Philip Howse, Matthew Oates, Mark Parsons and Martin Warren. Dick Seamons kindly drew my attention to some of the wonderful German moth names.

I am grateful to Richard Lewington for allowing us to use some of his incomparable drawings to illustrate Book Two, and to Beatrice Forshall for designing a lovely jacket in the spirit of the book.

I am grateful to The Stapleton Collection/Bridgeman Images for inclusion of two hand-coloured engravings from *Twelve New Designs of English Butterflies* (1742) by Benjamin Wilkes, and to the Natural History Museum/Bridgeman Images for the hand-coloured engraving by Maria

Sibylla Graff Merian from *Insects of Suriname* (1726). I am also grateful to the Linnean Society of London for permission to reproduce the various portraits featured in Book One, and thanks to The Map House for the geometric, hand-coloured engravings from *A Rare Depiction of Butterflies and Moths* (1764) by Benjamin Wilkes. I am grateful to Kate Diston, librarian at Oxford University Museum of Natural History, Andraea Deneau at the Linnaean Society and Julie Harvey at the Natural History Museum, for their kind help in tracking down literary sources and images. I am also grateful to Watkins and Doncaster (via the blog Nets, Pins and Things) for the wonderful photograph of collectors in the New Forest.

Finally, I thank the team at Little Toller, Adrian and Gracie Cooper, Graham Shackleton and Jon Woolcott for bringing the book to fruition; and Ruth Reisenberger for her diligent proofreading.

This book is dedicated to Michael McCarthy, a writer with the happy knack of always asking the right question. I am indebted to his warm friendship, generous spirit and endlessly enquiring mind over the years.

P. M.

2019

Little Toller Books

Anthology and Biography
ARBOREAL: WOODLAND WORDS
CORNERSTONES: SUBTERRANEAN STORIES
MY HOUSE OF SKY: THE LIFE OF J. A. BAKER

Field Notes
DEER ISLAND *Neil Ansell*
ORISON FOR A CURLEW *Horatio Clare*
SOMETHING OF HIS ART *Horatio Clare*
ON THE MARSHES *Carol Donaldson*
THE TREE *John Fowles*
SAVAGE GODS *Paul Kingsnorth*
LOVE, MADNESS, FISHING *Dexter Petley*
WATER AND SKY *Neil Sentance*
RIDGE AND FURROW *Neil Sentance*
KING OF DUST *Alex Woodcock*

Monographs
HAVERGEY *John Burnside*
LANDFILL *Tim Dee*
HERBACEOUS *Paul Evans*
EAGLE COUNTRY *Seán Lysaght*
SPIRITS OF PLACE *Sara Maitland*
MERMAIDS *Sophia Kingshill*
LIMESTONE COUNTRY *Fiona Sampson*
SNOW *Marcus Sedgwick*
BLACK APPLES OF GOWER *Iain Sinclair*
BEYOND THE FELL WALL *Richard Skelton*
SHARKS *Martha Sprackland*
ON SILBURY HILL *Adam Thorpe*

The Oliver Rackham Library
THE ASH TREE *Oliver Rackham*
THE ANCIENT WOODS OF THE HELFORD RIVER *Oliver Rackham*
THE ANCIENT WOODS OF SOUTH EAST WALES *Oliver Rackham*

Nature Classics
THROUGH THE WOODS *H. E. Bates*
MEN AND THE FIELDS *Adrian Bell*
THE MIRROR OF THE SEA *Joseph Conrad*
ISLAND YEARS, ISLAND FARM *Frank Fraser Darling*
THE MAKING OF THE ENGLISH LANDSCAPE *W. G. Hoskins*
THE PATTERN UNDER THE PLOUGH *George Ewart Evans*
A SHEPHERD'S LIFE *W. H. Hudson*
FOUR HEDGES *Clare Leighton*
DREAM ISLAND *R. M. Lockley*
THE UNOFFICIAL COUNTRYSIDE *Richard Mabey*
RING OF BRIGHT WATER *Gavin Maxwell*
IN PURSUIT OF SPRING *Edward Thomas*
THE NATURAL HISTORY OF SELBORNE *Gilbert White*

LOWER DAIRY, TOLLER FRATRUM, DORSET
W. littletoller.co.uk **E.** books@littletoller.co.uk